W9-CBO-871

The Consequences of Cuts

Richard P. Nathan, Fred C. Doolittle,
and Associates

The Consequences of Cuts

The Effects of the Reagan Domestic Program
on State and Local Governments

PRINCETON URBAN AND REGIONAL RESEARCH CENTER
Woodrow Wilson School of Public and International Affairs
Princeton University

Princeton Urban and Regional Research Center
Princeton University
Princeton, New Jersey 08544

Copyright © 1983 by
Princeton Urban and Regional Research Center
All Rights Reserved
Printed in the United States of America

ISBN 0-938882-06-6

Library of Congress Cataloging in Publication Data:
Nathan, Richard P.
  The consequences of cuts.
  Includes bibliographical references.
  United States—Appropriations and expenditures.
Grants-in-aid—United States. I. Doolittle, Fred C.
II. Title.
HJ2051.N165 1983 353.0072'5 83-60542
ISBN 0-938882-06-6

Distributed by Princeton University Press
Box AA
3175 Princeton Pike
Lawrenceville, N.J. 08648

Contents

List of Tables

Acknowledgments

This volume is in the truest sense a collaborative work. It is the product of a battalion. First and foremost in the order of march are the field researchers. The book is a compilation of analytical findings made in the field by an interdisciplinary team of forty-six field research associates who work on this study on a part-time basis. Their names and affiliations are listed on the following pages. All of the field associates are academic social scientists, primarily political scientists and economists, who reside in the areas for the fifty-four state and local governments included in the sample for this study.

In addition to the two indicated authors, the central staff includes five research assistants—two full-time employees and three graduate students at the Woodrow Wilson School. They are Laurie Angiolillo-Bent; John Lago; Jennifer Brand, MPA 1984; Marie Korn, MPA 1984, and Vivian Li, MPA 1983.

A number of outside readers also contributed valuable comments and suggestions. This includes members of the Advisory Committee for this study, whose names are listed later in this section, and Philip M. Dearborn, Paul R. Dommel, and Clifford A. Goldman. The manuscript was edited by David L. Aiken. Mary Capouya provided editorial support and reviewed the entire manuscript. A dedicated corps of skillful practitioners of the art and science of word processing produced the manuscript: Debbie Bill, Lori Davison, Michele Pollak, Helen Pringle, and Kathy Shillaber. Nan Nash managed this production process.

This recitation of people who have helped us would not be complete without an acknowledgment of the two foundations—the Ford Foundation and the Commonwealth Fund—that provided grants-in-aid to make all of this possible. We especially want to thank Susan V. Berresford and Shepard Forman of the Ford Foundation and Margaret E. Mahoney and Thomas W. Moloney of the Commonwealth Fund.

At Princeton University, the Woodrow Wilson School of Public and International Affairs has proved to be a happy home for this research, for which we thank Dean Donald E. Stokes, Ingrid W. Reed, and Agnes M. Pearson.

Richard P. Nathan
Fred C. Doolittle

Princeton, New Jersey
June 1, 1983

Field Associates

Arizona

John S. Hall
Professor of Public Affairs
Director,
Center for Public Affairs
Arizona State University

Joseph Cayer
Associate Professor of
Public Affairs
Arizona State University

Richard A. Eribes
Associate Professor of
Public Affairs
Arizona State University

California

John J. Kirlin
Professor of
Public Administration
Sacramento Public
Affairs Center
University of
Southern California

Cristy A. Jensen
Associate Director for
Academic Affairs
Sacramento Public
Affairs Center
University of
Southern California

Catherine H. Lovell
Professor of Administration
University of
California at Riverside

Dale Rogers Marshall
Professor of Political Science
University of
California at Davis

Ruth Ross
Assistant Professor
Center for Public Policy
and Administration
California State
University, Long Beach

Florida
John M. DeGrove
  Professor of
  Political Science
  Director, Joint Center for
  Environmental and
  Urban Problems
  Florida Atlantic University
Nancy E. Stroud
  Senior Research Associate
  Joint Center for
  Environmental and
  Urban Problems
  Florida Atlantic University
Edward Montanaro
  Executive Director
  Florida Advisory Council on
  Intergovernmental Relations
Robert Bradley
  Chief Analyst
  Florida Advisory Council on
  Intergovernmental Relations
Karen Fausone
  Analyst
  Florida Advisory Council on
  Intergovernmental Relations
Illinois
Charles J. Orlebeke
  Professor of
  Urban Planning and Policy
  University of Illinois
  at Chicago Circle
John N. Collins
  Associate Professor of
  Public Administration
  Director, Center for Policy
  Studies and
  Program Evaluation
  Sangamon State University

Massachusetts
Fred C. Doolittle
  Associate Professor
  John F. Kennedy School
  of Government
  Harvard University
Kathryn Haslanger
  Boston, Massachusetts
Eve Sternberg
  Cambridge, Massachusetts
Mississippi
Lewis H. Smith
  Professor of Economics
  Director, Center for
  Manpower Studies
  University of Mississippi
Stanley Herren
  Associate Professor
  of Economics
  University of Mississippi
Missouri
George D. Wendel
  Professor of
  Political Science
  Director, Center for
  Urban Programs
  St. Louis University
George Otte
  Assistant Professor
  of Urban Studies
  St. Louis University
E. Allan Tomey
  Instructor of
  Urban Economics
  St. Louis University
New Jersey
Richard W. Roper
  Director
  Program for
  New Jersey Affairs
  Princeton University

Nancy Beer
  Senior Research Assistant
  Program for
  New Jersey Affairs
  Princeton University
Martin Bierbaum
  Assistant Professor
  of Urban Studies
  Rutgers University, Newark
New York
Sarah F. Liebschutz
  Professor of
  Political Science
  State University of
  New York at Brockport
Irene Lurie
  Associate Professor of
  Public Administration
  State University of
  New York at Albany
Ohio
Charles F. Adams, Jr.
  Assistant Professor of
  Public Administration
  Ohio State University
Frederick D. Stocker
  Professor of Economics
  Ohio State University
Joseph M. Davis
  Associate Executive Director
  Federation for
  Community Planning
  Cleveland, Ohio
Patricia Barry
  Research Associate
  Federation for
  Community Planning
  Cleveland, Ohio
Oklahoma
R. Lynn Rittenoure
  Associate Professor
  of Economics
  University of Tulsa

Steve B. Steib
  Associate Professor
  of Economics
  University of Tulsa
Larkin Warner
  Professor of Economics
  Oklahoma State University
South Dakota
William O. Farber
  Professor Emeritus
  of Political Science
  University of South Dakota
Sue Brown
  Sioux Falls, South Dakota
Greg Redlin
  South Dakota
  Office of Budget and Finance
Rich Sagen
  Physical and
  Transportation Planner
  Sixth District Council
  Rapid City, South Dakota
Texas
Susan A. MacManus
  Associate Professor
  of Political Science
  University of Houston,
  Central Campus
Robert M. Stein
  Assistant Professor
  of Political Science
  Rice University
Vernon H. Savage
  Associate Professor of
  Finance and Economics
  Southwest Texas
  State University
Robert D. Wrinkle
  Associate Professor
  of Political Science
  Pan American University

Washington
V. Lane Rawlins
  Associate Provost
  for Administration
  Washington State University
Betty Jane Narver
  Research Consultant
  Institute for Public
  Policy and Management
  University of Washington

Lawrence Wohl
  Instructor of Economics
  Washington State University

Advisory Committee Members

Samuel Beer '
  Thomas P. O'Neill, Jr., Professor of American Politics
  Boston College
George F. Break
  Professor of Economics
  University of California at Berkeley
Martha Derthick
  Director of Governmental Studies
  The Brookings Institution
Mitchell I. Ginsberg
  New York City
  Former Dean, School of Social Work, Columbia University
  Former Administrator of Human Resources Administration
Edward M. Gramlich
  Professor of Economics
  University of Michigan
T. Norman Hurd
  Albany, New York
  Former Budget Director, New York State
Maynard H. Jackson
  Former Mayor of Atlanta
Francine F. Rabinovitz
  Professor of Public Administration
  University of Southern California
  Vice President, Hamilton, Rabinovitz & Szanton, Inc.
Robert D. Reischauer
  Vice President
  The Urban Institute
  Former Deputy Director,
  Congressional Budget Office

Allen Schick
   Professor of Public Affairs
   University of Maryland
   Former Senior Specialist
   Congressional Research Service
Elmer B. Staats
   Washington, D.C.
   Former Comptroller General of the United States
Richard H. Ullman
   Professor of International Affairs
   Woodrow Wilson School, Princeton University
Robert C. Weaver
   Emeritus Professor
   Hunter College, City University of New York
   Former Secretary
   U.S. Department of Housing and Urban Development
Aaron Wildavsky
   Professor of Political Science
   University of California at Berkeley

1. Introduction

The most notable achievement of the Reagan administration to date in changing the policies of the U.S. national government has been in the domestic area. Although Congress did not enact all of Reagan's grand design of "swaps" and "turnbacks" for shifting responsibilities and funding sources between the federal and state governments contained in his January 1982 state of the union message, the administration nevertheless has made fundamental changes in domestic policy and in implementing a new federalism.

The most important of these changes came in the administration's first year in office. The Omnibus Budget Reconciliation Act of 1981, which brought about far-reaching budget cuts and policy shifts, stands as the major domestic policy achievement to date of the Reagan administration. In this 1981 legislation, Reagan convinced Congress to take actions that had the following effects:

- Significantly cut domestic spending and trimmed the federal government's role in domestic program areas.
- Substantially changed welfare programs.
- Increased the proportion of federal grant funds that are channeled to the states and reduced the share paid to local units of government.

Each of these three main elements of Reagan's domestic program is discussed briefly below.

Table 1. *Federal Outlays for Grants-in-Aid, 1981–1982*
(millions of dollars)

Fiscal year	Total outlays	Grants for payments to individuals	Capital	Operating
1981	94,762	39,934	22,132	32,696
1982	88,194	40,744	20,480	26,970
Dollar change	−6,568	+810	−1,652	−5,726
Percentage change	−6.9	+2.0	−7.5	−17.5

Source: Executive Office of the President, Office of Management and Budget, *Budget of the United States Government, Fiscal Year 1984, Special Analyses* (Washington, D.C.: U.S. Government Printing Office, 1983), table H-7.

Reduced Federal Role

The long period of growth in the scope and cost of the domestic programs of the federal government that began with the New Deal came to an end in Reagan's first year in office. Instead of growth and innovation, the focus of federal grant programs is now on retrenchment. New spending initiatives are out of fashion.

In relative terms, the largest cuts made under Reagan occurred in the programs of greatest interest for this research—namely, grants to states and local governments and various local nonprofit organizations. Federal grants to states and localities declined by $6.6 billion between 1981 and 1982. This is the first time in twenty-five years that there has been a year-to-year decline in the absolute level of federal grants-in-aid to state and local governments. Federal grants declined in two of the three major categories shown in table 1.

Although the largest category in table 1 (grants for payments to individuals) rose in 1982, this 2 percent increase was well below the increases of the previous five years, which averaged 10 percent per year. Grants for payments to individuals were relatively stable despite the sharp rise in unemployment, and the increase was less than the rate of inflation. This represents a cut in spending below what would otherwise have been expended during the recession, as discussed in the entitlement grant section of this chapter and in chapter 3.

Welfare Changes

Although welfare programs have not been turned over to the states and localities, as Reagan proposed in 1982, existing federal welfare programs have been fundamentally altered.[1]

There are two main approaches or theories of national welfare policy. One emphasizes providing incentives for poor people to work. This approach would reward people who are trying to make it on their own by permitting them to keep a certain amount of the welfare benefits they would otherwise receive, in addition to their earnings. A second, more conservative, theory of welfare holds that because the welfare system encourages dependence, we should take steps to exclude poor people who are working, or who are able to work, from exposure to the welfare system.

In the 1970s, the first approach to welfare, the incentive approach, was ascendant. It has been embodied in changes in existing programs and in various plans for welfare reform. Both President Nixon's Family Assistance Plan and President Carter's Better Jobs and Income Plan exemplified this approach.

The Reagan administration has changed the nation's course on welfare. The administration has successfully advanced the second, work-oriented theory of welfare. Many of Reagan's ideas and proposals are based on his experience as governor of California, when he proposed reducing assistance to the working poor and requiring able-bodied adults to participate in workfare programs. These initiatives caused widespread controversy, both in the courts and in the political arena. As a result, they tended to fall short of their objectives. To a significant degree, what we are witnessing today is a much more successful effort to advance similar ideas in national policy by a president who had learned from his gubernatorial experience the problems involved in doing so.

1. Reagan's 1982 state of the union address proposed a "swap" whereby the federal government would take over the responsibility for medicaid (the program that provides health and medical assistance to the poor) and the states would take over responsibility for the aid to families with dependent children (AFDC) program, plus the food stamp program. The 1982 address also proposed "turnbacks" of existing federal programs to the states in exchange for the elimination of certain federal excise taxes. The negotiations to draft legislation for this "swap" and "turnback" plan fell apart in late 1982, and the plan as a result was not formally transmitted to Congress.

Role of the States

A third major element of Reagan's new federalism involves the role of the states. The states are the middlemen in American federalism. At the same time that the national government is reducing its role in domestic affairs, local governments, lobbying groups, and nonprofit organizations are increasingly looking to their state capitals for help.

In addition, the states are being tested by the Reagan administration through the adoption in 1981 of new block grants combining existing grant programs—many of which previously provided federal money directly to local governments or nonprofit organizations—into new and broader programs controlled by the states. The administration consolidated fifty-four previous "categorical" grants with total budget authority of $7.2 billion into block grants in 1981. Seven new block grant programs were created, and two existing block grants were modified. This consolidation process was used to justify reductions in spending of up to 25 percent in several of the new block grants.

Purpose of This Book

In this book, we examine how these and other changes that took effect in federal fiscal year 1982 affected state and local governments and the people they serve. The focus is on grants-in-aid to state and local governments and nonprofit organizations. In order to bring the material together in an effective way for the reader, we describe the specific character of the changes made in fiscal year 1982 in the discussion of how these changes affected the sample governments and how they responded to them. The analysis presented in this volume is based on information obtained as part of a multiyear study funded by the Ford Foundation and the Commonwealth Fund.

The research is being done in two phases. In the first phase, we examined the nature and impact of the changes in a sample of fourteen states and forty local governments during fiscal year 1982. The second phase will extend the research to fiscal years 1983 and 1984, so that the overall study will cover almost the entire period of the current presidential term of office.

Preliminary findings from the first phase of this research appeared in *Reductions in U.S. Domestic Spending: How They Affect State and Local Governments*, edited by John William

Ellwood and published in 1982.[2] That report analyzes in detail the Omnibus Budget Reconciliation Act of 1981 and presents our preliminary analysis of its impact on part of the sample—fourteen states and fourteen big-city governments—through the first quarter of federal fiscal year 1982 (October 1 to December 31, 1981). This book extends the earlier analysis, presenting more detailed findings for the entire sample of fifty-four jurisdictions and for the entire fiscal year (October 1, 1981 to September 30, 1982).

The series of field network evaluation studies, of which this research is a part, began more than ten years ago at the Brookings Institution with a field network evaluation study of the general revenue sharing program that was enacted in 1972. Similar studies have been undertaken since then at the Brookings Institution and at the Woodrow Wilson School, Princeton University. Field evaluation studies have been made of the community development block grant and the public service employment program that was a component of the Comprehensive Employment and Training Act (CETA). A set of uniformly organized case studies has also been conducted on the effects of all federal grants in selected big cities in 1978.[3] These earlier studies assessed the effects of federal aid as it was growing and at its peak; this new study is being made as grants to states and local governments are shrinking.

Summary of Main Findings

We concentrate in this book on the degree to which, and the ways in which, states and localities have replaced federal funds. This subject has important implications for one of the basic aims of the Reagan presidency—to reduce the size and scope of government in the national economy, particularly in social program areas. It already appears that in these basic terms the Reagan presidency

2. New Brunswick, N.J.: Transaction Books.

3. For information on the earlier studies, see Richard P. Nathan and Charles F. Adams, Jr., and Associates, *Revenue Sharing: The Second Round* (Washington, D.C.: The Brookings Institution, 1977); Richard P. Nathan, Robert F. Cook, V. Lane Rawlins, and Associates, *Public Service Employment: A Field Evaluation* (Washington, D.C.: The Brookings Institution, 1981); Paul R. Dommel and Associates, *Decentralizing Urban Policy* (Washington, D.C.: The Brookings Institution, 1982); James W. Fossett, *Federal Aid to Big Cities: The Politics of Dependence* (Washington, D.C.: The Brookings Institution, 1983); and Richard P. Nathan, "The Methodology for Field Network Evaluation Studies," in Walter Williams et al., *Studying Implementation: Methodological and Administrative Issues* (Chatham, N.J.: Chatham House, 1982).

has made notable progress. While we cannot present a final analysis at this time, because changes and state and local adjustments still continue, a summary of the main findings presented in this volume follows:

1. The most pronounced effects of the Reagan program have been on people, especially the working poor. These effects stem from cuts and changes in entitlement grants (AFDC, medicaid, food stamps, and school lunches) as well as in operating grants for such purposes as jobs and job training, compensatory education, and health and social services.

2. For state and local governments, the cuts were not as large as was expected when the 1981 budget reconciliation act was being debated. Local governments, in particular, overestimated the cuts. State and local government officials were more concerned with the deep recession and resulting fiscal problems than with the federal aid cuts in federal fiscal year 1982.

3. Few cuts were replaced with state and local funds. Most federal aid cuts were "ratified," that is, passed along to the recipients of the federally aided benefits and services.

4. Replacement was highest in three states in the sample—Oklahoma, New York, and Massachusetts. They were found to have used new revenues to replace between 10 percent and 25 percent on a net basis of the cuts in federal aid made in fiscal year 1982. Five states—Arizona, Florida, New Jersey, California, and South Dakota— replaced smaller amounts of federal aid, in their case less than 10 percent of the cuts.

5. Six state governments in the sample realized net savings of state funds as a result of the 1982 federal aid cuts. They are Illinois, Mississippi, Missouri, Ohio, Texas, and Washington. Much of the savings in state spending occurred under the AFDC program—not as a result of deliberate state action, but because, as persons were removed from the AFDC rolls, the required state matching contribution was reduced.

6. State governments on the whole were more affected than local governments by the fiscal year 1982 cuts. They have the main responsibility for federally aided entitlement programs, which tended to be the focus of the early effects.

7. The local governments of large cities in the sample that replaced the highest percentages of the cuts were those in Orlando and Los Angeles. Three other cities—Cleveland, Rochester, and Houston—replaced smaller amounts of federal aid cuts. Some cuts affecting large cities were replaced by overlying county governments, others by special districts, and others by the city itself.

8. Suburban and rural governments have been much less affected by federal grants than large cities. Some of the suburban and rural jurisdictions studied experienced increases in federal aid in certain programs in fiscal year 1982. These increases occurred primarily because the new block grants spread out funds to a larger number of jurisdictions than the previous categorical grants, which had been more concentrated on large cities and economically hard-pressed jurisdictions. Suburbs in the inner ring of metropolitan areas, which face social and economic conditions much like older and distressed cities, were much more seriously affected by the cuts than wealthier and less densely populated suburban communities.

9. Rural communities tend to receive very few federal grants. Often the aid they receive is limited to general revenue sharing funds, which were not affected by the reconciliation act. Overlying local governments in rural areas are likely to be more affected—but not greatly affected—by federal grants.

10. States and local governments used various delaying and coping tactics to put off the effects of the fiscal year 1982 cuts. Several states used carryover federal grant funds under the block grant programs established in 1981. For local governments, the changes resulting from the new block grants were smaller than at the state level in 1982, but as carryover funds are used up and states set new priorities, changes will be felt. Local officials often found that deregulation at the federal level under block grants led to new and in some cases more restrictive state regulations.

11. Although on the whole the replacement by state and local governments of the 1982 federal aid cuts was modest, it tended to occur most frequently in well-off places and on the part of governments that are generally liberal. Replacement also tended to be highest under federally aided programs that involve politically popular health and social services and for capital grants. In the case of capital grants, some jurisdictions raised new funds in anticipation of cuts that did not occur.

Many of the effects of the cuts and changes made in fiscal year 1982 are still to be felt. To follow up on these issues and also study the effects of other and more recent changes, the field research will continue for fiscal years 1983 and 1984. The study as a whole will thereby cover the full period of the current presidential term of office. Special studies, based on the field data, are also being conducted on the effects of the Reagan domestic program in selected policy areas and in relation to major institutions of American federalism. Reports are currently planned on the effects of the Reagan domestic program in the health area, on welfare programs, under the new block grants, and on the role of state governments in American federalism. Other special studies are being planned that would combine the field data from this study with the data from previous field evaluation studies.

This book contains seven chapters. Chapter 2 discusses the research approach used; it describes the analytical framework developed to classify state and local responses to the fiscal year 1982 federal aid cuts and explains the method by which the research was carried out. The appendix describes the report form used by the associates. Chapter 3 examines the responses to federal aid cuts by the fourteen state governments in the sample for this study; chapter 4 examines the cuts and responses for the fourteen large cities studied; and chapter 5, for the twenty-six suburban and rural jurisdictions in the sample. Chapter 6 is a special analysis by one of the field associates, Catherine Lovell of the University of California, Riverside, of the effects of changes made by the Reagan administration in regulations and administrative processes under federal grants-in-aid. Chapter 7 draws together the main lessons from this analysis and proposes a theory of the behavior of state and local governments in response to cuts in federal grants-in-aid.

2. Studying the Effects of Federal Aid Cuts

Researchers who study the effects of cuts in federal grants to state and local governments face a number of formidable problems. One is the variety of types of federal aid programs; another is the vast difference in the functions, finances, and politics of the governments that receive federal grants. This chapter discusses these and other difficulties and how we have endeavored to deal with them. It first describes the method used in this research, then discusses the types of grants and the changes that were made in each in 1981, and finally presents a framework for analyzing state and local responses to the changes.

Research Approach

The biggest problem faced in research on the effects of federal grants-in-aid is the diversity of the jurisdictions that receive federal support. Cuts play out differently in a growing, recently settled region than in an older area with declining population and employment. The fiscal condition of recipient jurisdictions has a major effect on the behavior of state and local governments under federal grants. The political culture of a community also is important. Some governments have chosen to participate extensively in programs funded by federal grants, adding funds from their own sources and setting up federally aided programs on a permanent and continuing basis. Other jurisdictions have participated only minimally in federally aided programs.

There is no existing centrally available data set that can be used to assess all of the factors that affect the behavior of state and local governments under federal grants. The U.S. Bureau of the Census publishes data on state and local government finances, but these

data provide little detail on federal aid. Using them to study state
and local reactions to federal policy changes is difficult; for many
purposes, it is impossible.

Budget data also pose problems. Federal budget data are uniform for the whole country, but they tell us little about which governments receive federal aid, and nothing about what they do with
it. State and local budgets sometimes show how much federal aid
is received and how it is spent, but different governments have different methods of reporting such data. Only someone familiar with
a particular government's political and financial systems can
obtain the data necessary to analyze its response to changes in federal aid levels and policies. In short, it is necessary to analyze
financial and program data at the state and local levels in order to
understand and assess the effects of the Reagan administration's
domestic policy changes.

In this study we use the field network evaluation methodology,
which has been used over the last ten years to evaluate a variety of
federal grant programs. The research approach has five key elements:

1. In each jurisdiction, a field associate analyzes the effects of the
    federal policy or policies being studied. Associates normally
    hold an academic appointment in a political science or eco-
    nomics department and work part-time on this research. All
    have an interest in applied social science research and partic-
    ipate in the development of the research design. In preparing
    the analysis, an associate interviews officials of government
    and nonprofit agencies and examines both unpublished and
    published records and reports containing program and fiscal
    information and statistics.

2. A central research staff, in consultation with all of the field
    associates, develops a common analytical framework and
    reporting format for the associates to use in developing and
    writing up their findings.

3. Information is gathered at several times over a period of years
    in order to analyze the effects of federal policy changes on a
    longitudinal basis. Such a research design maintains continu-
    ity while at the same time allowing for the consideration of
    new issues as they arise.

4. The analysis focuses on the nature of the actual changes in federally aided programs in each local area, the effects of these changes, and how the grantee government responds to them.

5. A central staff coordinates the research and prepares reports, such as this one, which summarize the field analyses and present generalizations across the sites and over time.

The sample of governments for this study consists of fifty-four jurisdictions—fourteen state governments and, within those states, fourteen large cities and twenty-six smaller cities and suburban and rural governments. The jurisdictions are listed in table 2. The states and local governments were chosen to provide a representative cross section of governments in different regions, of different population size, with differing fiscal conditions, government structures, and politics.

The first phase of this study was organized to enable us to provide a timely summary analysis of how states and local governments responded to the cuts and changes in federal grant programs during the year they took effect. Field associates conducted their research during fiscal year 1982. In identifying cuts and analyzing their effects, field associates collected the best information available in the summer and fall of 1982.

As we discovered in previous research and again in this study, uniform, detailed, and definitive figures on federal aid do not exist. The budget and program data that are available have to be carefully scrutinized; in many cases they have to be adjusted to apply to the time period of a particular study, in this one, October 1981 to September 1982. Furthermore, over the course of the year, funding allocations often change, even in a normal year without program upheavals such as occurred in 1982. In still other cases, adjustments are made in earlier estimates after a given fiscal year has ended. The figures on budget cuts used in this volume are as of the fall of 1982; the field associates and central staff made adjustments in these figures only in very special cases where large and important changes were made in budget data after September 30, 1982. The research is continuing into fiscal years 1983 and 1984, which will enable us to take into account final budget data for the sample jurisdictions for the 1982 federal fiscal year period.

Table 2. Jurisdictions in Sample

State	1980 Population	Region	Large cities	1980 population	Suburbs	1980 population	Small cities and rural jurisdictions	1980 population
Arizona	2,718,215	West	Phoenix	789,704	Scottsdale	88,482	Casa Grande	14,971
California	23,667,902	West	Los Angeles	2,966,850	El Monte	79,494		
					Redlands	43,619		
Florida	9,746,324	South	Orlando	128,291	Winter Park	22,339	Winter Garden	6,789
Illinois	11,426,518	N. Central	Chicago	3,005,072	Robbins	8,853	Lincoln	16,327
Massachusetts	5,737,037	Northeast	Boston	562,994	Chelsea	25,431	Middleton	4,135
Mississippi	2,520,638	South	Jackson	202,895			Grenada	12,648
							Tupelo	23,905
Missouri	4,916,686	N. Central	St. Louis	453,085	Webster Groves	23,097	Washington	9,251
New Jersey	7,364,823	Northeast	Newark	329,248	Orange	31,136		
New York	17,558,072	Northeast	Rochester	248,741	Greece	81,367		
Ohio	10,797,630	N. Central	Cleveland	573,822	Cleveland Heights	56,438	McConnelsville	2,018
Oklahoma	3,025,290	South	Tulsa	360,919	Bixby	6,969	Wilburton	2,996
South Dakota	690,768	N. Central	Sioux Falls	81,343			Rapid City	46,492
							Yankton	12,011
Texas	14,299,191	South	Houston	1,595,138	Katy	5,660	Weslaco	19,331
Washington	4,132,156	West	Seattle	493,846	King County	1,269,749	Walla Walla County	47,435

Source: U.S. Bureau of the Census, 1980 Census of Population, vol. 1, General Population Characteristics (Washington, D.C.: U.S. Government Printing Office, 1982), chap. B.

Types of Effects of Federal Grant Changes

This study deals with the following types of effects of changes in the level and character of federal grants:

1. *Fiscal effects*—Changes in the levels of state or local government spending and taxation as a consequence of changes in the level or character of federal grants.
2. *Programmatic effects*—Changes in the distribution of federal aid funds by functional area and type of service.
3. *Incidence effects*—Changes in the share of federally aided public services and benefits going to people in one group compared with another. The groups are usually defined by income, but can be defined by race or neighborhood or in other ways.
4. *Institutional effects*—Changes in the way decisions are made about how to allocate federal grant funds, reflecting the amount of influence and authority exercised by different types of public officials and interest groups.
5. *Regulatory effects*—Changes in state and local policies and procedures brought about by regulatory changes under grant-in-aid programs at the federal level, either to deregulate or to add new regulations.

This book concentrates on two main questions:

- *What specific programs and services were cut, and when, in the sample jurisdictions?*
- *How did the sample governments respond to these cuts?*

Both of these questions are very hard to answer. We have taken pains to spell out carefully when and where the cuts actually occurred, and how the sample governments responded. Our focus here is on the *services* reduced as a result of federal aid cuts or in some cases replaced by state and local government out of their own funds. Other books and reports planned for this project focus on particular policy areas—for example, health and welfare—and on how the cuts and changes made in 1981 affected specific institutions.

Federal Grants and How They Were Changed

There are three main types of federal grants: entitlement, operating, and capital. The sections below describe each type and discuss the ways they were affected by the cuts and related changes that took effect in fiscal year 1982.

Entitlement Grants

Entitlement grants are made to states and localities, which in turn make transfer payments to families and individuals. These payments can be in cash or in kind, such as those for medical care, food stamps, and school lunches.

Typically, state and local governments are reimbursed by the federal government for some portion of the entitlement payments they provide to eligible persons. A key characteristic of these programs is that all persons eligible for aid must receive it; state and local governments cannot regulate caseloads by appropriation actions.

The largest entitlement grants are aid to families with dependent children (AFDC), medicaid, and food stamps. Some analysts do not classify food stamps as a grant-in-aid, because the federal government pays 100 percent of the cost of the stamps. However, we include the food stamp program in this study, because the stamps are paid to state and local governments, which in turn distribute them to individual recipients. In addition to administering the food stamp program, states and localities pay a portion (approximately half) of the administrative costs of this program out of their own funds.[1]

The 1981 reconciliation act tightened the eligibility rules for federal entitlement programs (AFDC and medicaid), thus reducing the number of people served. The total costs of these programs are shared by the federal government and the state or local government that administers them, so the federal government and the administering governments shared in the savings realized in fiscal 1982.

These savings are hard to identify, however. In some jurisdictions, the recession caused many newly eligible people to apply for these programs. As a result, these jurisdictions as well as the federal government spent more in fiscal 1982 than they had in 1981. Nevertheless, spending in 1982 was lower than it would have been under the old eligibility rules, because the reconciliation act changes decreased the number of eligible persons or families below what it otherwise would have been.

---

1. Two of the largest federal entitlement programs—social security and medicare—are administered directly by a federal agency, the Social Security Administration. A third, unemployment compensation, is administered by the states but is financed by earmarked payroll taxes. This study focuses on grants to state and local governments and hence does not analyze these programs.

Most states have estimates of the number of people who were cut off from AFDC or medicaid, or who received lower benefits because of the 1981 changes. Because a relatively small proportion (10 to 15 percent) of the recipients removed from the rolls returned to the programs within six to twelve months,[2] the numbers of case closings and benefit reductions due to the 1981 policy changes are a good approximation of the minimum size of the cuts. Some states produced estimates of the expected effect of the current recession on the caseloads had there been no 1981 changes, allowing us to refine our estimate of the net effect of those changes.

Operating Grants

Operating grants are paid to states and localities to support such service programs as education, health, social services, housing, and job training. This group of grants includes revenue sharing, block grants, and narrower categorical grants dealing with a single program or program area. Many of the services financed by these grants are provided by special-purpose governments and nonprofit organizations.

Operating grants are of two main types: *formula* grants allocated to states or local governments on an automatic basis, specified in the law or regulations, and *project* grants, for which a federal agency considers individual applications for particular activities or projects.

In the case of formula grants, associates generally used the fiscal year 1981 level of operating grants as the basis for estimating the anticipated 1982 grant, often simply reporting the difference in funding between 1981 and 1982. For some formula grants, however, associates reported that the recipient jurisdictions had not spent or committed all the funds from previous years and that these balances were carried forward into fiscal 1982. Because our concern is with funds available to provide services in fiscal year 1982, we take note of these carryover funds in our analysis. If a recipient government used these funds in fiscal 1982 to maintain services, the effect was to delay the impact of the federal cut.

Where a number of previous categorical grants were combined to create a new block grant, as in the new health and education

2. This finding is based on a special canvass conducted for this study, and is consistent with the findings of other studies. This return rate is generally in line with the "normal" return rate.

block grants, the old categorical programs often did not operate on the same funding cycle. Some were formula grants distributing annual payments at fixed times; others were project grants, with funds awarded throughout the year and for varying periods. Associates had to estimate the full-year effect of the changes as the new block grants were phased in and the old project grants expired.

Despite cuts in the overall funding level for a new block grant, some jurisdictions experienced increases in aid because of the overlap of funds still available under the previous categorical grant and the money from the new block grant, distributed for the full year on October 1, 1981. In other cases, a jurisdiction received more aid under one of the new block grant programs than it had under previous categorical programs, even though total spending in a particular state was reduced. This happened because of the grant distribution system adopted by that state.

Capital Grants

An important distinguishing feature of federal grants for capital purposes is the long interval between the time funds are appropriated and when they are actually spent. This interval affects the way state and local governments respond to changes in national policies relating to capital grants. The biggest federal grants to states and localities for capital purposes are for highways, mass transit, housing, and wastewater treatment facilities. The 1981 changes affect only new awards; current construction activity is a function of past grant awards,

Most capital grants are awarded for specific multiyear projects, and many are project grants awarded through a competitive process. Even without changes in total federal funds, grant awards to a jurisdiction for capital purposes typically go up or down from one year to another because projects vary in size and previous projects reach completion. A jurisdiction might not apply for a new award in some years, perhaps because it was in the midst of a project or because it did not have pressing capital needs.

For capital programs where federal funds are distributed on a formula basis, the analysis is similar to that for operating grants. Capital grants that operate on a project basis, however, present a harder task. If a jurisdiction's proposal had progressed through the approval process to the point that an award seemed likely but funding was subsequently denied, and if there was a clear link to the 1982 budget act, the associate counted this denial as a cut. Under this narrow definition of a cut, few jurisdictions experienced identifiable losses in the twelve-month period studied for this report. The main effects of the fiscal year 1982 changes in capital grant programs will come in future years.

State and Local Responses to Federal Aid Cuts

We have classified the responses of state and local governments to the 1982 cuts and changes in federal grants into two main categories: (1) maintaining service levels fully or partially in the face of federal cuts, and (2) ratifying or passing through the cuts in the form of service reductions. These basic categories comprise a range of responses as defined below. This is the analytical framework used in the next three chapters to examine the responses of the sample jurisdictions to the cuts made in 1981.

Policies to Maintain Service Levels

1. *Replacing lost federal funds through increased state and local spending.* This type of response applies to cases where new funds are devoted by state and local governments to a federally aided program, allowing the continuation of services despite a federal cut. Spending can be increased directly for the program being cut, as when a government increases its own spending for social services supported by the social services block grant to make up for a federal cut. An increase can also occur in a related program offering a substitute service, as when a recipient government increases general relief expenditures to aid families removed from the AFDC and food stamp rolls as the result of federal changes in eligibility. In some instances, revenue sources that can only be used for limited purposes were tapped to cover the cuts; in others, increased tax revenues provided the needed revenue for replacement. Another possible source of replacement of federal aid is private funds or funds provided by nonprofit organizations. We found only scattered instances of this type; all were local efforts of relatively narrow scope. Many nonprofit organizations were cutting back in fiscal 1982 after being hit hard by the federal cuts, primarily in operating grants.

2. *Imposing or increasing fees.* In many of the sample jurisdictions, users were required to pay higher fees for services, such as wastewater treatment, bus or subway rides, health and various other social services, and school lunches, as a consequence of federal aid cuts. The added revenue helped to finance continued service. The net effect of these policy changes depends on the elasticity of demand for the service involved. In some cases, fewer

people use a service as prices rise. The decrease in a service level will depend on the characteristics of the service, the alternatives available, and the size and distribution of the price rise.

3. *Spending carryover funds or one-time windfalls from over-lapping funding periods.* This response was found to be most common under the new block grants. It allows service providers to protect service levels in the short run. Jurisdictions that spent their carryover balances postponed the impact of the cuts; they will be unable to protect services in this way in the future.

4. *Shifting other federal funds from related programs.* Some jurisdictions responded to the 1982 federal aid cuts and changes by shifting funds to maintain services in what they regard as high-priority areas and cutting lower-priority programs. This process was facilitated in the new block grants contained in the 1981 reconciliation act. This does not mean that cuts were avoided, only that some federally aided services were continued (in full or in part), and cuts were made in other areas.

5. *Increasing efficiency.* Even if funds decline, service levels can be maintained if federal aid is used more efficiently. The Reagan administration argued that increased efficiency and the elimination of fraud and abuse would lessen—even elimi-nate—the impact of some federal funding cuts on service levels. Many jurisdictions sought to cut costs in federally aided programs by means of changes in operational procedures and administrative systems. They reorganized departments, made changes intended to provide services more efficiently, and increased their oversight and control over organizations under contract with them to provide services. An effort is made in this volume to cite illustrative cases where these types of changes were made; further attention will be given to this subject in the subsequent field analyses.

Policies Cutting Service Levels

6. *"Ratifying" the cut under conditions where other revenue and service efficiency are unchanged.* Where no steps are taken to provide other revenues or increase efficiency, a cut in federal aid translates into a cut in services. In entitlement programs, the link can be a direct and immediate one between cuts in federal funding and reduced caseloads and benefit levels. In service programs, the link between funding and the number of people served is not as easily observed; organizations can reduce the number of people served or attempt to serve the same number of people with fewer resources by reducing the scope or quality of services.

7. *"Compounding" the federal cuts by cutting state or local spending in addition to the amount of the federal aid reduction.* States or local governments may consciously decrease their own spending and thus compound federal aid cuts as grant revenue declines. In jurisdictions where the Reagan program of cuts is popular, government officials may take this opportunity to cut federally aided programs that have only weak local support. Compounding the federal cuts could also be seen as a contribution to the president's battle against "excessive" government spending.

The focus of this report on the 1982 field data is on the first-order effects of the cuts and changes made in federal grants in Reagan's first year in office. Later analyses, as part of this research program, will probe the longer-run fiscal and economic effects of these policy shifts.

Organization of the Analysis

The 1982 cuts and changes in federal grants need to be differentiated in terms of the types of governments and organizations that they affected. Certain entitlement programs, block grants, and some capital programs go primarily to state governments. Other grants go directly from the federal government to local governments, as do a number of operating and capital grants. In addition, some services at the local level are supported by federal block grants, which are distributed by the states to local governments and nonprofit organizations. Most local governments do not receive entitlement grants beyond the child nutrition program for school meals, though some counties do administer federally aided welfare programs, in which case they receive federal aid funds via the state for this purpose. Nonprofit organizations receive federal funds by allocations from state governments or cities, or directly from the federal government. They also provide services that are federally aided under contracts with state and local governments.

In light of this diversity in the routing of funds under different federal grants, we have organized the discussion of cuts by jurisdictional groupings. Table 3 lists the most important grant programs affected by the 1981 reconciliation act and shows the type of government or organization that receives these federal funds. It also shows the amount of total spending, and the percentage reduction in budget authority in 1982 (see notes to the table for details). This table provides a useful key for the analysis of cuts and responses at the state level in chapter 3, and at the local level in chapters 4 and 5.

Table 3. *Change in Budget Authority of Federal Grant Programs, by Type of Recipient*

Program	Type	1982 Budget authority Millions of dollars	Percentage change from CBO baseline[a]
GRANTS TO STATES FOR PROGRAMS ADMINISTERED PRIMARILY BY STATES			
Medicaid	Entitlement	17,624	-5
Food stamps	Entitlement	10,280	-16
Federal aid to highways	Capital	8,279	+5
Aid to families with dependent children	Entitlement	5,461	-17
Social services block grant	Operating	2,400	-23
State employment service	Operating	757	-5
Maternal and child health block grant	Operating	374	-25
Trade adjustment assistance	Entitlement	306	-83
Preventive health block grant	Operating	82	-36
Youth conservation corps	Operating	0	-100
Highway safety	Capital and operating	-73[b]	-137
GRANTS TO STATES PRIMARILY DISTRIBUTED TO LOCAL GOVERNMENTS OR NONPROFIT AGENCIES			
Child nutrition	Entitlement	2,847	-31
Low-income energy assistance block grant	Operating	1,875	-17
Education block grant	Operating	470	-38
Alcohol, drug abuse, and mental health block grant	Operating	432	-37
Community services block grant	Operating	348	-41
Primary care block grant	Operating	248	-30
Special milk	Operating	28	-78
GRANTS TO STATES AND LOCAL GOVERNMENTS AND NONPROFIT AGENCIES			
Community development block grant	Capital and operating	3,456	-13
Compensatory education	Operating	2,914	-26
CETA training	Operating	3,037	-46
Economic development	Capital and operating	199	-68

Table 3, continued

Program	Type	1982 Budget authority Millions of dollars	Percentage change from CBO baseline[a]
Energy Conservation	Capital and operating	145	-83
CETA public service employment	Operating	0	-100
GRANTS TO LOCAL GOVERNMENTS OR NONPROFIT AGENCIES			
Assisted housing	Capital and operating	16,367	-43
Mass transit	Capital and operating	3,495	-31
Wastewater treatment[c]	Capital	2,400	+50
Public housing operating subsidy	Operating	1,490	+20
Urban development action grant	Capital	440	-35
Education impact aid	Operating	437	-50
Housing rehabilitation loan fund	Capital	0	-100

Source: John William Ellwood, ed., *Reductions in U.S. Domestic Spending: How They Affect State and Local Governments* (New Brunswick, N.J.: Transaction Books, 1982), part 2.

a. Change is measured from Congressional Budget Office current policy baseline for 1982. This baseline is calculated by estimating what level of spending would have been needed in fiscal 1982 if the federal government's policies had remained unchanged from the previous year but spending were increased to keep pace with inflation. The baseline figures shown here were those available to Congress when it considered the fiscal 1982 budget, and show the size of the cuts Congress thought it was making. Spending levels reflect supplemental appropriations made after the reconciliation act during late 1981 and early 1982.

b. The reconciliation act reduced current-year authority by $100 million and also rescinded $173 million in prior-year contract authority.

c. Wastewater treatment grants originally had a 1981 budget authority of $3.3 billion before a rescission of $1.7 billion. Grants are made directly to local governments, but the amount of grants in a state is limited by an annual allocation of funds.

3. State Governments:
Cuts and Responses

As the middle level in American federalism, states face new pressures from the national government, which is cutting aid, and from local officials, who are demanding more financial support. State governments in 1982 faced other problems as well. The economic recession was deeper than had been predicted, and voters in many states were expressing resentment toward state spending by supporting constitutional and statutory prohibitions against increases in spending and taxes. This was the economic and political context in which state officials made the responses to federal aid cuts reported in this chapter.

The overall fiscal context is also important to this analysis. Federal aid is one of the several revenue sources for state governments. Despite the many changes in the federal aid system, the proportion of federal aid as a component of state government finances has been remarkably constant since 1960. As table 4 shows, federal aid to states grew substantially during the postwar period; however, since state spending also grew rapidly, federal aid has remained at about 20 percent of total state expenditures. Federal aid plays a different role in different state government functions. In education, the largest category of state spending in 1981, federal aid accounted for 14 percent of state spending; while in the second largest category of state spending, public welfare, federal aid accounted for 56 percent of state expenditures, as shown in table 5. For highways, the third largest category, federal aid was 39 percent of state expenditures. For all other categories, federal aid amounted to 13 percent of expenditures.

The fourteen states in the sample include three northeastern states, four North Central states, four southern states, and three western states. The three most populous states are included in the

Table 4. *Federal Aid to the States and State Expenditures*

Year	Federal aid (millions of dollars)	State expenditures (millions of dollars)	Federal aid as percentage of expenditures
1950	2,275	15,082	15
1960	6,382	31,596	20
1970	19,252	85,055	23
1975	36,148	158,882	23
1981	67,868	.291,527	23

Source: U.S. Bureau of the Census, *Historical Statistics on Government Finances and Employment* and *State Government Finances,* annual issues (Washington, D.C.: U.S. Government Printing Office).

Table 5. *Federal Aid by Major State Government Functions, 1981*

Expenditure category	Federal aid (millions of dollars)	State expenditures (millions of dollars)	Federal aid as percentage of expenditures
Education	14,100	96,921	14
Public welfare	28,892	51,463	56
Highways	9,369	25,439	39
All other	15,507	117,704	13
Total	67,868	291,527	23

Source: U.S. Bureau of the Census, *State Government Finances in 1981* (Washington, D.C.: U.S. Government Printing Office, 1982).

sample—California, New York, and Texas. Five states in the sample were below 5 million in population in 1980. The two fastest-growing states in the nation (Arizona and Florida) are also in the sample, which was structured to present a cross section of fiscal and economic conditions and governmental structure.

For state governments, the biggest federal aid cuts in 1982 came in entitlement programs. These cuts were important because of the size of the AFDC, food stamp, and medicaid programs: Small percentage cuts in these programs translated into large dollar declines in federal aid. The smaller entitlement programs—child nutrition, refugee assistance, and trade adjustment assistance—had large percentage cuts nationally, although only the changes in the child nutrition program were important in all

Table 6. *Frequency of Mention on List of Five Largest Cuts for State Governments*

Program	Type of program	No. of states
Social services block grant	Operating	13
CETA	Operating	12
Aid to families with dependent children	Entitlement	9
Food stamps	Entitlement	8
Federal highways aid	Capital	5
Medicaid	Entitlement	5
Child nutrition	Entitlement	5
Education block grant	Operating	3

the states under study. Many operating grants, including most of the block grants, had cuts of from 10 to 25 percent—more in some cases—in most of the states in this study. The public service employment component of the Comprehensive Employment and Training Act (CETA) was eliminated.

Table 6 indicates the number of the sample states that included a program in the ranking of the five largest dollar cuts. Two operating grants lead the list: the social services block grant and the CETA program. Four entitlement programs are included in the table, as is one capital grant, the federal highway aid program, and another operating grant, the education block grant.

Most state governments were unable or unwilling to maintain service levels in the face of the federal aid cuts. Most of the funding cuts, especially in the entitlement programs and in the public service employment program, were ratified, that is, passed through as service reductions. Operating and capital grants on the whole tended to fare better than entitlement programs. In a limited number of programs, some states used their own funds, shifted other flexible federal grants, or applied carryover funds to protect service levels.

The net effect of the 1982 cuts and changes in federal aid was that the cuts primarily affected poor people receiving transfer payments and services. Those on the margin of income eligibility for means-tested programs were most affected. Most of these people lived in households in which someone worked, but brought in wages just above the poverty level.

This chapter amplifies these conclusions. It first reviews the impact of the reconciliation act on key programs, examining the size of the cuts and the responses of state governments. This section discusses different types of programs in the order of the importance of cuts: (1) entitlement grants, (2) block grants, (3) other operating grants, and (4) capital grants. The second section summarizes the responses of state governments, using the framework presented in chapter 2. The third and final section presents a state-by-state description of the cuts and responses.

Entitlement Grants

Four entitlement programs received major cuts in federal aid in most of the states in this study: aid to families with dependent children (AFDC), medicaid, food stamps, and child nutrition. In a few states with special situations, cuts in refugee assistance and trade adjustment assistance were also important. Table 7 summarizes the cuts for each program.

Aid to Families with Dependent Children

The reconciliation act made a larger number of major changes in the substance of the AFDC program than had been made by the welfare reform efforts of three previous presidents. The bill did the following:

1. Allowed states to require certain recipients to work in public agencies and for private firms in exchange for welfare payments.

2. Decreased the amount of earnings and other income that is disregarded in calculating how much assistance a recipient should receive. (Formerly the first $30 in earned income plus one-third of the amount over that had been excluded in the calculation of benefits.)

3. Imposed an absolute income ceiling on eligibility, so that no one earning more than 150 percent of the state standard of need could receive aid.[1]

1. Each state calculates its own standard of need reflecting its evaluation of a level of income needed to live in the community. The state may set this standard below the federal poverty line (forty-seven states did so in 1982) and may also pay benefits below its standard of need.

Table 7. *Entitlement Programs: Estimated Change in Federal Aid, by State, Fiscal Year 1982*

Aid to families with dependent children

Reduced 10% to 24%
Florida ($8 million)
Massachusetts ($40-45 million)
Mississippi ($5 million)
Missouri ($15-20 million)
Ohio ($55 million)
Oklahoma ($15-20 million)
Texas ($10-15 million)

Reduced less than 10%
Arizona ($500,000-1 million)
California ($60 million)
Illinois ($35-40 million)
New Jersey ($15-20 million)
New York (NA)
South Dakota ($500,000)
Washington ($6-10 million)

Medicaid

Reduced less than 10%
California ($50 million)
Florida (NA)
Illinois ($60 million)
Massachusetts ($15 million)
Mississippi ($4 million)
Missouri (NA)
New Jersey ($15 million)
New York ($30 million)
Ohio ($45 million)
Oklahoma ($7 million)
South Dakota ($1 million)
Texas (NA)
Washington ($2-5 million)

No program
Arizona

Food stamps

Reduced 10% to 24%
California ($60 million)
Massachusetts ($10 million)
New Jersey ($60 million)
New York ($200 million)
Texas ($50-60 million)

Reduced less than 10%
Arizona ($3 million)
Florida ($25 million)
Mississippi ($22 million)
Missouri ($1 million)
Ohio ($20 million)
Oklahoma ($6 million)
South Dakota (NA)
Washington (NA)

Child nutrition

Reduced 25% to 49%
Massachusetts ($21 million)

Reduced 10% to 24%
Arizona ($3 million)
Florida ($34 million)
New Jersey ($20 million)
South Dakota ($1 million)
Texas ($36 million)
Washington ($10-12 million)

Reduced less than 10%
California ($20 million)
Illinois ($1 million)
Mississippi ($6 million)
Missouri ($3 million)
Ohio ($12 million)
Oklahoma ($6 million)

No significant change
New York

Note: The estimates of losses for aid to families with dependent children and food stamps cuts are based on estimates of the number of people removed from the rolls as a result of the various changes in eligibility rules. In most states, federal aid in these programs increased because of the recession. The discussion of the medicaid changes in this section explains the difficulty in calculating the cuts for that program. Child nutrition cuts are based on 1981 compared to 1982 federal aid.

4. Ended payments to strikers, students over eighteen, and women pregnant with their first child until the sixth month of pregnancy.

5. Required that a portion of a stepparent's income be treated as available for support of an AFDC stepchild.

6. Required states to use a retrospective accounting method, under which a grant is based on the recipient's actual income in the previous month rather than the expected income in the coming month. Recipients must report their income each month.

These changes were aimed at cutting program costs by removing families from the rolls. The Reagan administration estimates that nationally the changes made about 10 percent of the caseload ineligible and lowered benefits for another 7 percent.[2]   Cuts in AFDC funding in the states in the study, shown in table 7, range from a high of just under 25 percent in Oklahoma to less than 10 percent in seven states, including low percentages in California and New York.

Three factors account for most of these differences in AFDC cuts. First, since the cuts were accomplished by limiting eligibility for those with earnings and with other sources of support, differences in the characteristics of recipients in different states led to different effects. A 1979 survey of AFDC recipients found that the proportion of households with earnings varied from 7 percent in New York, Ohio, and Texas to over 20 percent in Massachusetts, Mississippi, and Missouri.[3]   The cuts in AFDC in the latter states were among the largest in the sample in percentage terms. In addition, starting in 1982, the income of stepparents in AFDC households was counted in calculating eligibility and benefits; this change had the greatest impact in the southern states in the sample.

Litigation also affected the rate at which, and the way in which, the 1982 AFDC changes went into effect. The resulting administrative delays in implementing the federal changes in California decreased the amount of the federal cuts there. The state legislature adjourned in September 1981 without implementing the fed-

2. L. Demkovitch, "Reagan's Welfare Cuts Could Force Many Working Poor Back on the Dole," *National Journal*, January 2, 1982, pp. 18–23.

3. U.S. Social Security Administration, Bureau of Research and Statistics, *AFDC Recipient Characteristics Study, 1979: Part II, Financial Characteristics* (Washington, D.C., 1979). The study did not include data for Oklahoma.

eral changes. In October, during a special session that had been called to deal with reapportionment, the legislature enacted a statute requiring the state welfare department to issue emergency regulations implementing the federal changes. A state court soon thereafter enjoined enforcement of the new rules because the counties had not been given enough time to implement them properly. The full list of new rules was not implemented until April 1982; court challenges continued after that date.

The final reason for differences among the states in the effect of the 1982 AFDC changes is that, in a matching grant program such as AFDC, the state government pays a specified percentage of assistance costs and can control these costs by setting the benefit level under the program. Some states made changes in their programs, discussed below, that increased state and federal spending on assistance—in effect, restoring some of the federal cut.

Households with a working member were most affected by the changes in the AFDC program. In most of the states studied, the ceiling on maximum total income, set at 150 percent of the poverty line, and the elimination of the $30 plus one-third earnings disregards in calculating benefits were the two most important changes.

Most of the cuts in federal spending for AFDC were ratified by states. This outcome, in fact, was in many cases difficult for states to avoid. The result was that a number of the states in the sample ended up spending less of their own funds than they would have spent in the absence of the reconciliation act. A look at the mechanics of the AFDC program explains these outcomes. The state and federal governments share the costs of AFDC benefits; the proportion provided by the federal government depends on the state's per-capita income relative to the national average. When Congress tightened federal eligibility rules, caseloads dropped and federal *and state* spending declined below the levels they otherwise would have reached.

Several types of state action could restore state spending to what it would have been without the reconciliation act changes. First, the state could provide aid on its own to those cut off by the new federal rules. In New York, California, Ohio, and Florida, some of the former AFDC recipients were eligible for existing state programs, such as fully state-funded general relief or emergency assistance. Other states in the sample had no such program in place, and none created new programs of this kind. In fact, New York moved to restrict eligibility in general relief to limit the number of certain groups of former AFDC recipients who could receive benefits and to limit the spending increase for that program, but still ended up increasing state AFDC spending.

States could also change the AFDC eligibility rules under their control to bring some of the former recipients back onto the program and in the process increase benefits for some of those who remained on the rolls. This would increase state *and federal* spending. One of the key 1982 eligibility changes removed all households with incomes that were greater than 150 percent of the state-determined standard of need. By raising this standard of need, states could bring some or all of those terminated, plus other new households, onto the program. Seven states in the sample did this to varying degrees: Florida, Illinois, New York, Massachusetts, Mississippi, Missouri, and Ohio.[4]

States could also change the AFDC program to compound the federal cuts. Two states—Missouri and Washington—ended the optional unemployed-parent program providing aid for two-parent families. (Most AFDC households are headed by single women.) Washington cut its standard of need.

The changes in federal aid under the AFDC program, along with state responses to these changes, resulted in nearly every state in the sample spending less of its own funds on AFDC or substitute programs than it would have without the reconciliation act. New York was the only exception. It increased its standard of need and funded substitute general relief for selected groups; the result was that it maintained state spending and probably replaced a small part of the federal cut.

Medicaid

This, the largest federal grant-in-aid program, was not cut by a large percentage in most states, though the dollar decline in federal aid often was substantial. Medicaid cuts are especially difficult to estimate. Program costs, and hence federal aid, are sensitive to the level of unemployment, so the 1981–82 recession increased spending. In addition, unlike AFDC, the costs per recipient are to a large extent beyond the control of the state. Recipients choose how often to use medical services. Also, medical cost increases have driven up program costs substantially.

---

4. In New York, the state raised the standard of need just before the federal changes were passed. The standard had not been raised for many years; the increase was principally an attempt to make up for past inflation. In Ohio, state law requires an annual cost-of-living adjustment.

The changes made in medicaid in the reconciliation act reduced expenditure growth in several ways. AFDC recipients are automatically eligible for medicaid. Hence, because the AFDC rolls were reduced, medicaid caseloads dropped below what they would have been otherwise. States were also given more discretion in limiting the medical services covered by medicaid, and were encouraged to increase efforts to control the cost of services.

The major method of reducing federal medicaid expenditures, accounting for nearly half of the estimated federal savings, was a reduction in the federal government's matching share of medicaid costs. As with AFDC, the federal government's share of spending on benefits depends on each state's per-capita income relative to the national average. A wealthier state has a lower federal matching rate than a poorer state; as of fiscal year 1981, the average federal share was 56 percent. The reconciliation act requires the federal share to be reduced by 3 percent in fiscal year 1982, 4 percent in fiscal year 1983, and 4.5 percent in fiscal year 1984.

States can avoid this loss of aid in two ways. First, one percentage point of the reduction can be waived if the state implements a program to review hospital costs; a second percentage point is forgiven if the state's unemployment rate is more than one-and-a-half times the national average; and a third percentage point is waived if the state reduces fraud and abuse by a certain amount. Second, if a state controls spending so that federal medicaid expenditures are below a specified target, the state is entitled to a dollar-for-dollar offset against the reduction up to the difference between the federal medicaid expenditures and the target.[5] However, the total amount recovered through this method can not exceed the amount of the reduction. In 1982, states did not know whether they had stayed within the ceiling and would have the federal cut restored. The numbers in the table thus should be seen as preliminary estimates of the cut.

Sorting out the state response is just as difficult. Most states spent more on medicaid in fiscal year 1982 than in 1981, and often the increase exceeded the federal cut shown in table 7. Medical care cost increases are crucial in understanding these increases. These increases do not mean the states replaced the federal cuts;

5. The targeted amount for fiscal year 1982 was 109 percent of the 1981 federal payment. The reconciliation act specified that the targets for fiscal years 1983 and 1984 are to be set by the secretary of Health and Human Services and based on the increase in the medical care category of the consumer price index.

state spending would have risen by more than it did without the 1982 changes.

Though estimates of the cuts and state responses in medicaid are of necessity imprecise, it is possible to group states into categories that illustrate types of responses. In some states, such as Illinois, Massachusetts, Missouri, Ohio, and Texas, the caseload cuts caused by the AFDC changes were large, the recession did not dramatically increase the caseload, and cost containment had some impact. In those states, spending, according to our analyses, was below what it would have been without the reconciliation act.

Four states (Oklahoma, Florida, California, and South Dakota) appear to have increased their spending in response to federal aid cuts. In Oklahoma and Florida, the federal matching rate dropped both because of changes made in the reconciliation act and because the state's per-capita income increased relative to the national average. In both of these cases, state spending increased to cover the entire drop in federal aid. In California and South Dakota, savings caused by cuts in AFDC caseloads accounted for relatively small percentages of total spending on this program, and were probably exceeded by increases in state spending.

According to the associates' reports, the remaining states spent on medicaid roughly what they would have in the absence of the reconciliation act. They saved money because of the drop in the number of recipients resulting from AFDC cuts, but the savings were approximately balanced out by the legislated drop in the federal matching rate.

The changes in medicaid also provided the states with new authority to operate the program more efficiently. Most states made changes in the administration of the medicaid program. One notable example of the types of administrative changes made in 1982 was California's new system for negotiations with hospitals leading to contracts for the services provided to medicaid recipients. Each contract specifies the daily rate the hospital will charge to treat a medicaid patient. Once this system is operating, recipients will have to go to a participating facility and choose a doctor or clinic from among those participating in the program.

Food Stamps

The reconciliation act attempted to lower food stamp costs in much the same way as it limited AFDC spending, by tightening eligibility for those with other incomes and by imposing new administrative requirements. The act made the following key changes:

1. Imposed an income ceiling of 130 percent of the federally defined poverty level.

2. Cut the proportion of an applicant's earnings that is disregarded in calculating eligibility and benefits from 20 percent to 18 percent.

3. Required that all people living together in the same household apply as a single unit regardless of whether they prepare or purchase food together.

4. Reduced or delayed increases that otherwise would have been made in food stamp benefits due to increases in the cost of living. These changes accounted for about half the savings in food stamps in fiscal year 1982 attributable to the 1981 reconciliation act.

Though food stamp cuts were large in most states, their importance is a function of the size of the program rather than large percentage cuts; only five states had cuts of 10 percent or more. The food stamp program operates with the same eligibility rules and benefit levels in all states; differences in the cuts realized reflect differences in the characteristics of a state's population. States with a high proportion of working recipients were hardest hit.

In addition, the way the AFDC cuts were made also affected the food stamp program. AFDC recipients are automatically eligible for food stamps. The relationship between the two programs was found to have affected the impact of the food stamp cuts. Households removed from AFDC by the 1982 changes in many cases had to reapply for food stamps. Many did not do so; this contributed to the decline in the food stamp caseload in a number of the states studied.

States uniformly ratified the cut in the food stamp program; no state increased its own spending to cover the food stamp cuts. In fact, it would have been very hard to figure out a way to do so. The food stamp program is seen by many as a federal program, and properly so. The federal government pays all of the assistance costs and a portion of the administrative costs. Some states may have indirectly replaced a small portion of the food stamp cuts through increases in state-financed general assistance, though the information available suggests that such increases were not large. The greatest response to the food stamp cuts came at the local level, primarily from nonprofit organizations expanding emergency feeding programs, as is discussed in chapter 4.

Child Nutrition

The reconciliation act cut subsidies for school meals and lowered the income eligibility for the most heavily subsidized meals. The associates reported that in all states but Massachusetts, the reduction in spending for school meals brought about by the 1981 reconciliation act was less than 25 percent; in six states it was estimated to be less than 10 percent. This program was among the five with the largest dollar cuts in five of the states. The impact of these cuts, as discussed in chapters 4 and 5, is actually felt at the local level by the school districts that receive the money and the students who receive the meals.

Only Oklahoma increased state spending to replace the federal cut in aid for child nutrition. The result in all states but Oklahoma was an increase in the price per meal paid by needy students and a decrease in the number of subsidized meals served.

Refugee Assistance

A major controversy involving federal entitlement grants arose in several of the sample states because the federal government limited the length of time refugees would be eligible for a special federally financed assistance program. The program reimburses states for the full costs of AFDC, social services, and medicaid provided to refugees. Refugees are not required to satisfy the normal eligibility requirements; if they satisfy income tests, they are eligible for services because of their refugee status.

Until 1982 this aid was provided for up to thirty-six months. In an effort to cut program costs, the federal Department of Health and Human Services issued a regulation in 1982 limiting this aid to eighteen months. The regulation offered states the option of receiving federal reimbursement for a second eighteen months if they provided aid to refugees under a state general assistance program. Since general assistance benefit levels are normally much lower than AFDC, federal costs were cut.

These changes had their greatest effect in the states with large numbers of refugees and no general assistance program. Washington, with Indochinese refugees, and Florida, with Caribbean refugees, are in this category, and they confronted difficult problems. Refugees were cut off from assistance, job training, and medical and social services at a time of high and rising unemployment. Local governments attempted to provide emergency food, shelter, and services, as discussed in chapter 4, but many refugees received no assistance. Government officials in the affected states protested what they saw as an abdication of federal responsibility.

In the aftermath of these protests, Congress in March 1982 enacted a special program of discretionary grants for aid to new entrants. This aid could be used for health, employment, and social services, but not for cash assistance. It could only be used to help recent arrivals cut off as a result of the eighteen-month rule and not the general refugee population. Florida received nearly all of this money because of the concentration of new refugees there, the state's lack of a general relief program that would qualify for the regular federal refugee assistance, and the social problems of refugees in that state. This grant partly, but not fully, reimbursed state and local governments for services to refugees.

Trade Adjustment Assistance

This federal entitlement grant program provides cash assistance, job training, job-search assistance, and relocation expenses to workers who lose jobs in industries unable to meet foreign competition. The reconciliation act tightened eligibility for the program by requiring more proof that foreign competition was the cause of unemployment, restricted cash assistance to the period after unemployment compensation benefits were exhausted, and shifted the focus of the program to encouraging the search for new employment. Program outlays nationwide were cut by more than 80 percent.

In most states in the sample, few workers were affected and the decline in federal aid was negligible. The changes were important in Arizona, New Jersey, and New York among the sample states. Arizona copper mines have faced stiff foreign competition, and its miners were receiving trade adjustment assistance. In New Jersey, auto workers lost benefits, while in New York, auto, clothing, and toy manufacturers were the key industries affected.

No state moved to replace lost trade adjustment benefits, and the cuts were ratified. The New York associates reported that the program was seen as unfair because it supported one type of unemployed worker at a fairly high level of income while others were not assisted or received much less support.

Table 8. *New or Changed Block Grants in 1981 Reconciliation Act*

Grant	Number of programs consolidated	Final FY 1982 budget authority (millions of dollars)
Social services	3	2,400
Low-income energy assistance	1	1,875
Small-cities community development	1	1,037
Elementary and secondary education	29	470
Alcohol, drug abuse, and mental health	3	432
Maternal and child health	7	348
Community services	1	348
Primary health care	1	248
Preventive health and health services	8	82
Total for nine block grants	54	7,240

Block Grants

A major purpose of block grants is to remove the restrictions imposed under categorical grants, giving states and local governments more control over the use of federal aid funds. The reconciliation act created seven new block grants and modified two existing block grant programs. Table 8 shows the number of programs consolidated and 1982 funding for each.

The greatest effect of these changes was in the health field, where the reconciliation act combined twenty-one categorical grants into four block grants for:

1. *Alcohol, drug abuse, and mental health,* which supports community mental health centers and alcoholism and drug abuse treatment and prevention programs;
2. *Maternal and child health,* which finances programs for crippled children, genetic testing, counseling and family planning, and lead-paint poisoning prevention;
3. *Preventive health,* which combined existing programs for rodent control, hypertension control, emergency medical services, and health education, and added a new initiative in rape prevention, and

4. *Primary care*, which finances community health centers.

In addition to these health programs, the act created three other block grants.

1. The *community services block grant* abolished the Community Services Administration, and replaced the previous program of direct grants to local community action agencies with block grants to the states.

2. The *elementary and secondary education block grant* combined twenty-nine small programs into one block grant going to the states.

3. The *community development block grant* was modified to give states the option of taking over administration of the small-cities portion of the program, leaving the existing federal-local program unchanged for large jurisdictions.

The two existing block grants affected by the 1981 reconciliation act were the social services block grant and the low-income energy assistance block grant. The act made relatively minor changes in administrative and program requirements in these programs. In each, the states already administered the program, and the funding cuts were the most important changes made in 1982.

The new block grants established in the 1981 reconciliation act were implemented at differing rates. The alcoholism, drug abuse, and mental health program, the maternal and child health program, and the preventive health block grant program were assumed by most states early in fiscal year 1982. All states had already assumed administration of the social services and low-income energy assistance program; most assumed the new community services block grant program. None of the sample states began administration of the small-cities community development program at the beginning of the fiscal year because of delays in the issuing of the federal regulations. Ten of the sample states picked up this block grant during fiscal year 1982. The education block grant began in July 1982, with most states assuming administration during fiscal 1983. None of the sample states assumed the primary care block grant because of the continuing regulatory role of the federal government under this program and the lack of federal cost-sharing for state administrative expenses. In addition, a 1982 court order called into question the federal application process for the program.

The sections that follow describe what was cut for each block grant program affected by the reconciliation act and explain how the states in the sample responded. Table 9 shows the approximate size of the cut for each of the block grant programs described in these sections.[6]

Health Block Grants

Cuts in funding for the health block grants averaged between 20 and 35 percent nationwide. Under the alcohol, drug abuse, and mental health program, associates in half the states reported funding cuts of 25 percent or more. Under the maternal and child health program four states experienced cuts of 25 percent or more; and under the preventive health block grant program five states had such cuts; nearly all the remaining states had cuts of more than 10 percent under these programs. (This section does not discuss the primary care block grant because it was not in operation during fiscal year 1982.)

The full effects of these funding cuts tended not to be felt during fiscal year 1982, because most health block grant programs had a cushion of carryover funding. Carryovers often occurred in the health programs because previous project grants operated on a different fiscal-year basis from the new block grants.

In nearly every state in the sample, carryover funding was available in at least one of the health block grants. The effects of cuts in the alcohol, drug abuse, and mental health block grant—which had the largest percentage cut of the health block grants—were cushioned in eleven of the fourteen states. As an extreme example, Florida and Arizona had carryover funding about four times as great as the 1982 cut in this program. In Missouri, funding carryovers amounted to slightly more than the 1982 cut, and in seven states they were nearly equal to the cut. In the preventive health block grant, carryovers exceeded the cuts in three states, equaled the cuts in four others, and partly made up for the cuts in another four states. The maternal and child health pro-

6. As the table shows, the extent of funding changes varied widely from state to state for these programs. Rather than being clustered around the average of the overall nationwide cut for a particular program, states range from deep percentage cuts to funding increases. This variation occurred because the categorical programs incorporated into the new block grants had made grants covering varying periods. Some grants covered one year, others shorter or longer periods. This means the annual allocations of funds vary from year to year, so comparisons of the 1981 allocation with 1982 do not necessarily yield the national percentage change. Furthermore, some of the new block grants did not allocate 1982 funds based on the states' 1981 share of funds under the programs consolidated. Other distribution factors were used, such as population, low-income population, and school-age population.

Table 9. *Block Grants: Estimated Change in Federal Aid,*
by State, Fiscal Year 1982

HEALTH BLOCK GRANTS

Alcohol, drug abuse, and
mental health
Reduced 25% to 49%
Massachusetts ($7 million)
Mississippi ($3.7 million)
Missouri ($2.1 million)
New York ($21 million)
Ohio ($11 million)
Oklahoma ($2.8 million)
South Dakota ($1.3 million)
Reduced 10% to 24%
Arizona ($1.7 million)
California ($7-9 million)
Florida ($3 million)
Illinois ($1.8 million)
New Jersey ($4 million)
Washington ($1.1 million)
Level funding
Texas[a]

Maternal and child health
Reduced 25% to 49%
Arizona ($860,000)
Florida ($1.3 million)
Illinois ($4.4 million)
Mississippi ($1.8 million)
Reduced 10% to 24%
California ($3.8 million)
Massachusetts ($1.4 million)
Missouri ($1.2 million)
New Jersey ($2 million)
New York ($5 million)
Ohio ($2.1 million)
South Dakota ($200,000)
Texas ($2.7 million)
Washington ($1.1 million)
Reduced less than 10%
Oklahoma ($150,000)

Preventive health
Reduced 50% or more
Oklahoma ($500,000)
Reduced 25% to 49%
Arizona ($400,000)
Florida ($2.2 million)
Massachusetts ($800,000)
Ohio ($2 million)

Reduced 10% to 24%
California ($636,000)
Illinois ($200,000)
Missouri ($300,000)
New Jersey ($500,000)
New York ($1 million)
South Dakota ($50,000)
Texas ($540,000)
Washington ($1.1 million)
Reduced less than 10%
Mississippi ($400,000)

OTHER BLOCK GRANTS

Social services
Reduced 10% to 24%
Arizona ($3.7 million)
California ($58.2 million)
Florida ($16.8 million)
Illinois ($30 million)
Massachusetts ($19 million)
Missouri ($14 million)
New Jersey ($19 million)
New York ($59 million)
Ohio ($10.5 million)
Oklahoma ($7.2 million)
South Dakota ($1.9 million)
Texas ($17 million)
Washington ($20 million)
Increased funding
Mississippi ($207,000)

Community development—
small cities
Increased funding
Arizona ($714,000)
California ($1.4 million)[b]
Florida ($2 million)[b]
Illinois ($1.3 million)
Massachusetts ($4 million)
Mississippi ($3.6 million)
Missouri ($2.7 million)
New Jersey ($1.3 million)
New York ($1.8 million)[b]
Ohio ($4.7 million)
Oklahoma ($2 million)
South Dakota ($940,000)
Texas ($7.3 million)[b]

Table 9, continued

Washington ($260,000)

Community services
Reduced 50% or more
Arizona ($7.5 million)
California ($33.8 million)[c]
South Dakota ($900,000)

Reduced 25% to 49%
Florida ($3.3 million)
New Jersey ($4.3 million)

Reduced 10% to 24%
Illinois ($3 million)
Massachusetts ($900,000)
Mississippi ($1.2 million)
Missouri ($1.6 million)
Ohio ($3.1 million)
Oklahoma ($700,000)
Washington ($3 million)

Reduced less than 10%
New York ($3 million)[b]

No significant change
Texas[b]

Education
Reduced 50% or more
Arizona ($5 million)
Mississippi ($6 million)

Reduced 25% to 49%
Florida ($6.4 million)
New York ($23 million)

Reduced 10% to 24%
California ($13 million)

Illinois ($5.3 million)
New Jersey ($2.9 million)
Ohio ($6 million)
Texas ($3.9 million)

Reduced less than 10%
Washington ($5 million)

Increased funding
Massachusetts ($400,000)
Oklahoma ($1.4 million)
South Dakota ($850,000)

No significant change
Missouri

Low-income energy assistance
Reduced less than 10%
Massachusetts ($1.4 million)
Oklahoma ($900,000)

Increased funding
Arizona ($890,000)
California ($5 million)
Illinois ($4.4 million)
Mississippi ($350,000)
Missouri ($7 million)
New Jersey ($4.4 million)
New York ($5.7 million)
Ohio ($5 million)
South Dakota ($3.5 million)[a]
Texas ($2.6 million)
Washington ($5.6 million)

No significant change
Florida

a. Includes carryover.
b. State did not assume administration of the program.
c. California received an unusually large grant in fiscal year 1981, thus distorting the percentage change and dollar cut.

gram had small carryovers in seven states.

All states with carryover funding used the money to protect service levels. Most states with small carryover funding chose to commit it all to 1982 services. Some states with larger amounts of carryover funds developed a multiyear plan that allowed service providers to adjust gradually to the cuts. In California, for example, the state took over the maternal and child health block grant while previous categorical programs were still providing funds. This overlap resulted in a one-time $3.2 million windfall, even as the shift to the block grant reduced the annual funding allocation from about $21 million under the categorical grants to $17 million. The state chose to allocate $1.5 million of the $3.2 million windfall to services to be provided in state fiscal year 1982 and the rest in fiscal year 1984. The full effects of the 1982 cuts will not be felt until nearly two years after they were made. By that time, the state will no longer have a cushion to ease the effects of the cuts, and will be forced either to reduce services or to find alternative sources of funding.

Some states replaced a part of the federal aid cuts under the block grants with increases in their own spending covering a small part of the cuts made. Massachusetts, Illinois, and Mississippi replaced a small part of the cuts in the alcohol, drug abuse, and mental health program, but all other states ratified them to the extent that carryover funding was not available. In preventive health, Florida fully replaced the federal cuts while Arizona slightly increased state spending. Four states—Massachusetts, New York, Oklahoma, and Florida—increased state spending on maternal and child health programs, but Missouri and Texas cut state spending, compounding these federal cuts.

The impact of the funding reductions in block grants on the actual provision of services varied from program to program.[7] In the alcohol, drug abuse, and mental health and preventive health programs, carryover funds protected service levels in many states, but cuts did occur. The evidence available so far suggests that the program components hit hardest by the adjustments made in response to spending cuts under the block grants were health outreach, health education, and other services that have a long-run payoff though little short-term impact. In the maternal and child health program, carryovers were not large, and service cuts were

---

7. This subject will be discussed in detail in a forthcoming health policy report, so it is discussed only briefly here.

most important and clearly manifest. In some states, such as Florida, income eligibility requirements were tightened; the range of available maternal health services was cut in a number of states.

Social Services Block Grant

This program provides funds to states for a variety of social services primarily for the poor. Services include child daycare, counseling, protective services for children and adults, and homemaker services. Most of these programs had previously been funded under title XX of the Social Security Act. The reconciliation act reduced funding and ended the requirement that states provide 25 percent matching funds.

Most states experienced relatively large funding cuts under the social services block grant. The lone exception, Mississippi, had a slight increase in funding. Social services cuts were among the largest in dollar terms for the block grants in nearly every state.

Four states increased state spending on social services. In Massachusetts, spending rose more than the federal cut; increased spending on social services was an important state priority due to criticism of the state's social service delivery system by advocates for children and the aged and by service providers. In Arizona, state spending rose slightly with funds earmarked for child protective services. In New Jersey, the legislature and the governor agreed on a $6 million increase in state spending to cover about one-third of the federal cut. In New York, state spending on social services rose because New York City increased its social service spending beyond the expected level, forcing the state to increase its spending to provide the required state match for the local spending. State spending on social services dropped slightly in Oklahoma and California. The California cut must be viewed in context. The state has been providing money from its own sources to support local social services in an amount equal to nearly 60 percent of the federal aid it has received. Since 1981, the state has continued to allocate substantial amounts of its own funds for these services despite the elimination of the federal matching requirement.

Social services also benefited from the transfer of funds from other federal and state programs. Six states shifted funds to social services from the low-income energy assistance block grant. California shifted funds into the social services program to cover about 15 percent of its large ($58 million) cut. In Florida, shifts covered about the same proportion of the cut, and the state used a small reserve fund to help maintain services. Missouri covered about one-fourth of the cut with fund transfers, New Jersey about one-third, and New York about 40 percent.

Despite the replacement and shifting of funds, the cuts under the social services block grant in most states were still substantial and services were affected. Daycare services frequently were cut; associates reported cuts for this service in Massachusetts, New York, Texas, and South Dakota. Outreach, advisory services, and preventive programs also were cut in several states.[8]

Small-Cities Community Development Block Grant

Until the reconciliation act took effect in fiscal year 1982, the U.S. Department of Housing and Urban Development (HUD) administered the small-cities portion of the community development block grant (CDBG) program directly. The department made discretionary grants to cities that had less than 50,000 population or that were outside large metropolitan areas. The reconciliation act gave states the option of administering the small-cities portion of the CDBG, with wide discretion in how to distribute these funds.[9] HUD continues to provide community development block grants directly to large cities and urban counties on a formula basis.

All of the states in the sample, except for California, New York, Florida, and Texas assumed administration of the small-cities block grant during federal fiscal year 1982. However, federal regulations for the program were not issued in final form until halfway through the federal fiscal year, delaying start-up.

The reconciliation act increased the proportion of federal funds earmarked for the small-city portion of the CDBG program from 25 to 30 percent at the same time reducing the amount allocated for the entitlement portion of the program, which provides federal funds to larger jurisdictions. All the states in the sample received an increase in the total statewide allocation for the small-city portion of CDBG. Most states distributed these small-city funds on a discretionary basis, reviewing applications for grants from local governments and awarding funds according to the state's assess-

8. A later report on the impact of the 1982 federal aid cuts on families and children will provide more detailed information on these service impacts.

9. The significance of this expansion in the states' roles will be studied in later rounds of this research project, along with other institutional changes brought about by the new block grants.

ment of the relative need of the community and the merit of the project or projects described in its application. Ohio stands out in the sample since it chose to administer small-city CDBG funds on a formula basis to all eligible localities. The state's formula distributed funds to 220 cities; allocations were based on population, income, and employment characteristics. Many states earmarked a portion of their small-city funds for communities with special needs.

Community development block grant funds for small cities are used for housing, public works, and economic development projects. Though most states have not yet put their stamp on the program because of the delay in issuance of federal regulations and the requirement that multiyear commitments by the Department of Housing and Urban Development be honored, some associates noted changes in the program mix. Several associates reported instances where states gave priority to grants for economic development projects as opposed to housing, which had been a HUD priority. The associate for Ohio reported,

The state's emphasis is on activities related to economic development. Downtown redevelopment is an example. Housing is expected to receive less emphasis. This priority reflects the policy of Governor Rhodes's administration that this is the most effective way to reduce unemployment.

The field associates for Arizona and South Dakota reported that their state government emphasized public works projects, particularly water and sewer facilities.

In addition to the uses of small-cities block grant funds, a major issue for this research involves their distribution, specifically the extent to which state governments spread these funds out in a way that reduces the degree to which they were targeted on distressed jurisdictions under HUD administration. Even during the first year, associates indicated that state administration had produced a wider geographic distribution of these funds. A number of states set minimum and maximum levels on individual grants and funded projects of one year's duration. Both types of changes facilitate the wider distribution of this federal aid.

Community Services Block Grant

This block grant is for community-based programs that provide health, nutrition, housing, employment, and other services to low-income persons. Many of the community action agencies that administer these funds date back to Lyndon Johnson's "war on poverty," initiated in the mid-1960s. Prior to fiscal year 1982, funds for community action agencies were provided by the Community Services Administration. The reconciliation act reduced the funding for these services and assigned control of the distribution of these funds to the states.

Associates in Arizona, California, and South Dakota reported the greatest cuts, over 50 percent, although most cuts were under 25 percent.[10] Only Oklahoma replaced any of the community services cut. In Ohio, Oklahoma, and Massachusetts, carryover funds partly cushioned the impact of this cut, but in most states its impact on service was immediate.

The shift to state administration is likely to bring long-run changes. Some states have already adopted fund allocation systems that shift community service dollars out of big cities. This happened in Illinois, Massachusetts, Missouri, New York, and Ohio. Most community action agencies in big cities that in the past had looked to Washington for funding had been inactive in state politics. This lack of state political ties helps to explain the shift in funding under this program and the fact that the states have not replaced federal cuts.

Several associates reported that state administration may also affect the services provided by community action agencies. In Massachusetts, the emphasis under state administration has shifted away from community organizing and advocacy to direct service provision for social services and energy conservation. A similar new emphasis on services was found in South Dakota and California. In Missouri, the governor urged community action agencies to spend more money on prevention of child abuse. For community action agencies in most states, the cuts led to major reductions in funding, cuts in staff, a need to build new political relationships, and changed program directions.

Elementary and Secondary Education Block Grant

This block grant program consolidated twenty-nine small programs into one block grant with funds distributed on the basis of school-age population. The size of a state's cut depended on previous participation in the categorical programs, especially the programs providing aid for districts implementing school desegregation plans. Cuts ranged from over 50 percent in Arizona and Mississippi to less than 10 percent in Washington. Massachu-

10. Some states, for example California, got unusually large allocations in 1981, leading to unusually large cuts.

setts, Oklahoma, and South Dakota had increases.

All states ratified the cut. The most important program effects of these changes occurred at the level of local school districts and are discussed in chapters 4 and 5.

Low-Income Energy Assistance Block Grant

Under this program, set up in 1980 during a period of sharp rises in the cost of home heating fuel, states make grants to households and public housing projects to help them meet their fuel expenses. The reconciliation act eased restrictions on a state's distribution of these funds, and slightly increased appropriations for the programs.

Associates reported small cuts for Oklahoma and Massachusetts and little significant change in funding for Florida. All the other states received an increase in funding compared to the previous year. Only Arizona and Washington experienced substantial cuts. There was considerable uncertainty about the funding level for this program over the year; several associates mentioned late allocations and delays in getting funds.

The only state to increase spending on energy assistance was Massachusetts. Many of the sample states took advantage of the new authority allowing fund transfers out of this program to other federally aided programs. They shifted funds to other programs with bigger cuts, especially the social services block grant and the energy conservation (weatherization) program. Associates from several states also reported that in 1981 their states had problems distributing all their available fuel assistance funds to eligible households, because of the late fund allocations, difficulties in publicizing the program, and low levels of application by persons eligible to apply. The shifts of funds out of this program in 1982 undoubtedly indicated that state officials regarded other programs as having a higher priority.

Institutional Changes Related to Block Grants

The new block grants created in 1981 confronted states with a politically difficult task—deciding how to allocate reductions. The previous categorical programs had funded governmental and nonprofit agencies that had a strong political stake in continuing their operations.

Understandably, state officials in most states put off making any decisions as long as possible. One way to do this was to use carryover funds to ease the impact of the transition to reduced funding levels. In the meantime, the states established various types of advisory committees and task forces to work out policies and procedures for administering block grant programs in future years. These groups were seen as a means to "educate" the agencies that had been providing services and other interest groups on the "hard choices" that would have to be made. The task forces also co-opted these agencies and interest groups by giving them a share of the responsibility for making these choices.

California is a good example of a state that used this delay and consultation strategy. A more unusual approach was that of Missouri, which moved quickly to set new spending priorities and administrative arrangements. The following capsules describe these two cases.

Block Grants in California

Block grants were not a priority issue in California during fiscal year 1982 because the governor and the legislature were preoccupied with the problem of how to stretch shrinking state revenues to cover expenditures. The amount of funding cuts involved in federal block grants was dwarfed by the state's own revenue reductions brought about by the recession and by the effects of citizen initiatives that limited tax increases.

Into the leadership vacuum left by the governor and the legislature stepped a coalition of organizations representing the people served by the currently funded programs. The coalition was formed after a handful of well-informed activists and state lobbyists began to publicize the likely effects of the new federal block grant policy. This coalition sought to protect currently funded programs from radical program changes. The coalition also hoped to make changes in a way that would provide a channel for constituent participation. A few members of the state legislature actively supported the coalition, most notably the chairman of the Assembly Ways and Means Committee, who introduced bills on behalf of the coalition. As a result of the coalition's efforts, a task force was formed in January 1982 to advise the governor and legislature on block grant issues.

Gov. Jerry Brown, a Democrat, and the Democratic-controlled legislature allowed the task force to take the lead on block grant issues, and further distanced themselves from the issues by delaying assumption of the block grants as long as possible, so that the federal government would continue to operate the programs and bear the brunt of any criticism of cuts.

The California block grant task force became the communication center on block grant issues. The appointment of a new state secretary of Health and Welfare in February 1982 also gave focus to the block grant issue, since the secretary was interested in helping to coordinate and develop state block grant policy. In spring 1982, the task force presented its recommendations, which included:

• Making pro-rata reductions to existing, eligible programs;

• Making no transfers between block grants in state fiscal year 1982–83;

- Making no replacement of federal money with general funds; and
- Imposing administrative cost caps on both state and local agencies.

This conservative approach gave state agencies a transition period in which to integrate block grant programs and procedures into existing systems. It also provided nonprofit agencies and county governments time to evaluate how funding cuts would affect their programs and to secure program support for the next budget year.

The mandate of the task force was extended until July 1984 and its responsibilities were expanded. The task force was directed to continue to prepare block grant policy recommendations for the legislature. Block grants were expected to generate more interest in state fiscal year 1982–83. The California associate anticipated that the administration of block grants might begin to be changed in 1983–84, especially if the state fiscal base continued to erode.

Block Grants in Missouri

Missouri's reaction to the federal block grant program was not like the hesitant California response. By the end of the first year of the block grants Missouri had made substantial changes to reorient its administration of block grant programs.

Missouri shared two problems experienced by California during this period. One was extreme fiscal stress, which meant that federal funding reductions were overshadowed by funding cutbacks at the state level. The other was a legal constraint on spending. A 1980 amendment to the state constitution limited increases in state spending to the rate of increase in personal income. In January 1983 the Missouri Supreme Court ruled that the state had exceeded this limit in fiscal year 1982 and ordered the state to return funds to taxpayers.

Despite these problems, at the initiative of the governor, who supported the shift to block grants, state officials devoted considerable attention to developing state block grant policy. The effort to develop a coherent policy was most apparent in the health block grants. The director of social services, working closely with the governor, scheduled hearings with citizen representatives and health care providers to discuss state block grant policy. Advisory committees composed of representatives from "service" providers and the state Division of Health made policy recommendations to the legislative oversight committee on block grants. The Division of Health used the opportunity offered by the administrative changes in block grant programs to set new priorities, shifting resources to small towns and rural counties that lacked public health programs. This shift took funds away from programs serving low-income, predominantly black populations in Kansas City and St. Louis.

State health officials drew up plans to take federalism one step further by shifting responsibility for health programs to the county level. The state implemented a plan to do away with state rules targeting preventive services to certain population groups, giving counties discretion to provide preventive services as they chose as long as minimum standards were met. The state health division wanted to go even further, ending all categorically funded health programs and channeling all funding through counties. The

Division of Health ran into opposition on this plan, particularly from the state legislative oversight committee on block grants, which wanted to retain some control over the allocation of the maternal and child health block grant.

Despite the effort to increase county involvement and discretion with block grant funds, some of the money was also used to fund state health division positions that had been lost because of state revenue shortfalls.

Allocation Decisions Related to Block Grants

As indicated, most states put off making decisions about allocating block grant funds by using carryover funds and by setting up task forces to give advice on future policies. Another reason allocational changes were slow to emerge is that the reconciliation act constrained states' ability to make changes in allocations in some block grant programs. These constraints reflected hard-won victories at the national level for supporters of a particular program component or type of service organization. For example, under the alcohol, drug abuse, and mental health block grant, Congress mandated that states continue grants to all community mental health centers that had received operating grants in 1981. In the community services block grant, 90 percent of the funds were earmarked for existing community action agencies.[11]

Under two block grant programs, however, most states moved relatively quickly to make allocation decisions. In the community services block grant, states had to allocate major funding cuts and had the flexibility to act because most community action agencies lacked significant political clout at the state level. Under the elementary and secondary education block grant, local school districts pressed state officials for the detailed financial information they needed to draw up budgets for the coming school year, creating political pressure on state officials to decide quickly on the allocation of these funds. The following capsules describe state actions on these two programs.

---

11. This 90 percent requirement does not apply to individual community action agencies. It applies to all the community action agencies that had received federal funds in the previous year as a group. This left considerable room for discretion on the part of state officials.

Allocating Community Services Block Grant Cuts

Because community service funds go to organizations providing services to low-income people, the number of such people in a jurisdiction was almost always one of the allocation formula factors used by the states. In many states, however, community action agencies in large cities had been receiving a higher percentage of funds than their city's proportion of the state's poverty population. This occurred partly because larger professional staffs enabled big-city community action agencies to become more successful in grantsmanship and partly because of the political power of the big cities in Washington. When the new block grant changed the distribution system, community action agencies in smaller cities and towns sought to change fund allocations at the expense of big cities. Many states shifted to distribution formulas that gave heavy weight to the poverty count, and as a result big-city community action agencies lost funding.

Some states set aside part of the 1982 grant for a one-year transitional grant to the largest community action agencies; Massachusetts used some carryover money for this purpose. Despite these adjustments, the impacts were substantial. The Chicago community action agency's share of state community service funds, for example, went from 70 percent in 1981 to 55 percent in 1982 and 40 percent in 1983. Boston's community action agency will lose $1 million once the $500,000 transition grant ends.

Some states postponed decisions. New York and California waited until October 1982 to assume the block grant, and New Jersey passed through all cuts in a pro-rata fashion for 1982.

Education Block Grant Distribution Formulas

Different school districts participated to widely varying degrees in the programs that were merged into the education block grant, of which all but four were discretionary project grants. Districts that were implementing school desegregation plans had particularly benefited from several programs that had operated under the Emergency School Aid Act, all of which were merged into the block grant.

Because of such past differences, the introduction of this block grant program set the stage for a struggle in many states over how the state would distribute these funds among school districts.

The states in the sample made very different decisions that reflected different views on the purposes of this federal aid for education. Some states saw it as compensatory aid for poor districts or disadvantaged students while others chose to use the funds for general support for education. Those taking the first approach used various poverty-weighting factors in the distribution formula, while those adopting the second approach came closer to spreading funds evenly according to the number of students in a school district.

Many of the states in the sample adopted formulas that mixed the two approaches. In Massachusetts, the new formula distributes 40 percent of the funds based on enrollment and 60 percent based on the number of students from AFDC families. In New York, the state chose to use a formula similar to the normal state educational aid formula, which provides pupil aid in inverse proportion to a district's wealth per pupil, with high-cost pupils given a higher weight. In Washington, the new formula weights enrollment (50 percent), number of students in racially isolated schools (10 percent), community income (15 percent), number of bilingual students (5 percent), number of minority students (10 percent), and number of high-achieving students (5 percent). Mississippi gives $7.60 per student, with 5 percent of the program funds going to school districts with a high percentage of high-cost students. Florida divided the funds based on program cost factors and the cost of living in each district.

Other Operating Grants

Many of the important changes in operating grants made in 1981 were brought about as a result of the changes just described in the block grants. However, other changes were made in federal grants for operating programs. The most significant changes were in the employment and training field. Deep cuts were made in funding under the Comprehensive Employment and Training Act (CETA). State employment services were also hit with large cuts; however, these cuts were in substantial measure restored later in the fiscal year.

Funds under the CETA program were distributed by the U.S. Department of Labor to "prime sponsors." A prime sponsor could be a state or local government, a regional organization, or in some cases a nonprofit organization. Most prime sponsors were responsible for a particular geographical area, such as a city, a county, or a multicounty area; in most states the prime sponsor for the "balance of state" (typically a state government) covered those portions of the state not covered by any other prime sponsor. The prime sponsor allocated CETA funds to agencies or nonprofit organizations that provided services.

Congress eliminated the public service employment portion of CETA in 1981 and significantly reduced the remaining spending for training programs and labor market assistance. Late in 1981, the CETA program as a whole was abolished, and replaced by a new program, the Job Training Partnership Act. The new act provides funds to state governments (not to local prime sponsors) and is limited to training. This legislation was based heavily on proposals made by the Reagan administration. It went into effect at the beginning of fiscal year 1983. Its effects on the sample governments and its relationship to other parts of the Reagan domestic program will be considered in the continuation of this research.

Public Service Employment

This program, authorized under CETA, began in 1973. It was initially intended to provide work experience in public agencies for disadvantaged persons; a component was later added for aid to workers temporarily unemployed because of a recession. The program underwent many changes, the most significant of them in 1978 when Congress passed restrictions intended to target the entire program more heavily on poor and low-skilled workers. These restrictions made the program much less valuable to state and local governments. These governments were interested in the services they could obtain from the subsidized workers and wanted workers with experience and skills. After the 1978 changes, many state and local governments allocated large proportions of public service workers to nonprofit organizations rather than using them in their own agencies. As a result, by 1981 the program had lost many of its governmental defenders and was vulnerable to the Reagan administration's proposal to eliminate it. It had always been controversial because of allegations that local governments had used subsidized workers improperly for "leaf-raking" jobs, for political purposes, and to substitute for regular employees. At the urging of the Reagan administration, Congress rescinded much of the program's funding early in 1981; the reconciliation act passed in July 1981 did away with the funding that remained.[12]

With the elimination of the CETA public service jobs program, every state lost a large amount of federal aid. Table 10 lists the amount of public service employment funds lost by the state governments in the sample. Federal aid going directly to local governments that acted as prime sponsors is not included in the discussion in this chapter. The cuts at the state level in the CETA public service jobs program shown in table 10 are measured after the 1981 rescissions.

No state made any effort to save the public service employment program by replacing the federal cut or shifting other funds to the aided activities. The program's elimination was felt most by the workers whose jobs ended and by the nonprofit organizations for which many of them worked.

---

12. For background, see Richard P. Nathan, Robert F. Cook, V. Lane Rawlins, and Associates, *Public Service Employment: A Field Evaluation* (Washington, D.C.: The Brookings Institution, 1981).

Table 10. *Other Operating Grants: Estimated Change
in Federal Aid, by State, Fiscal Year 1982*

CETA public service employment[a]	CETA training[a]
	Reduced 50% or more
	New York ($141.8 million)
Program eliminated	Washington ($15 million)
Arizona ($6.7 million)	
California ($14.4 million)	Reduced 25% to 49%
Florida ($10.2 million)	Arizona ($3.2 million)
Illinois ($19.2 million)	California ($16 million)
Massachusetts ($13.4 million)	Florida ($9.4 million)
Mississippi ($15.5 million)	Massachusetts ($10.7 million)
Missouri ($11.5 million)	Mississippi ($9.4 million)
New Jersey ($3.7 million)	New Jersey ($6.3 million)
New York ($101.2 million)	South Dakota ($1.6 million)
Ohio ($20.3 million)	
Oklahoma ($6.2 million)	Reduced 10% to 24%
South Dakota ($2.1 million)	Illinois ($11.7 million)
Texas ($10.1 million)	Missouri ($6.4 million)
Washington ($18 million)	Ohio ($10.6 million)
	Oklahoma ($3.6 million)
	Texas ($7.8 million)

a. Balance-of-state prime sponsor and governor's discretionary grant; 1981 comparison figures are after the rescissions.

CETA Training Programs

The CETA program in 1982 also supported job training for adults and a variety of youth programs, including summer programs. The reconciliation act reduced funds for these activities. Training for adults was cut by 38 percent, year-round youth employment and training by 39 percent, and summer youth employment by 27 percent. Only the Job Corps, providing training for youths in residential centers, and the private-sector initiatives program, designed to encourage involvement of private businesses, were spared; these two components had budget increases.

Two associates reported cuts of more than 50 percent in CETA training programs, seven reported cuts of from 25 to 49 percent, and five reported cuts of 10 to 24 percent. These figures are for the balance of state and the governor's discretionary grant portion of the program, and are calculated after the 1981 rescission. Oklahoma and South Dakota had sufficient carryover funds to maintain services at 1981 levels.

Only three states chose to replace any of these federal cuts by increasing spending or to maintain services by shifting funds: Cal-

ifornia, Massachusetts, and New Jersey set up new training programs or expanded existing efforts. These new state training programs are not exact substitutes for the programs that were cut; they
are open to residents of the entire state, not just those in the
CETA-defined balance-of-state area. Given the unpopularity of
CETA, officials in all three states sought to distinguish their new
training efforts from CETA.

Massachusetts expanded a small existing state training program
in 1982. The Bay State Skills Center was a favorite project of Governor King and of officials in companies in the growing high-technology industry. The center provides training in technical skills
for expanding industries.

New Jersey enacted legislation for an $8 million training pro-
gram for displaced workers and former welfare recipients. Again,
state officials stress that this is not a response to the CETA cuts,
but rather to cuts in federal programs overall and declining economic conditions in the state.

California established a major new training program,
"Investment in People," but funded it by shifting $55 million a
year out of the unemployment insurance trust fund rather than by
increasing state spending. Increases in the payroll tax in 1975
augmented the surpluses in this fund, and state officials decided
that financing training with some of the excess funds would be an
appropriate way to alleviate unemployment in the state. The training is aimed at providing displaced workers and welfare recipients
with marketable skills. Though state officials did not label this initiative as a substitute for lost CETA training funds, it provides
some similar services.

State Employment Services

The state employment services program provides labor market
and job-counseling assistance to unemployed persons. It is federally funded but administered by state governments. Under the
reconciliation act, states experienced cuts in funding of nearly
one-third for employment services, although a supplemental
appropriation reduced the cuts to about 10 percent. Because the
funding restoration came late in the year, many states already had
laid off workers and cut services to stay within the severely
reduced earlier appropriation.

Most of the sampled state governments had laid off significant
numbers of employment service workers as a result of the initial
federal cuts. In Illinois, 500 employment service workers were

laid off. New Jersey dropped 364 people, but managed to keep all of its branch offices open. Mississippi closed sixteen local offices and eliminated 422 employees. New York State planned to lay off about 650 out of 4,000 employees. Florida closed sixteen local employment service offices and cut staffing by more than 25 percent when it closed twelve branch offices.

State officials and employees reacted strongly and vocally to these cuts. New Jersey employment service workers demonstrated at the state capitol in January to protest the cuts. However, the state's primary response to the funding cut was to ratify the layoffs and attempt to raise productivity standards by revising administrative procedures. The Texas associate reported that labor, minority, and state employee groups held large public protests and threatened litigation because of this cut.

Congress, as indicated, eventually restored a substantial amount of employment services funds, allowing many states to rehire workers and reopen offices. For example, the Texas Employment Commission reopened most of the fifty-nine local offices that had been closed, and the state rehired most of the 900 laid-off workers after Congress restored the funds.

The large cuts in the CETA program coupled with funding uncertainty in state employment services led to major reorganizations of some state labor departments. In New Jersey, for example, the state Department of Labor reorganized its bureaus, combining staffs previously providing job-finding services to the general population and those serving disadvantaged groups.

Capital Grants

For most states, reductions in federal grants for capital programs were not among the largest cuts, either in percentage terms or dollar amounts. Cuts in capital grants take longer than others to make themselves felt. What is more, the 1981 reconciliation act made relatively few real and lasting cuts in this area.

The largest capital grant going to states, the federal highway program, experienced a slight increase in budget authority in 1982 as the result of the Federal Highway Aid Act of 1981, passed after the reconciliation act. Later, the Surface Transportation Assistance Act of 1982 raised the federal gasoline tax by five cents per gallon, in part to finance job-creating investments in highways and mass transit facilities. This act raised budget authority in 1983 and beyond.

Each year, in appropriation acts, Congress places a ceiling on the highway program, limiting the amount of contract authority from the current or previous years that can be obligated in that year. The reconciliation act reduced this ceiling for 1982, but this had only the effect of postponing outlays. Some associates reported declines in obligation authority received for 1982 under the federal highway aid program; in five states the fiscal year 1982 cuts in federal highway spending authority that could be used in 1982 were said to be among the largest cuts made (see table 11).

Mass transit capital grants were cut in 1982, although this only affected state governments with statewide transit authorities, including New Jersey. Moreover, this budget cut proved to be short lived. The Surface Transportation Assistance Act of 1982, referred to above, raised budget authority for mass transit aid programs in 1983 and future years.

Two other relatively small capital programs experienced large percentage cuts in funding at the state level in 1982—energy conservation and land and water conservation.

Also affected by the reconciliation act was the Economic Development Administration (EDA), which provides capital grants to support industrial and commercial development, and for economic development planning. Budget authority for EDA was reduced by more than 60 percent from the 1981 level, although actual outlays were not expected to drop significantly for fiscal 1982 because of the delays in spending for EDA construction projects. These are project grants distributed on a competitive basis. Because they fluctuate from year to year, it is difficult to isolate the impact of the 1981 changes in the study period.

Despite the relative stability of funding of federal capital grants compared to operating and entitlement grants, changes (or even the prospect of change) in these programs were very important at the state level in 1982. There was considerable apprehension that future cuts in capital grants to states would occur as the Reagan administration continued its efforts to reduce the federal deficit. Cuts in capital grants going to local governments also drew attention in several of the states in the sample. Moreover, the federal cuts that were made in these programs in 1982 came at a time when many states were seeking ways to finance new infrastructure, both at the state and local levels, in response to growing public concern about collapsing bridges, rutted roads, and inadequate water and sewer systems.

State government responses to the changes in federal capital grant programs varied widely by program. In the highway pro-

Table 11. *Capital Programs: Estimated Change
in Federal Aid, by State, Fiscal Year 1982*

Energy conservation	Federal aid to highways
Reduced 50% or more	*Reduced 10% to 24%*
Arizona ($1.6 million)	Arizona ($14 million)
Florida ($1 million)	Illinois ($60 million)
Massachusetts ($8 million)	Missouri ($33 million)
New York ($12 million)	New York ($73 million)
Oklahoma ($1 million)	
South Dakota ($2 million)	*Reduced less than 10%*
Texas ($6 million)	New Jersey ($15 million)
	South Dakota ($3 million)
Reduced 25% to 49%	
California ($7.6 million)	*Increased funding*
Illinois ($7 million)	Oklahoma ($5 million)
Mississippi ($1.6 million)	Texas ($1 million)
Missouri ($5 million)	
New Jersey ($5 million)	*No significant change*
Ohio ($7 million)	California Mississippi
Washington ($3 million)	Florida Ohio
	Massachusetts Washington

gram, several states increased their own spending commitments for highway construction and maintenance, but in most cases for reasons unrelated to the federal cuts. In Arizona, state spending rose as earmarked revenues from state vehicle taxes increased due to an increase in the tax rate. This increase equaled about two-thirds of the $14 million cut in authorized federal spending for highways in 1982. In New York, additional state spending commitments for highways were approved as part of an overall effort to improve the state's infrastructure. The new funds are for increased state aid to local governments, with an emphasis on urban areas. Texas increased its spending for highways under its highway funding system, whereby a construction index is used to adjust state highway spending automatically.

The most immediate result of the reduction in economic development funds was cuts in planning activities and in the activities of regional development commissions. New York chose to replace lost federal funding for state economic development planning with state funds; Mississippi, Oklahoma, and South Dakota ratified these cuts. The Ozark Regional Commission, serving parts of Missouri and Oklahoma, lost all of its economic development authority funding. The states used some small-cities community development block grant funds and other small federal grants to support the commission in its phase-down period.

Cuts or the threat of cuts in capital grants to local governments also produced state responses. Massachusetts and New York increased aid to local mass transit districts, partly out of a desire to improve services and partly from the concern that federal support would decline.[13] New York and Massachusetts both operate large state housing assistance programs; they increased spending in the face of cuts in capital grants and mortgage assistance under federal housing programs.

The wastewater treatment program is a special intergovernmental fiscal arrangement. The program provides grants to local governments for the planning, design, and construction of facilities, but there is a statewide annual ceiling on grant awards, and the state must approve all proposals for local project funding. In many states, the state government plays an active role under this program and covers a portion of the cost of federally aided projects. When the reconciliation act eliminated the grants to localities for planning and design and reduced the portion of a project the federal government would fund after 1984, several states reacted. Massachusetts set up a new program to pay for the planning and design of projects, providing grants to local governments that would be repaid if they received construction grants from the federal government. Florida did not replace the federal cut, but received approval from the federal Environmental Protection Agency to spread the federal funds to more projects by lowering the federal matching percentage for each individual project and increasing the portion local governments must pay. The Oklahoma associate reported that state officials were considering increasing state aid to local governments.

New Jersey is considering a new program proposed by Gov. Thomas Kean for financing wastewater treatment and other capital needs through an "infrastructure bank." The bank would be capitalized by several sources, including federal wastewater treatment grants, and would provide low-interest loans to communities seeking financing for major construction projects. Loan repayments, raised largely through user fees, would be reused for other projects. Before the bank can be set up, the federal Clean Water Act

13. New Jersey operates a statewide transit system; state mass transit subsidies increased, reflecting higher costs and reduced federal aid.

must be amended to allow the use of wastewater treatment grants as loans. The governor cites growing capital needs and cuts in federal capital programs in arguing for this proposal.

Summary by Types of State Responses

As discussed in chapter 2, government responses to a federal aid cut can range from replacing the cut to compounding it. This section, by way of summary, discusses the most common responses found for the sample governments. The responses are basically of three types: (1) replacement with general revenue or earmarked taxes; (2) various delaying and shifting tactics that continue the federally aided services from existing revenue, either on a temporary or long-term basis; and (3) ratification of the cuts, either by simply passing through the federal aid reduction or by compounding the cut. Ratification in matching grant entitlement programs can result in state savings as well. Compounding is defined as a conscious, discrete state or local decision to reduce spending on federally aided programs or activities by an amount greater than the federal aid cut, hence reducing the level of state and local funds devoted to this service at the same time federal aid is cut.[14]

Table 12 summarizes state responses by focusing on the net effect of the 1982 federal aid cuts. It groups the states by the extent to which their overall spending on federal programs that were cut in fiscal year 1982 either increased or, in some cases, decreased, compared with the level that would have occurred without the 1982 cuts.

Though most states replaced at least some cuts, the states in the sample can be divided into three groups. In some, spending on the affected programs increased by 10 percent or more of the total amount of the cuts; these states are shown as "highest net replacement" states. Other states are shown as making "some net replacement" (net replacement of less than 10 percent of the amount cut). The final group of states consists of those states that replaced none or few of the cuts and realized net savings of state funds as a result of other federal aid reductions. These states are shown as having net savings as a result of the 1982 federal aid cuts.

The net percentage replacement and savings figures associated with the ratings shown here are presented as ranges. Greater pre-

---

14. These three groups subsume the seven response categories discussed in chapter 2. We did not find important examples of user fees being increased to offset federal aid cuts at the state level.

Table 12. Net Fiscal Effect of 1982 Federal Aid Cuts

State	Programs in which cuts were partially or fully replaced	Federally aided programs in which state spending declined[a]
Highest Net Replacement (10% to 25%)		
Oklahoma[b]	Child nutrition Community services Maternal and child health block grant Medicaid	Aid to families with dependent children Low-income energy assistance Social services block grant
New York	Aid to families with dependent children Assisted housing Economic development Highways	Food stamps outreach
	Mass transit Maternal and child health block grant Social services block grant	
Massachusetts	Alcohol, drug abuse, and mental health block grant Assisted housing Education block grant Land and water conservation Low-income energy assistance Mass transit	Aid to families with dependent children Child nutrition Medicaid
	Maternal and child health block grant Primary care block grant Training Social services block grant Wastewater treatment	

Table 12, continued

State	Programs in which cuts were partially or fully replaced	Federally aided programs in which state spending declined[a]
Some Net Replacement (Less than 10%)		
New Jersey	Mass transit Social services block grant	Aid to families with dependent children
Florida	Education impact aid Maternal and child health block grant	Medicaid Preventive health block grant
Arizona	Education impact aid Highways	Preventive health block grant Social services block grant
California	Medicaid	Aid to families with dependent children
South Dakota	Medicaid	Aid to families with dependent children Child nutrition Social services block grant
		Aid to families with dependent children Economic development planning

Table 12, continued

State	Programs in which cuts were partially or fully replaced	Federally aided programs in which state spending declined[a]
Net State Savings		
Illinois	Alcohol, drug abuse, and mental health block grant	Aid to families with dependent children Highways Medicaid Wastewater treatment
Mississippi	Alcohol, drug abuse, and mental health block grant	Aid to families with dependent children
Missouri	None identified	Aid to families with dependent children Energy conservation Highways Maternal and child health block grant Medicaid
Ohio	None identified	Aid to families with dependent children Medicaid

Table 12, continued

State	Programs in which cuts were partially or fully replaced	Federally aided programs in which state spending declined[a]
Texas	None identified	Aid to families with dependent children Maternal and child health block grant Medicaid Social services block grant
Washington	None identified	Aid to families with dependent children

Note: Net replacement is calculated by subtracting the amount of compounding plus savings from the ratification of entitlement cuts from the total amounts of replacement. The replacements ratings shown here are then determined by dividing net replacement by the total amount of federal aid cuts. "Net savings" indicates total state spending on federal programs that were cut was less than the expected level had the reconciliation act not been passed.

a. A decline is measured against the expected level without the reconciliation act. See text for details.

b. Oklahoma also increased state spending on tuition assistance for higher education in response to federal spending cuts that were later mostly restored.

cision is not possible because of the types of structural, data, and timing problems discussed in chapter 2.

Replacement

In general, the states in the sample made only modest efforts to replace the federal cuts. The most active state was Oklahoma, where we estimate that on balance one-fourth of the federal funding cut was restored. In addition, Oklahoma sharply increased state tuition grants in response to federal cuts that were later restored. Massachusetts and New York restored 10 to 20 percent of the funds on a net basis. Most states replaced much less than these three states. Five states—Arizona, California, Florida, New Jersey, and South Dakota—are classified as making some replacement. Six are shown as having net savings. Two of these states, Illinois and Mississippi, replaced some of the cuts in the alcohol, drug abuse, and mental health block grant, but this replacement was outweighed by savings in other programs. Four states—Missouri, Ohio, Texas, and Washington—made no effort to replace federal cuts and realized savings in some entitlement programs.

The programs in which cuts were most frequently replaced were operating programs, especially in social services and in the health field. Replacement of cuts in the social services block grant occurred in four states, while six states replaced cuts in one or more of the health block grants.

Some states also took steps to replace cuts in capital programs, even though most states did not actually experience cuts in capital funding in fiscal year 1982, and even though the cuts that did occur had little or no immediate impact on state activities. A few states even replaced some of the cuts in capital funds that go directly to local governments. Arizona and New York increased state spending on local highways, as did Texas, which also had a slight increase in federal aid. New York and Massachusetts increased state aid to local housing authorities. Similarly, Massachusetts increased state aid for the construction of wastewater treatment facilities, and Oklahoma and New Jersey considered adopting a larger role in the financing of such facilities.

It is apparent that some states expected future reductions in federal capital aid, and attempted to head off the effects of these cuts by immediately putting state money into the capital pipeline. These actions may turn out to have the paradoxical effect of increasing state spending to make up for some anticipated cuts that never actually materialize.

Cuts in entitlement programs were least likely to be replaced. Only New York replaced AFDC cuts, by raising the standard of need under AFDC and transferring some of the recipients who lost AFDC eligibility to the state-funded general relief program. No state replaced cuts in food stamps or trade adjustment assistance. Oklahoma replaced cuts in child nutrition programs, while four states replaced reductions in medicaid funding.

Delaying and Offsetting the Cuts

State and local governments took a number of steps to delay the effects of federal aid reductions either temporarily or in the long run. As noted in chapter 2, they could (1) shift state funds used for some programs to make up for cuts in other federally aided program areas, and (2) use carryover funds under a federal grant to delay the effect of a cut made in that particular grant in 1981. Of the two possibilities, the use of carryovers was by far the more frequent.

It is likely that federal officials were not aware that states would use carryovers as often and as heavily as they did. Many carryovers occurred because, when state and local governments took over the administration of a federal program (as in the case of a block grant), they received a letter of credit for the amount they were entitled to use for the full twelve-month period of fiscal year 1982, if they acted on October 1, 1981. (Letters of credit under the new block grants were in this way also used on a partial-year basis.) Many jurisdictions and nonprofit institutions were still operating under the previous categorical grants that still had time to run. They were thus able to use carryover funds effectively to delay the effect of the cuts in these programs. The ultimate impacts of the cuts in funding under the new block grants are an important topic for the continuing field research.

The new block grants also provided greater authority for shifting funds. The most important result of this type of change, as noted earlier, was the transfer of funds from the low-income energy assistance block grant to the social services block grant and the energy conservation program.

Chapter 2 also identifies administrative improvements as a way to offset the effects of cuts. There are many examples in the field reports of reorganization measures, layoffs of middle managers, and tightened administrative procedures that were said to be a response to the Reagan program. Such actions, Reagan officials argued, would enable federal aid cuts to be absorbed without reductions in services. At this stage in the analysis, we are not able to assess the effects of these kinds of changes. This is an important topic for the continuing research.

Ratifying and Compounding Cuts

Allowing a federal cut to cause reductions in service levels was by far the most common response of state governments to the 1982 cuts. All states ratified the cuts in AFDC, food stamps, trade adjustment assistance, the community services block grant, state employment services, and public service employment. Most states ratified the cuts in medicaid, all the remaining block grants, and the training portions of the CETA program.

Cuts in entitlement programs were the most likely programs to produce savings in state funds, i.e., reductions in state spending that would not have occurred in the absence of the 1981 reconciliation act. As shown in table 12, all states except New York had net savings due to the reconciliation act under the AFDC program. Five states had savings under medicaid. Two states cut spending in the social services block grant program, though in one of them, California, state spending continued to be high compared to other states.

Individual State Descriptions

Most states did not develop a comprehensive, planned response to federal aid cuts; rather, they reacted to a change in a particular policy area as the change became apparent. This section contains individual descriptions of the states in the sample, describing their fiscal condition and how they responded to the key cuts in federal aid.

The descriptions are presented in the order of the net replacement ranking described above. Table 13 summarizes the important federal aid cuts for each state, showing percentage cuts and dollar amounts.

Oklahoma

Though Oklahoma's financial condition remained strong during federal fiscal 1982, the state came under increasing pressure as the year progressed. The effects of the recession began to take their toll on the state's manufacturing industry. High interest rates and sluggish wheat and cattle prices depressed Oklahoma's agricultural sector. Farm liquidations were running at relatively high

Table 13. *Major Changes in Federal Aid to States*

State	Major cuts	
	By percentage	*In millions of dollars*
Arizona	*Reduced 50% or more* CETA public service employment Community services block grant Education block grant Energy conservation	Federal highway aid, 14.3 CETA[a], 10 Community services block grant, 7.5 Education block grant, 5 Social services block grant, 3.7
	Reduced 25% to 49% CETA training Refugee assistance Trade adjustment assistance	
	Reduced 10% to 24% Child nutrition Federal highway aid Health block grants Social services block grant	
California	*Reduced 50% or more* CETA public service employment Community services block grant Economic development planning	Food stamps, 60 Social services block grant, 58 AFDC, 60 Medicaid, 50 Community services block grant, 34
	Reduced 25% to 49% CETA training Energy conservation	
	Reduced 10% to 24% Education block grant Food stamps Health block grants Social services block grant	
Florida	*Reduced 50% or more* CETA public service employment Energy conservation	Child nutrition, 34 Food stamps, 25 Cuban refugee program, 19 CETA[a], 19 Social services block grant, 17
	Reduced 25% to 49% CETA training Community services block grant Education block grant Refugee assistance	

Table 13, continued

| State | Major cuts | |
	By percentage	In millions of dollars
	Reduced 10% to 24% AFDC Child nutrition Health block grants Social services block grant	
Illinois	*Reduced 50% or more* CETA public service employment Special milk Youth conservation corps	Medicaid, 60 Federal highway aid, 60 AFDC, 35–40 CETA[a], 31 Social services block grant, 30
	Reduced 25% to 49% Energy conservation	
	Reduced 10% to 24% CETA training Community services block grant Education block grant Federal highway aid Health block grants Social services block grant	

Massachusetts	*Reduced 50% or more*
	CETA public service
	  employment
	Energy conservation
	Land and water
	  conservation
	Youth conservation corps
	Special milk
		AFDC, 40–45
		Child nutrition, 21
		CETA[a], 24
		Social services block
		  grant, 19
		Medicaid, 15

	Reduced 25% to 49% CETA training Child nutrition	
	Reduced 10% to 24% AFDC Community services block grant Food stamps Health block grants Social services block grant	
Mississippi	*Reduced 50% or more* CETA public service employment Education block grant	CETA[a], 25 Food stamps, 22 Social services block grant, 7 Education block grant, 6 Child nutrition, 6
	Reduced 25% to 49% CETA training Energy conservation	

Table 13, continued

	Major cuts	
State	*By percentage*	*In millions of dollars*
	Highway safety	
	Reduced 10% to 24% AFDC Community services block 　grant Compensatory education Health block grants	
Missouri	*Reduced 50% or more* CETA public 　service employment Economic development 　planning Highway safety Youth conservation corps	Federal highway aid, 33 Wastewater treatment, 24 CETA[a], 18 AFDC, 15–20 Social services block grant, 14
	Reduced 25% to 49% Energy conservation Wastewater treatment	
	Reduced 10% to 24% AFDC CETA training Community services 　block grant Federal highway aid Health block grants Medicaid Social services block grant	
New Jersey	*Reduced 50% or more* CETA public service 　employment Trade adjustment 　assistance Youth conservation corps	Food stamps, 60 Trade adjustment 　assistance, 25 Child nutrition, 20 Social services block grant, 19 AFDC, 15–20
	Reduced 25% to 49% CETA training Child nutrition/special milk Community services 　block grant Energy conservation	
	Reduced 10% to 24% Education block grant Food stamps Health block grants Social services block grant	

Table 13, continued

| State | Major cuts | |
	By percentage	In millions of dollars

New York	*Reduced 50% or more*
	CETA public service
	  employment
	CETA training
	Economic develop-
	  ment planning
	Education impact aid
	Energy conservation
	Trade adjustment
	  assistance
		CETA[a], 243
		Food stamps, 200
		Trade adjustment
		  assistance, 84
		Federal highway aid, 73
		Social services block
		  grant, 59

	Reduced 25% to 49% Education block grant Special milk	
	Reduced 10% to 24% Employment service Federal highway aid Food stamps Health block grants Social services block grant	
Ohio	*Reduced 25% to 49%* CETA public service employment Energy conservation Health block grants	AFDC, 55 Medicaid, 45 CETA[a], 31 Food stamps, 20 Social services block grant, 11

	Reduced 10% to 24%
	AFDC
	CETA training
	Community services
	  block grant
	Education block grant
	Social services block
	  grant	

Oklahoma	*Reduced 50% or more*
	CETA public service
	  employment
	Energy conservation
		AFDC, 15–20
		CETA[a], 10
		Social services block
		  grant, 7
		Medicaid, 7
		Food stamps, 6

	Reduced 10% to 24%
	AFDC
	CETA training
	Community services
	  block grant
	Health block grants
	Social services block
	  grant	

Table 13, continued

| State | Major cuts | |
	By percentage	In millions of dollars

South Dakota	*Reduced 50% or more*
	CETA public service
	    employment
	Community services
	    block grant
	Energy conservation
	Land and water
	    conservation
		CETA[a], 3.7
		Federal highway aid, 3
		Social services block grant, 1.9
		Air transportation, 1.7
		Land and water
		    conservation, 1.6

	Reduced 25% to 49% CETA training	
	Reduced 10% to 24% Child nutrition/special milk Health block grants Social services block grant	

Texas	*Reduced 50% or more*
	CETA public service
	    employment
	Energy conservation
		Food stamps, 50–60
		Child nutrition, 36
		CETA[a], 18
		Social services block
		    grant, 17
		AFDC, 10–15

	Reduced 10% to 24% AFDC CETA training Child nutrition Education block grant Food stamps Health block grants Social services block grant	

Washington	*Reduced 50% or more*
	CETA public service
	    employment
	CETA training
		CETA[a], 33
		Social services block
		    grant, 20
		Child nutrition, 12
		AFDC, 6–10
		Refugee assistance, 6

	Reduced 25% to 49% Energy conservation	
	Reduced 10% to 24% Community services block grant Health block grants Social services block grant	

Note: The cuts listed here were identified by the associates as causing major program changes. A few involve programs of special interest in the state, but they are not discussed in the text of the report. Some programs with large percentage cuts nationally, such as the youth conservation corps, were so small in some states that the associate did not identify the change as major.

a. Figures for CETA are for balance-of-state prime sponsors and for governor's discretionary fund.

levels during the year. The state also faced financial pressure as a result of the downturn in the oil and natural gas industries. Revenue from the state's gross production tax on oil and natural gas continued to rise but at a slower rate than they did in the previous year. Proceeds from the state's sales tax also grew at a slower rate. Despite these growing fiscal pressures, the state was able to end its 1982 budget period on June 30, 1982 with a $279 million surplus. In preparing the state's 1983 budget, Oklahoma's legislature planned to draw from this surplus to replace some of the federal cuts.

Government retrenchment was popular in Oklahoma, and there was little political support for using the surplus to make up for all the federal cuts. Instead, state replacement of federal funds was taken up after competing claims had been honored. Part of the surplus was used to cut the personal income tax by increasing personal exemptions. The governor took little part in developing the state's response to the cuts; the legislature took the lead. When that body took up the issue of replacement of federal cuts, about $16.6 million in general funds was available. In March 1982, the chairman of the state House Appropriations and Budget Committee polled all legislators on their preferences for the use of funds, and the Legislative Fiscal Office constructed an elaborate ranking of the results. After considering the rankings and a variety of other factors, legislative leaders developed a bill providing $6.6 million for tuition grants for higher education, $6 million for the school lunch program, $2.7 million for health programs, and the remaining $1.3 million for a wide range of programs. The legislature also increased spending on community services, though this action was not part of the formal "federal makeup" bill described above.

Several large programs administered by the state Department of Human Services, such as AFDC, the social services block grant, and medicaid, were not competing for state makeup money from the general surplus, since the department is financed by an earmarked sales tax. However, state spending on AFDC and social services actually decreased. The 25 percent decline in AFDC spending here was among the largest percentage cuts in the nation. State spending on medicaid increased, because the federal reimbursement rate declined as state per-capita income rose.

New York

The economy of New York was hit by the recession, but suffered less than the nation as a whole. In 1981, the state had enacted tax relief for business and individuals and a package of tax increases designed to finance aid to local mass transit. State budget projections assumed correctly that the state's unemployment rate would stay somewhat below the national average. The battle over the state budget for the period beginning April 1982 was protracted and dramatic, but revolved around issues for the most part unrelated to the federal cuts. The dispute between Democratic Gov. Hugh Carey and the legislature concerned the governor's proposals for state tax increases and the legislature's desire to increase expenditures without levying new taxes. After the governor had vetoed several spending bills, the legislature temporarily capitulated. However, after the fiscal year began, the legislature successfully passed supplemental appropriations. These led the governor to announce an austerity program consisting of a hiring freeze, a ban on nonessential construction, and the impoundment of state university funds.

The Reagan cutbacks were not a major issue in the debate. The governor publicly stated that he would neither replace nor compound the federal aid cuts with changes in state spending. The legislature on the whole followed a similar approach. Despite this public stance, the state did change its spending in ways that maintained services in the face of cuts.

In most cases, the motives for action were state policy concerns, not federal cuts. State changes in the AFDC program, made before the federal cuts, raised the state's standard of need, which raised state and federal spending above what it otherwise would have been. Though the state did tighten eligibility conditions for its general relief program, some of those removed from AFDC rolls were eligible for state-financed relief.

The two largest increases in state spending, for mass transit and highways, were part of a long-term effort to improve the infrastructure of the state. Though the primary impetus for these increases was state concern over declining public services and the need to be competitive economically, the prospect of declining federal aid in these areas was also important. The state funds will finance slightly different projects, but they are similar enough to the federal projects to help maintain service levels. Other smaller replacement efforts came in the social services block grant program, assisted housing, economic development planning, and the maternal and child health block grant.

Massachusetts

Massachusetts in 1982 was enjoying economic growth based on high-technology manufacturing and a thriving service sector. The state's unemployment rate was the lowest of the ten major industrial states and well below the national average. The state government has taken on new responsibilities since the passage in 1980 of Proposition 2 1/2, a stringent property tax limitation measure, with state aid to local governments up dramatically since 1981. Though the state fiscal year 1982 ended with a small deficit and the state's bond rating is low, tax revenues have withstood the recession without major shortfalls, and the state income tax rate was lowered slightly in 1982.

The state was slow to respond to the Reagan cuts, partly because of confusion about the nature of the federal changes. The difference in budget years also delayed the state response; state fiscal year 1982 was three months old before the federal changes hit. When the 1982 state budget was prepared in the winter and spring of 1981, no one knew what would result from the coming battle between President Reagan and the House of Representatives. In addition, Gov. Edward King, a conservative Democrat, supported the Reagan program, was proud to be President Reagan's favorite Democratic governor, and was not interested in making a wholesale commitment to covering lost federal funds.

Other more liberal citizens and members of state government took a different view of proper state policy and eventually prevailed. The state's social service, health care, and assisted housing providers were long established, well organized, and politically well connected. They found key committee chairpersons in the legislature sympathetic to their arguments. As the year went on, President Reagan's coattails got shorter, Governor King's influence waned, and the legislature took over the budget process, as it has often done.

The state budget for its fiscal year 1983 included much more replacement of lost federal funds than initially proposed by Governor King. The state spent less of its own money on AFDC, because federal changes in eligibility rules led to large declines in total spending in that program, which is supported equally by the state and federal governments. Massachusetts replaced many other federal cuts, however. The state has a long history of involvement in social services, health care, housing and urban renewal, and public assistance. Much of the replacement came in the form of increases in state spending for existing state programs, many of which provide aid to local governments or nonprofit agencies. Noticeably absent from the list of programs receiving state replacement is the community services block grant, which received a 10 percent cut in federal funds statewide. The community action agencies and their clients were unable to muster political support for the program and debated the distribution of the smaller amount of money instead of pushing successfully for state replacement.

New Jersey

Changing state finances and leadership in New Jersey played an important part in shaping the state's response to the Reagan program. In June 1981, Democratic Gov. Brendan Byrne was nearing the end of his second term in office with state treasury balances of about $140 million. Governor Byrne and the Democratic legislature decried the Reagan cuts and their prospective impact on New Jersey. In January 1982, a new Republican governor, Thomas Kean, took office just as the deepening recession began to cause shortfalls in the state's tax revenues. Governor Kean and the legislature reached an impasse over a strategy to balance the state's budget, and layoffs began. Finally, pressure to meet school financing needs, increase mass transit aid, and balance the budget resulted in an agreement in late December 1982 to increase state taxes.

The state's first real response to the federal cuts came in the fiscal year 1983 budget, prepared early in 1982. The departments requested about $57 million to replace federal cuts. The governor's budget pared this to about $40 million. The legislature reduced the governor's figures still further. A package of support for social services was agreed upon. In addition, the state began a new program to train displaced workers and former AFDC recipients. New tax measures were passed in December 1982 and were used in part to increase subsidies for the state mass transit system. The increase in state transit aid was a response to current and anticipated federal reductions as well as to rising costs in the statewide system.

Florida

State government in this fast-growing jurisdiction was dominated by a coalition of moderates and conservatives. Under the
state's unusual executive branch organization, the strong cabinet
and the governor developed the state's response to the cuts. A legislative committee on the cuts urged that every effort be made to
maintain minimum necessary levels of support in entitlement programs, but the governor and his cabinet decided to ratify most cuts,
leaving the local governments to bear much of the political heat for
service cuts. The state increased its sales tax, effective in the middle of 1982, and used half of the proceeds to increase aid to local
governments, so cities and towns did have some flexibility.

Florida eventually covered some of the cuts with new state
funding. For AFDC, state spending was cut back little, if at all.
The standard of need was increased in fiscal year 1983, bringing
some former recipients back on the rolls; moreover, a rising per-
capita income caused the state's portion of program costs to go up
in 1982. Refugee assistance and child nutrition, two other entitlement programs, received substantial funding reductions, which
the state did not replace. The state did allocate some funds to the
preventive health and maternal and child health block grants to
cover some of the funding cuts. State spending on medicaid also
rose to counter a drop in the federal matching rate. Finally, the
cuts in educational impact aid were severe in some localities, and
the state responded to this politically important cut with an
increase in aid. The most common state response was a combination of shifting funds across programs, using carryover funds,
implementing cost-cutting measures, and adding small amounts of
new state money in an effort to maintain service levels.

Arizona

In this conservative state, the Reagan program of cuts in federal
spending was popular. State officials, anticipating eventual
declines in federal aid, had always been careful to avoid dependence on federal funding for any basic operation of state government. Gov. Bruce Babbitt, a Democrat with an interest in
federal/state relations, led the state in developing a response to the
federal cuts, though the legislature was increasingly interested in
federal grant policy. In 1981 the economy was strong and the state
government's fiscal condition was good, but by mid-1982 the
recession had reached Arizona. Rising unemployment and tax revenue shortfalls caused concern.

Most federal cuts were ratified. State aid formulas did result in some increased state spending in education. State education aid was based on total revenue from other sources, so as federal aid declined, state aid automatically increased. Increases in the tax revenues allocated to the state highway budget also substituted for lost federal highway revenue. In 1981 and 1982 the state had increased the gasoline tax to finance highway programs. Finally, the state allocated a small amount of additional money to child protective services and increased spending on public health programs, indirectly helping to cover some cuts in the programs incorporated into the new health block grants. The main public assistance entitlement programs were not drastically affected in 1982. Because Arizona's AFDC program provides very low benefits primarily to those without other sources of income and because the state did not even have a medicaid program until October 1982, the federal changes cutting off the working poor had little impact there.

California

California's fiscal fortunes have reversed in the recent past. The state surplus of 1978 had evaporated by state fiscal year 1982, leaving the state struggling to balance its budget. California's severe fiscal stress was largely due to a series of tax limitation measures. In 1978, Proposition 13 limited the property tax rate to 1 percent of full market value. This applied to local governments, but affected the state because local officials successfully called on the state to bail them out with extra aid payments in fiscal year 1979, when the rate reduction took effect. One subsequent tax measure was adopted that limited increases in governmental appropriations (Proposition 4 in 1979). By 1981 the state surplus was gone, but voters, not yet satisfied, adopted two more measures limiting revenue in June 1982: Proposition 7 fully and permanently indexed the state personal income tax, and Proposition 6 abolished the state inheritance and gift tax.

The recession weakened the state's ability to absorb these revenue losses as well as to continue to aid local governments in offsetting their loss of property tax revenues. The federal budget cuts equaled only a small fraction of the state budget cuts necessitated by the state's fiscal crunch. The state legislature was able to balance expenditures with revenues only by using one-time, stopgap measures.

California has a history of strong participation in income-security programs, and the liberal Democrats who dominated state-level offices wanted to maintain that tradition. Democrat Gov. Jerry Brown had an ambivalent reaction to the Reagan domestic program. Ideologically he opposed many of the cuts, but he did not want to replace federal funds and thereby support Reagan's arguments. Brown allowed the strong, well-informed, and professionally staffed state legislature to take the lead in responding to the federal budget reductions and block grant programs. The legislature, caught between statutory revenue limits and the state's worsening fiscal stress, could not replace lost federal money with state funds. These severe fiscal constraints prevented the state from replacing funds for any program except medicaid.

Political concerns as well as fiscal concerns affected the state's reaction to the Reagan domestic program. In order to maintain as large a distance as possible between the Reagan budget cuts and the state government, the state delayed picking up block grants as long as it could— until July 1982.

South Dakota

South Dakota is the least populous and most rural state in the field sample. Forty-nine of the state's sixty-six counties have fewer than 10,000 people; twenty-five of the counties have fewer than 5,000 people. Because it is a predominately rural state, state government plays an important role in delivering public services.

For most of federal fiscal year 1982, an overriding concern in the state was its depressed agricultural economy. Farm prices declined; interest rates and costs increased. Unemployment among the state's Indian tribes was high and rising.

Throughout the recession, the state government faced few financial problems and was able to maintain a balanced budget. Receipts from the sales tax, the state's principal revenue source, were slightly lower than expected; nevertheless, state revenue increased over the previous year. South Dakota does not have a personal income tax. The state has a conservative political climate; limits have been placed on state and local government spending and taxes.

The effects of federal aid cuts were not serious in fiscal 1982. Carryover funds helped delay the impact of some of the cuts; state officials tended to be more concerned about future cuts in federal aid than they were about the effects of the cuts made in fiscal year 1982. Confronted by a lagging economy and apprehensive about future cuts, the state did little to replace the 1982 cuts in federal aid, and there was little public support for such efforts. Republican Gov. William Janklow, who dominated the political scene, is a strong fiscal conservative and Reagan supporter. He opposed the replacement of lost federal aid; the legislature, which was two-thirds Republican, took the same position.

Federal aid changes had only a minor effect on entitlement programs because of the state's low benefits and small proportion of working recipients. AFDC eligibility restrictions translated into small savings for the state and federal government. The budget for the state fiscal year 1982, which ended June 30, 1982, was enacted before the reconciliation act, and it relied on projected monthly AFDC participation rates that were higher than the actual rates. The savings that resulted from the lower caseloads were used along with available fund balances to offset increased medicaid costs.

South Dakota received an increase in federal funds under the low-income energy assistance block grant. State officials used this increase to raise grant payments to eligible individuals. In addition, $900,000 in federal aid was transferred to the state weatherization program, which was cut in 1982.

The state received nearly $2 million, or 21 percent, less under the social services block grant, compared to the previous year. Like most other states in the sample, South Dakota continued to provide matching funds for the social services block grant, though the state was no longer required to do so.

State and local officials were especially concerned about reductions in the federal highway program. The state has one of the highest ratios of highway miles per resident. South Dakota's obligation ceiling under the federal highway program was only 5 percent lower than the previous year's level. However, officials were concerned about the possibility of future federal reductions in spending for secondary roads. As one way to avoid problems in this area, the state legislature considered increasing the allocation of state and federal highway funds to the counties and giving them greater responsibilities for the construction and maintenance of roads. This policy change, in devolving responsibility to localities, was not adopted.

Illinois

As the recession deepened during 1982, state-level issues came to dominate the political scene, and the state's policy response to the federal aid cuts was greatly influenced by these events. When the cuts were first enacted, the state government was living with fiscal restraints but expected to make it through the year without eliminating state balances. During the election campaign for governor, incumbent Republican James Thompson argued that the state budget was in good shape. Soon after his reelection, he announced what many had suspected: a large state deficit that forced him to propose further cuts in spending and an increase in taxes.

The governor supported the Reagan domestic program and sought to demonstrate that it would work well in Illinois. Party control of the legislature was split, with Republicans a majority in the House and Democrats a majority in the Senate. The Senate, led by its Democratic president, took the lead in asserting the legislative role in implementing the new block grants, thus limiting the role of the Republican-led executive branch.

Cuts in AFDC and a large number of operating grants were felt in Illinois in 1982. All of the new block grants underwent major cuts except the CDBG small-cities program and the low-income energy assistance program, which received increases. Carryover funds were important in lessening the immediate effect of the cuts. In the energy conservation institutional grant program and in refugee aid, carryover funds completely made up for the lost revenue in 1982. For the youth conservation corps, carryovers covered about half the cuts. For health programs, carryovers made up the entire cut in the maternal and child health and preventive health block grants and about half the cut in the alcohol, drug abuse, and mental health program. There was no new funding for assisted housing construction programs in 1982, and federal highway aid was cut nearly 20 percent. Funding increased in 1982 for compensatory education, air transportation facilities, as well as for the two block grants noted above.

Because of the state deficit, federal cuts received little attention. Cuts in entitlement programs were passed through, and nearly all the cuts in operating grants fared no better. The only exception came in the alcohol, drug abuse, and mental health program, where the state increased spending on the state-financed mental health centers, providing substitute services to federally funded community mental health centers. For wastewater treatment, the state imposed a freeze on bond sales that finance the state part of the program to reduce current and future interest costs. In the highway program, the state decreased earmarked revenue for the program, forcing a decline in its matching funds for the federal allotments.

Mississippi

In this poor state, many residents rely on federal entitlement programs for a portion of their income and AFDC eligiblity restrictions had an important effect in the state. Food stamp cuts were also important, amounting to about 9 percent of 1981 funding. Mississippi was unusual for the size of the cuts in the new education block grant and the compensatory education program. Previous large grants under the superseded categorical programs and the elimination of concentration grants in the compensatory education program (targeting aid to low-income areas) meant that the state suffered large percentage cuts in 1982. Carryover funding for the highway safety program and maternal and child health program covered about half the 1982 cut, while carryovers covered the entire cut in the health block grant. The CDBG small-cities program, the low-income energy assistance block grant, and the social services block grant had small increases in funding in 1982.

In Mississippi, the governor usually plays a relatively minor role in policymaking, while the legislature is relatively powerful. The Democratic governor, William Winter, focused his attention on publicly supported kindergartens, and unsuccessfully sought legislative support for this project. He did not attempt to replace lost federal money in educational programs. The block grant programs, however, provided Winter with the opportunity to increase his decision-making authority relative to that of the state legislature, particularly for programmatic decisions.

Mississippi's conservatism was reflected in an explicit state policy against using state revenue to replace federal cuts. For the most part, the policy was observed. An increase in alcohol tax revenues earmarked for alcoholism programs allowed the state to increase these services, and this partly made up for federal cuts. In all other programs, the state either cut funding (AFDC) or left it unchanged. In AFDC, the state did raise the standard of need significantly, starting in state fiscal year 1983. Officials anticipated that this increase would add about as many AFDC cases as were cut off by the 1982 changes. Despite this increase in state need levels, state spending on the program still declined during 1982.

Missouri

The already serious fiscal problems faced by the state government of Missouri were exacerbated by the recession. During 1982, a planned surplus in the state budget evaporated, and a $100 million deficit was forecast in its place. Republican Gov. Christopher Bond emphasized expenditure cutbacks; his program included a 10 percent cut in the current budget for almost all state agencies. The governor, who dominated the budget process, refused to back tax increases and supported the policy changes made by the Reagan administration to reduce the costs of aid to families with dependent children and medicaid programs.

The state's troubled fiscal condition and its history of generally conservative policies shaped its response to the federal cuts.

Despite the recession, which resulted in new cases on the AFDC rolls, state spending for that program declined by $5.6 million, or 8 percent. This was due both to the reduction in the caseload caused by the federal changes and the decision of the state to suspend its AFDC program for families with two parents. Following Reagan's "safety net" philosophy, the AFDC savings realized in 1982 were assigned to help pay for an increase in welfare benefits for "truly needy" families who remained on the AFDC rolls.

The state's medicaid program, which had grown dramatically over the past five years, was a major state concern. Officials were looking for ways to curb medicaid spending. In addition to the cuts produced as a result of federal policy changes, an array of cost-containment measures were adopted in federal fiscal year 1982, including tightened guidelines for state reimbursements for nursing homes and hospitals and a requirement that medicaid recipients get a second opinion for certain surgical procedures. State and federal actions combined to reduce the state's medicaid expenditures in 1982 by $19.8 million, or 4 percent.

Missouri received a $14.1 million (22 percent) cut in funding under the social services block grant. On the other hand, federal funding for the low-income energy assistance block grant increased by $7 million. The state transferred $4.3 million of these funds to offset some of the cuts in social services. The cuts that were finally made in social services affected such activities as legal services for the elderly, children's summer camps, and day-care.

Over half of the federal aid to Missouri for social services is spent under contracts with local governments and private agencies. During federal fiscal year 1982, the state adopted the policy that the largest share of the cutbacks in social services should be in services directly administered by the state, rather than those contracted for with local governments and private agencies.

With state administration of the community services block grant, a 15 percent cut was made in the funding for all but four of the state's community action agencies, compared with their support in the previous year. Furthermore, the state strongly encouraged community action agencies to set aside 10 percent of their funds to support services for abused and neglected children; these programs lost federal funds due to the cuts in the social services block grant.

During federal fiscal 1982, state officials were especially worried about federal reductions in highway aid, but they were concerned even more about the slowdown in the accumulation of earmarked state revenues for highway construction. As a result of this slowdown, the state faced the prospect of not being able to come up with the necessary matching funds for the state's allotment of federal highway grants.

Ohio

When the federal cuts occurred, Ohio was in the midst of a long period of economic hardship. The recession had an especially severe effect on the state's manufacturing industry. Unemployment remained well above the national average. The state government faced a severe fiscal crisis that overshadowed the effects of federal aid reductions. Adoption of the state budget for 1981–1983 did not occur until November 1981, five months into the biennium. State fiscal problems persisted throughout the initial year of the Reagan domestic program. Despite two recent tax hikes supported by Republican Gov. James A. Rhodes, who had previously been a staunch opponent of increased taxes, state officials in January 1983 faced the prospect of a $300 million deficit.

Through the summer and fall of 1982, caseloads in AFDC, food stamps, medicaid, and general relief programs exceeded projected levels. To add to these difficulties, tax revenues were running below the estimates used to plan the state's 1981–1983 budget. Though economic recovery had been projected for the fall of 1982, it did not occur.

In this context, the federal budget cuts were a comparatively minor problem, and it was almost inevitable that the state replaced little federal aid. Federal cuts in AFDC and medicaid were ratified. This produced savings for the state in comparison with the outlays that would have been made without the Reagan changes; however, state spending under both programs increased because of the recession.

The welfare caseload data for Ohio is especially interesting. Federal changes in AFDC eliminated or reduced benefits for over 42,000 families, but because of the worsening economy, the caseload remained at approximately 200,000 in 1982, slightly higher than in 1981. Ohio's general relief program increased by 25,000 cases during the year. The state pays 75 percent of the costs of this program; counties pay the remainder. State officials traced about 12 percent of the increase in the general relief caseload to people who had become ineligible for AFDC benefits due to the Reagan changes. The most important changes in AFDC that caused the general relief caseloads to rise were the provisions eliminating benefits for pregnant women and reducing eligibility for two-parent families.

Federal policy changes also had a major effect on Ohio's medicaid program. Total expenditures for the program increased between state fiscal years 1981 and 1982, reflecting rising health care costs and caseloads. Though state and federal expenditures for the program increased by over $200 million, the increase is less than it would have been if the 1982 federal changes in domestic policy had not occurred. Because AFDC recipients are categorically eligible for medicaid, a total of 28,000 AFDC cases dropped from the rolls (plus 6,500 applicants who were denied benefits) did not receive medicaid benefits in 1982 as a result of the changes in eligibility rules. A similar drop occurred in the supplemental security income program. Six thousand disabled workers were removed from the rolls as a result of federal eligibility changes; they also lost their medicaid benefits.

Ohio lost $10.5 million in the cuts to the social services block grant. While the state did not replace any of this aid, it continued to provide matching funds for the block grant, even though the federal government had dropped the matching requirement in 1981.

For the community services and most of the health block grants, federal carryover funds helped offset some of the effects of the cuts, delaying their impact beyond 1982. The state received a $5 million increase under the low-income energy assistance block grant. Portions of these funds were transferred to weatherization programs, which were cut as a result of the elimination of the CETA public service employment program. In addition, about 18 percent of the low-income energy assistance block grant funds were used for the first time to help support an emergency assistance program. The program helped protect households from utility shutoffs by providing one-time grants. State funding for this program decreased during the year.

State administration of the education block grant resulted in the spreading of federal funds. Under the education block grant, urban school districts that in previous years had been successful in receiving large discretionary federal grants for desegregation purposes (e.g., Cleveland) were especially hurt. Smaller districts, which had been less active in applying for funds for the programs consolidated into this new block grant, received federal aid under state administration of the block grant.

Ohio's administration of the small-cities community development block grant also resulted in the spreading of funds. This spreading effect was much greater in Ohio than in other states. Unlike other states in the sample, Ohio decided to administer small-cities block grant funds for community development on a formula basis. Over 200 small communities in Ohio are eligible for funding, a much larger number than received aid in the other states in the sample.

Texas

The state of Texas had been enjoying favorable economic conditions, primarily because of a boom in the petroleum industry. Between 1977 and 1981, total state revenue increased by 82 percent and expenditures grew by 72 percent, the net result being an increase in state fund balances. During this five-year period, most of the growth in state revenue resulted from increases in selective sales and natural resource severance taxes. Revenue from the state's severance tax on oil production increased rapidly in this period; the largest increase occurred in 1980 and 1981 as a result of the decontrol of oil prices. Although Texas was under little financial pressure at the outset of fiscal 1982, it came under increasingly greater pressure as the year progressed.

Texas traditionally has provided a low level of state services, and has been a low-tax state. The state has neither a personal nor corporate income tax. The governor of Texas in 1982, Republican William P. Clements, Jr., supported federal efforts to cut domestic spending. Changes in entitlement programs, like other federal aid reductions, were ratified. The state cut its own spending for social service programs, compounding the federal cuts.

Texas, like Mississippi, stands out among states in the sample for the firm position it took against replacing lost federal aid. The legislature meets biennially, and was not in session in 1982. The budget for state fiscal years 1982 and 1983 was passed in May 1981, approximately two months before Congress approved the reconciliation act. When the legislature enacted the 1981–83 budgets, it specifically adopted provisions that prohibited the use of state funds to finance federal aid shortfalls and also prohibited the state from absorbing federally funded positions or participating in new federal programs. In addition, the legislature decided against state participation in three of the newly established block grants—community services, small-cities community development, and primary health care.

Federal aid cuts took on a new light in Texas in the fall of 1982. The slump in the petroleum industry and the effects of the national recession hit Texas toward the end of the year. The state's budget came under increasing pressure, and there was growing concern about the effects of cuts in federal aid for social programs. State revenue continued to rise, but at a reduced rate. State unemployment, though still below the national average, increased as a result of a slowdown in oil drilling. A further problem was caused by worsening economic conditions in Mexico and the devaluation of the peso; the state faced a sharp increase in the migration of illegal aliens from Mexico. As a result of these changes, the associate reported that the legislature for the first time since 1971 faced considerable pressure for a tax increase to meet service needs.

Washington

In September 1981, shortly before the initial implementation of federal grant reductions, Washington State's revenue forecasts were revised downward by $650 million. The total state budget was approximately $6.5 billion, so this 10 percent revenue shortfall posed serious problems. Because state law requires a balanced budget over each biennium, this forecast, and the even more dismal reality that followed, set off a series of state budget reductions and tax increases. In the midst of that turmoil, the federal budget reductions were a relatively minor problem.

The proposed process for handling both state and federal budget reductions was to allocate funds to programs with higher priorities, as set by the state agencies. While this suggests the possibility of cross-program substitution, the actual process was much less flexible. In most cases the federal cuts were simply passed along, program by program, with resultant reductions in AFDC, medicaid, special educational services, job training, refugee assistance, and preventive health programs. This reduction was made easier by the fact that Washington State had always maintained a separation, both politically and fiscally, between federal and state funds.

Because of pass-through practices, the state actually saved money by applying the new federal eligibility standards to the AFDC program, and there was very little replacement in any program. While the lack of replacement is related to the state's fiscal crisis, that is not the sole cause. Washington's political climate is conservative, and historically federal and state programs have been separated. Thus, there was little fiscal substitution when the federal grants were expanding, and there is little replacement now that they are being reduced.

Concluding Comments

The jury is still out on the way in which the role of state governments will change—if it will—in response to the retrenchment in national social programs by the Reagan administration. In our history there have been periods of state innovation and leadership on social issues. While the current setting does not seem propitious for the reemergence of this role, there are stirrings and efforts at reassessment underway, which could have long-run implications for American government.

So far, the main story line is that, in the midst of the unexpectedly deep recession, the state governments studied made only modest efforts to step into the breach created by federal government retrenchment in social programs. The recession may be the main reason for this, and the picture may change as economic conditions improve and, in particular, as the cuts made under Reagan's new block grants take hold. Another important mitigating consideration is that, after 1981, Reagan's success in rolling back social programs declined sharply; a number of the cuts made at the national level have been restored by federal actions, as in the case of transportation (in the 1982 act that raised the gasoline tax) and in the 1983 emergency job-creation legislation. Still another important point concerns the way the cuts were made. The most important effects in the social program area were the result of changes in entitlement programs (AFDC, food stamps, medicaid), which were enacted in a way that, as a practical matter, is very hard for states to countermand. The basic eligibility and grant-calculation structure of the AFDC system, for example, is determined in federal law. The changes made in this structure in 1981 required states to remove certain people from the rolls under new rules that apply in all states and that cannot be directly changed in any one state within the context of the AFDC program.

The situation described in detail here supports a verdict that President Reagan's domestic program, in the areas studied, has been successful so far in reducing the role and scope of government in the U.S. economy. Cuts have been made in social programs—that is, relative to what would otherwise have happened in these policy areas under pre-Reagan policies—and the replacement of these cuts by state governments, which have the lead role in the areas most affected, has been modest at most. The situation at the local level, to which we turn next, points to the same conclusion.

4. Large Cities:
Cuts and Responses

The United States is unique among the nations classified as "federal" in that the central government makes large grants-in-aid directly to local governments. This is not the case in other federal nations, and was not the case in the United States up until the 1960s. Many politicians, including Ronald Reagan, favor a return to—or at least a move closer to—the earlier two-level model whereby federal grants, to the extent they are provided, go to state governments.

Ironically, the Republican administrations of Nixon and Ford took major steps to expand direct federal grants to local governments. The major ones enacted during this period were the revenue sharing program (now exclusively paid to localities) and several block grants, notably the Comprehensive Employment and Training Act (CETA) and the community development block grant. Direct federal aid to local governments was about 2 percent of total local government expenditures during the 1950s. With the Great Society programs, it rose to 4 percent in 1970. The Nixon-Ford years brought a sharp increase to 10 percent in 1975. In 1980, direct federal aid stood at 8 percent of total local expenditures. (Direct federal aid to city governments alone was a slightly higher percentage of local expenditures over this period.)

On the whole, state aid is a more important source of outside funds for local governments than federal assistance. It has accounted for slightly more than 30 percent of all local government expenditures since 1960. However, an unknown, but significant, portion of state aid is actually federal aid passed through the state governments to local governments.

In sharp contrast to its Republican predecessors, the Reagan administration has consistently adhered to the older two-level model of U.S. federalism in which federal aid goes exclusively to state governments. Its original proposals for block grants in 1981 called for $15 billion in consolidations, with most restrictions eliminated, and with all of the funds going to state governments. Although the 1981 reconciliation act fell considerably short of these proposals, the seven new block grants that the act created did, as the previous chapter indicates, transfer authority for considerable amounts of federal grant funds from local governments and nonprofit organizations to the states. This chapter discusses how the changes in block grants and direct federal aid in 1982 affected the large cities in our sample.

Large Cities in the Sample

The sample of large cities for this study captures the structural diversity of American federalism. Table 14 lists the cities in the sample by population and indicates the importance of overlying local governments as service providers. This structural characteristic is very important for understanding federal grants. As a general rule, for large cities in the sample, the larger the city's population, the more important are overlying governments and special districts; the city governments in four of the smaller cities provide most local services.[1]

In Los Angeles, the county role is especially comprehensive. The county administers AFDC, food stamp, and medicaid programs; Los Angeles County also provides locally financed general assistance benefits, health services, and social services. In Rochester, Monroe County provides all of these services plus administering the low-income energy assistance and wastewater treatment programs. On the other hand, in Jackson, Newark, Sioux Falls, and Tulsa, nearly all locally provided services are provided by the city government.

Because in many large cities federal funds go to several governments and not just the city itself, it is not surprising that few of the large cities developed a coordinated response to the federal cuts; the response came from the numerous recipients of the aid.

---

1. Population is not the only important variable; state laws, political institutions, and economic conditions are also important variables that may, in fact, be stronger explanations of the differences noted here. The region in which the city is located does not explain the importance of overlying governments. The Southeast, Northeast, North Central, Southwest, and West are all represented among the cities with important overlying local governments that appear in the third column of table 14.

Table 14. *Population and Role of Overlying Local Governments and Special Districts in Large Cities*

| Population | Role of overlying local governments and special districts in service delivery | | |
	Weak	Medium	Strong
Less than 500,000	Jackson Newark Sioux Falls Tulsa	Seattle St. Louis	Orlando Rochester
500,000 to 1,000,000		Boston Phoenix	Cleveland
More than 1,000,000			Chicago Houston Los Angeles

In Cleveland, for example, the city dealt with cuts in capital programs, the school board sought to cover education cuts, and the county addressed social service and health cuts. In Boston, a sharp drop in property tax revenues caused by Proposition 2 1/2, implemented in 1981, created a situation in which every department fended for itself in addressing the federal cuts. Top city officials were occupied with the fiscal problems created by the tax cut.

Another important institutional consideration in the response of large cities to federal aid cuts has to do with the role of the courts. Courts have recently become important in local resource-allocation decisions; the sample includes cities under court order to maintain or expand several types of services. These court orders prevent local officials from cutting services even when faced with federal aid reductions. In Boston, the school district and the housing authority are under court receivership; the schools are required to maintain efforts to desegregate and the housing authority is under order to improve public housing services. In St. Louis, Cleveland, and Seattle, the schools are also under desegregation orders. A desegregation order was also in effect in Los Angeles until recently.

The cities in the sample cover the spectrum of fiscal conditions. Boston, Los Angeles, Rochester, and St. Louis face serious fiscal problems; Houston, Orlando, Phoenix, Tulsa, and Sioux Falls are classified as having low or no fiscal stress, while Chicago, Cleveland, Jackson, Newark, and Seattle are in the middle range.[2]

The following sections describe how the federal cuts affected local governments and other service providers in the sample of large cities. This chapter is organized, as was chapter 3, by program type. Operating grants are discussed first because of the large cuts in programs operated under CETA. They are followed in order of importance by entitlement grants, block grants, and capital grants.

The most important points in the analysis are the following:

1. Cuts in CETA dominated the local effects of the 1982 budget cuts. Hardest hit were lower-income and working poor persons—the same group that was most affected by cuts in AFDC, food stamps, and medicaid, as discussed in chapter 3. Cuts under CETA also had substantial impacts on nonprofit organizations.

2. Cuts and changes in entitlement programs did most harm to large cities with a high proportion of low-income recipients. As demand increased in these cities for food and other forms of emergency income assistance, agencies providing social services tried to respond. Nonprofit organizations operating emergency food programs were able to attract increased private contributions in several cities.

3. Relatively little change was seen at the local level as a result of the creation of new block grants, though less money was available under most of these grants than under the previous categorical programs. In 1982, most local officials still viewed the new block grant programs as collections of individual programs, not as unified programs.

4. Several of the sample states shifted federal aid funds away from large cities to rural areas and smaller communities, particularly under the new block grants.

5. Like their state counterparts, local officials were uneasy about the prospect of future cuts in capital grants, and tried to anticipate such cuts, even in cases where it was not clear whether any cuts would occur.

2. Chapter 7 contains a detailed definition of these fiscal stress ratings.

Operating Grants

The reduction in CETA funds was the biggest operating grant cut for the large cities in the sample. For other operating grants, the experience of cities varied. Under the compensatory education and the education impact aid programs, funding cuts were large in a few cities and negligible in others. Table 15 shows the changes for operating grant programs, other than block grants, for the large cities in the sample.

CETA

CETA funds go to local prime sponsors; every city in the sample (except Orlando and Seattle) was a prime sponsor under CETA in 1981.[3] All CETA prime sponsors lost their funding for public service employment. Nine cities in the sample lost 25 to 50 percent of their CETA training funds. The total loss for these cities ranged from $52 million for Chicago to $2.1 million for Jackson. (These figures compare fiscal year 1982 allocations with fiscal year 1981 allocations after rescissions were made in winter 1981.)

Most local governments ratified the CETA cuts. CETA had always been viewed by local governments as a federal program; little local political support for it existed. The Phoenix associate stated,

Most of the decline in federal aid between the 1979–80 budget and the 1982–83 budget can be accounted for by the decline in CETA. City officials contend that the city acted as an agent for the federal government in the delivery of CETA programs and that CETA responsibilities are not local responsibilities.

Some jurisdictions did make small-scale efforts to continue some CETA services. The summer youth program received the most local support. In Houston, the city continued the summer youth program on a much reduced scale after the loss of funds. This action reflects the political strength of the minority groups that are the main beneficiaries under this program. In Chicago, community development block grant funds were used to finance a summer job program. In Boston, city and private-sector officials raised money to expand a summer job program started before the cuts.

The CETA cuts prompted local employment and training agencies to change the mix of services they offered, emphasizing those with a quick payoff or low cost. Associates in Boston, Jackson, Cleveland, and Seattle reported increased emphasis on develop-

---

3. The county was the prime sponsor for Orlando and Seattle.

Table 15. *Operating Grants: Changes in Federal Aid*
for Large Cities, Fiscal Year 1982

CETA public service
employment

Program ended
Boston ($5.4 million)
Chicago ($37 million)
Cleveland ($10.5 million)
Houston ($5.5 million)
Jackson ($1.2 million)[a]
Los Angeles ($23.8 million)
Newark ($7.6 million)
Orlando/Orange County
 ($2.5 million)[a]
Phoenix ($3.3 million)
Rochester ($2.6 million)
St. Louis ($9.1 million)
Seattle ($7.6 million)[a]
Sioux Falls ($262,000)
Tulsa ($1.4 million)[a]

CETA training

Reduced 25% to 49%
Boston ($3.5 million)
Cleveland ($4.3 million)
Houston ($4 million)
Los Angeles ($14.1 million)
Orlando/Orange County
 ($1.9 million)[a]
Rochester ($1.7 million)
St. Louis ($4.4 million)
Seattle ($5.9 million)[a]
Tulsa ($1.3 million)[a]

Reduced 10% to 24%
Chicago ($15.3 million)
Jackson ($900,000)[a]
Newark ($3 million)
Phoenix ($1.6 million)
Sioux Falls ($104,000)

Compensatory education:
Title I

Reduced 10% to 24%
Boston ($1.4 million)
Newark ($2.5 million)
Seattle ($500,000)
Sioux Falls ($71,000)

Reduced less than 10%
Chicago ($4 million)
Cleveland ($482,000)
Houston ($1.7 million)
Jackson ($190,000)
Los Angeles ($4 million)
Rochester ($350,000)
Tulsa ($106,000)

No significant change
Orlando
Phoenix (NA)
St. Louis

Impact aid

Reduced 50 % or more
Cleveland ($475,000)
Los Angeles ($1.4 million)
Rochester ($210,000)

Reduced 25% to 49%
Sioux Falls ($108,000)

No significant change

Boston	Orlando
Chicago	Phoenix
Houston	St. Louis
Jackson	Seattle
Newark	Tulsa

Note: For CETA, 1981 comparison figures are after the rescission.

a. Program was administered by an overlying government or consortium and was cut for entire prime sponsor.

ing job-finding skills and placement services, rather than training. In Seattle and Rochester, officials shifted their emphasis to shorter training courses in an effort to spread reduced funds. In Sioux Falls and Seattle, stipends to those in training programs were reduced or eliminated.[4]

Nonprofit organizations felt the CETA cuts in two ways: First, many such agencies relied on public service employment program participants, who often made up a significant share of an agency's work force. Second, several nonprofit agencies, such as the Urban League and Opportunities Industrialization Centers, used CETA funds to operate large training programs. Cuts in training funds forced many nonprofit organizations—especially those that are community based—to scale down or close their operations.

Many associates reported increased private-sector influence in the CETA program.[5] The private industry council component of CETA was relatively unscathed in the 1981 budget cuts. In addition, the overall decline in CETA funding led many prime sponsors to seek closer ties with private employers who might fund or administer training programs. In Boston and Rochester, for example, city officials obtained increased private support for training and summer programs. This increasing private-sector involvement changed the policymaking process for employment and training programs in some cities. The Tulsa associates reported that the local government could not make program decisions as independently as in the past, because it had to coordinate its decisions with private employers. In Rochester, the allocation of cuts among CETA services caused controversy; successful efforts by the private industry council to shift funds from training led to a conflict between business leaders and nonprofit training organizations.

4. Sioux Falls and Seattle eliminated stipends for trainees before Congress passed the new training law, which bars such stipends. The new law goes into effect October 1, 1983.

5. The role of private businesses was greatly increased under the Job Training Partnership Act of 1982, which went into effect at the beginning of federal fiscal year 1983.

Compensatory Education

School districts receive federal funds for compensatory education under what is now called "Chapter 1" of the Education Con-
solidation and Improvement Act. Before 1982, title I of the
Elementary and Secondary Education Act of 1965 provided grants
for compensatory education. The 1965 act also provided special
concentration grants in counties with a high proportion of children
from low-income families. Title I required that local school districts use federal funds to supplement, not replace, local funds,
and that the amount of state and local funds used in a title I school
be roughly equal to the average for all the district's schools.

In 1981, Congress renamed the 1965 statute, cut budget authority for the program by approximately 25 percent, eliminated concentration grants, and replaced many statutory requirements with
less specific language.

Compensatory education funds were cut for school districts in
at least eleven cities in the sample; in four of these districts, cuts
amounted to more than 10 percent. In Phoenix, figures were difficult to compile because of a multitude of small school districts. No
significant cuts were felt by two other large-city school districts.

Cuts in federal aid for compensatory education were ratified by
all but two of the large cities in the sample. In Tulsa, the school
district shifted part of a large increase in funds under the education block grant to maintain programs previously funded by the
compensatory education program. With a $186,000 increase in
education block grant funding, the Tulsa school district was able to
transfer slightly more than the compensatory education cut and
still increase funding for programs under the block grant.

The response of the Cleveland schools illustrates the importance of courts in determining the response of local governments
to federal aid cuts. Facing a court order to maintain desegregation
programs and educational services, Cleveland had to replace the
entire cut. The Cleveland associate reported the difficulties the
system faced in doing this:

The programs supported by federal funding were largely those the court ordered,
where retrenchment cannot be made. The school district has little or no power to
cut these programs. It was forced to refinance existing state emergency loans to pay
for these mandated programs. The school board estimates the system needs an
additional $30 million to operate at present levels—either through a tax levy or a
"windfall" settlement from the state. The city is suing the state to recoup 50 percent of the costs associated with desegregation, arguing that state policies contributed to the de facto segregation of the schools.

Because compensatory education is forward funded (that is, aid allocated in 1981 is used for services in school year 1981–82), most of the cuts made in federal fiscal year 1982 affected programs for the school year beginning in fall 1982. The preliminary indications were that about half the jurisdictions would serve fewer children and maintain the same levels of services per student, while schools in the other cities would opt to serve about the same number of children with fewer services per child. In Boston, Houston, and Sioux Falls, associates reported that schools are considering dropping schools, subjects, or grade levels from the program. The Newark and Chicago associates reported efforts to target services on the most disadvantaged students. Schools seeking to spread the funds more thinly planned to increase class size, eliminate teachers' aides in some cases, and in others substitute them for teachers for some functions.

Education Impact Aid

This program provides grants to local school districts as payments in lieu of taxes to help defray the cost of educating children whose parents live or work on federal property. The program distinguishes between "type A" children, whose parents both live and work on federal property, and "type B" children, whose parents either live or work on federal property but not both. Most type A children are children of military personnel or Indians living on reservations. Many type B children live in federally subsidized housing. The reconciliation act phased out aid for type B children over a three-year period; there was a 45 percent reduction in budget authority in 1982. Unlike most education aid, impact aid is not forward funded to the next school year; the cuts made in August 1981 affected the school year starting in September 1981.

The cut in this program did not affect most of the large cities in the sample, but those few that were affected lost a large portion of their aid. In Cleveland, for example, impact aid was cut by 88 percent; in Los Angeles, by 56 percent; and in Rochester, by 76 percent. Because the program provides unrestricted funds that are combined with general funds for school operations, it is difficult to untangle a district's response to this federal aid reduction. Most affected school districts appeared to have ratified the cuts. Cleveland presents a special case, since a court order there prevented the school district from ratifying this cut; emergency financing measures had to be resorted to in this case. Two states, Arizona and Florida, responded to this cut in federal aid to local governments by increasing state aid.

Entitlement Grants

Most local governments, and almost all municipal governments, are not involved in the direct administration and financing
of AFDC, food stamps, and medicaid; for them, the most important
impact of the cuts in these programs came in the form of increased
demands for locally provided services. The federal aid cut in an
entitlement program that most directly affected local jurisdictions
(in this case, local school districts) was for child nutrition. The cuts
in federal school meal subsidies led most school districts to raise
prices and caused some students from low-income families to drop
out of the program. In some cities support of refugees became a
local responsibility as federal assistance was cut off and refugees
sought alternative assistance.

AFDC, Food Stamps, and Medicaid

In the large cities in the sample for this study, four counties
(Los Angeles, Monroe for Rochester, Cuyahoga for Cleveland, and
Hinds for Jackson) administer the AFDC program and all but
Hinds administer medicaid. Counties in New York pay a higher
portion of the nonfederal share of AFDC assistance costs (50 percent) than in California (10 percent), Ohio (10 percent), or Mississippi (none). These county governments had changes in their own
local finances for AFDC and medicaid. However, because the two
programs, plus the food stamp program, which they also administer, are operated uniformly throughout the state, the counties have
no independent authority to change benefits, modify eligibility
rules, or in other ways respond directly to federal policy changes.

As persons removed from federally assisted programs sought
other support, some local governments tried to provide substitute
assistance. Often the substitute aid was in the form of social services, such as emergency health care or shelter, rather than cash
assistance. These indirect impacts of the 1982 federal policy shifts
for entitlement grants are very hard to identify. In Orlando, the
associate reported there were increases in the caseloads of locally
supported social services and health programs that could be linked
to the AFDC cuts. The Newark associate reported a small increase
in the general relief caseload. City officials in Los Angeles
expressed concern that federal cuts under AFDC, medicaid, and
food stamps would eventually lead to increases in caseloads in
locally financed assistance programs. In Cleveland and Rochester,
the associates reported noticeable increases in the general relief
caseloads, but found that former AFDC recipients were only a

small part of the increase; deteriorating economic conditions accounted for more of the caseload growth. The Seattle associate reported that increased demands were being placed on local health and social service programs.

Nonprofit organizations are heavily involved in administering many of the service and emergency programs that were called on to help poor people compensate for the loss of income support under federal entitlement grants. These organizations often provide the bulk of emergency food aid, an important, though indirect, replacement for welfare and food stamp cuts. This is the only area in which nonprofit organizations gained support and prominence as a result of the federal aid cuts; emergency feeding was an important augmented service in a majority of the large cities in the sample. Seattle and Cleveland had two of the largest emergency feeding programs. Federal cuts and a depressed local economy combined to bring hard times for poor persons in the two cities. In both cities, supporters of social programs worked to expand private and corporate giving for food and food distribution. Seattle area food banks served more than three times the number of people during the first six months of 1982 than in the comparable period of the previous year. In Cleveland, nonprofit organizations raised several million dollars to expand food distribution programs and to open new soup kitchens and meal centers. In addition, when a court found a local supermarket guilty of price fixing and ordered it to compensate residents of the five-county Cleveland area in the form of coupons redeemable for food, a community group launched a successful effort to have unredeemed coupons given to area food banks. A publicity campaign was undertaken to encourage people not to redeem the coupons unless they were in financial need.

Sunbelt cities also encountered public assistance problems. As the number of migrants from the North exceeded the number of jobs available, and as the recession came to the Sunbelt, many persons needed assistance. In Tulsa, this migration was said to have dramatically increased the demands facing nonprofit organizations that provide emergency assistance.

One of the most direct ways a change in a federal entitlement program affected localities concerns refugee assistance. As noted in chapter 3, federal changes in the refugee assistance program ended AFDC benefits for refugees after eighteen months, though federal funding was provided for general assistance benefits for refugees if such programs existed. In sites with large numbers of

refugees, such as Seattle and parts of Florida, where no general
relief program existed, federal funds were cut off and refugees
turned to the local government for aid. In Florida, the counties
provided health and social services to refugees and some emergency food and shelter. A supplemental federal appropriation for
refugees reimbursed the local government for part of this expense.

In Seattle, the reaction of the government and the refugees
illustrates a problem of providing income support at the local
level. With the end of federal support, the city expected many
people in the sizable Southeast Asian refugee population to turn to
the city for support. Plans were drawn up to redirect social service
and training programs to address the special needs of refugees.
The city waited for the increase in demand. When it came, it was
much smaller than expected. By piecing together the story from
refugees who did contact the city, officials discovered that some of
the refugees chose to move south to California in search of federally supported general assistance payments.

Child Nutrition Programs

Under the child nutrition programs, fiscal year 1982 brought
declines in federal subsidies for meals in school, daycare, and
summer recreation programs. In the largest of these programs, the
school lunch program, children from families below a certain
income level receive free food. Other children get lunches at a
reduced price; even children paying the "full price" receive some
subsidy. The reconciliation act cut most of the subsidy levels
under this program and lowered income limits for free and
reduced-price meals. The general subsidy was cut from 17.75
cents to 10.5 cents. The special subsidy for reduced-price meals
was cut from 71.5 cents to 58.75 cents. The commodity subsidy in
the form of low-cost foodstuffs dropped from 14.75 cents to 11
cents. On the other hand, the subsidy for free meals was increased
from 91.5 cents to 98.85 cents.

The effect of these changes varied from place to place depending on the characteristics of the schoolchildren, the response of
school districts, and the reaction of families to higher meal prices,
as shown in table 16. In every school district of the large cities
studied, administrators raised the price of meals rather than substitute local funds to maintain subsidies at the prior levels. Price
increases were greatest for higher-income students. In the school
districts of Boston, Cleveland, Rochester, and St. Louis, many students had previously received free meals, so the cuts made little

Table 16. *Child Nutrition: Changes in Federal Aid*
for Large Cities, Fiscal Year 1982

Reduced 10% to 24%	*Increased funding*
Los Angeles ($8.1 million)	St. Louis ($290,000)
Sioux Falls ($160,000)	
	No significant change
Reduced less than 10%	Cleveland
Boston, including special	Orlando
milk ($300,000)	Phoenix
Chicago ($3.27 million)	Seattle
Houston ($28,000)	Tulsa
Jackson ($100,000)	
Newark (NA)	
Rochester ($140,000)	

difference in the number of meals served and the total amount of federal aid. St. Louis actually had an increase in funding for child nutrition (see table 16) due in part to the increase in the subsidy for free meals. Other districts with a higher proportion of reduced-price and full-price student meals saw sharp declines in their federal aid.

Cuts in the related special milk program also hurt many school districts. (This program is discussed here in connection with the child nutrition programs, even though it is not an entitlement program.) Prior to 1981, the special milk program provided subsidies covering the full cost of milk for children receiving free lunches and a partial subsidy for other children. The reconciliation act sharply reduced milk program subsidies, eliminated subsidies to private schools, and restricted income eligibility in the remaining schools. No jurisdiction made up for these cuts in federal aid with local funds.

Block Grants

Most of the block grant money distributed to state governments eventually finds its way to local governments and nonprofit organizations. Several factors led to the widely differing amounts of cuts for the large cities in the sample shown in table 17. Differences in the proportions of reductions at the state level have already been discussed. Cities show even more variation because of differences in the ways states distributed the block grant funds. Declining population in some older large cities, most noticeably in St. Louis, caused large cuts in some programs, such as the community development block grant, where funds are distributed in part on the basis of population.

The social services block grant illustrates the difficulties involved in determining precisely the amount of federal aid cut at the local level under block grant programs. The Chicago associate described the Illinois situation as follows:

> The lead agency is the state Department of Public Aid; eight other state departments also operate portions of the social services block grant programs. The annual social service plan consists of programs to be undertaken by the nine agencies, operating through thousands of local governments and nonprofit organizations. Approximately three-fourths of the funds for the social services block grant are deposited in the state's general revenue account. The rest is allocated to agency accounts, where it is mixed with various types of local matching funds. Thus, social services block grant dollars lose identity at the state level and at the local level are frequently intermingled with other federal grants, United Way support, local government funds, fees, donations, and rummage sale proceeds. Social services block grant funds are not tracked geographically by the state, so I have no "fix" on how much is going to Chicago.

Though the Chicago example may be extreme, many associates reported difficulties in tracking block grant funds.

The following sections discuss the health block grants, the community development block grant, the community services block grant, and the elementary and secondary education block grant.[6] In table 17, which lists the cuts in block grants identified for each large city in the sample, cuts marked with asterisks are totals for an overlying government—normally a county, though in some cases a special district—that receives the funds and actually administers the program. Because it was not possible to separate out the funds spent by the overlying government for services in the city, the entire amount is reported.

Health Block Grants

In many of the large cities in the sample, the introduction of health block grants had no discernible impact in 1982. The slow pace of state implementation of the health block grants was described earlier. Many associates reported city officials still thought in terms of the superseded categorical programs. Local programs were described in terms of lead-paint poisoning preven-

---

6. The low-income energy assistance program is not discussed here, since the associates in all the cities in the sample except Houston reported level funding or increases. In Houston, there was a cut, but it was small.

Table 17. Block Grants: Changes in Federal Aid for Large Cities, Fiscal Year 1982

HEALTH BLOCK GRANTS

Alcohol, drug abuse, and mental health

Reduced 25% to 49%
Orlando (NA)*
St. Louis ($710,000)

Reduced 10% to 24%
Cleveland ($1.6 million)*
Houston ($30,000)*
Los Angeles, categorical mental health ($1.5 million)*

Reduced less than 10%
Boston (small cuts in categoricals)

Increased funding
Newark, drug and alcohol abuse ($50,000)
Sioux Falls ($140,000)

No significant change
Chicago
Jackson
Los Angeles, categoricals except mental health*
Phoenix
Rochester
Seattle
Tulsa

Maternal and child health

Reduced 50% or more
Cleveland ($110,000)*
St. Louis ($550,000)

Reduced 25% to 49%
Houston, categoricals ($798,000)*
Phoenix ($250,000)*
Seattle ($201,000)

Reduced 10% to 24%
Orlando ($50,000)*
Sioux Falls ($60,000)*
Tulsa ($98,000)

Reduced less than 10%
Boston (lead-paint poisoning and title V)
Los Angeles ($270,000)*

No significant change
Chicago
Jackson
Newark
Rochester

Preventive health

Reduced 50% or more
Houston, categoricals ($258,000)

Reduced 25% to 49%
Chicago ($220,000)
Cleveland, rodent control ($60,000), hypertension ($110,000)

Reduced 10% to 24%
Boston, rodent control ($150,000)
Newark ($600,000)
St. Louis ($150,000)

Increased funding
Phoenix, new hypertension program ($140,000)

No significant change
Jackson
Los Angeles*
Orlando
Rochester
Seattle
Sioux Falls
Tulsa

Table 17, continued

OTHER BLOCK GRANTS

Community development

Reduced 10% to 24%
Cleveland ($4.5 million)
Jackson ($500,000)
Phoenix ($1.1 million)
Rochester ($1.7 million)
St. Louis ($4 million)
Seattle ($2.7 million)
Tulsa ($740,000)

Reduced less than 10%
Boston ($300,000)
Chicago ($5.8 million)[a]
Houston ($860,000)
Los Angeles ($5.4 million)
Newark ($1.1 million)
Orlando (NA)
Sioux Falls ($110,000)

Community services

Reduced 50% or more
Sioux Falls ($40,000)

Reduced 25% to 49%
Chicago ($4.1 million)
Newark ($820,000)
Orlando ($310,000)

Reduced 10% to 24%
Boston ($500,000)
Rochester ($180,000)
St. Louis ($400,000)

Reduced less than 10%
Cleveland ($210,000)
Los Angeles ($120,000)

No significant change
Houston
Jackson
Phoenix
Seattle
Tulsa

Education

Reduced 50% or more
Rochester ($2.5 million)
Seattle ($3.3 million)

Reduced 25% to 49%
Cleveland ($3.7 million)
Jackson ($1 million)
Los Angeles ($2.6 million)
St. Louis ($2.6 million)

Increased funding
Boston ($190,000)
Sioux Falls ($150,000)
Tulsa ($186,000)

No significant change
Chicago
Houston
Newark
Orlando
Phoenix (NA)

* Cuts affected a program administered by an overlying county.

a. Chicago changed the beginning of its program year from October to July, permitting it to receive 1983 funds earlier than it otherwise would have. This lessened the impact of the 1982 cut.

tion, hypertension control, genetic screening, and so forth. Data on funding cuts, if available, often related to these categorical programs.

Under the alcohol, drug abuse, and mental health block grant, the changes in funding ranged from a large percentage cut for services in Orlando and St. Louis to small increases in Newark (for drug and alcohol abuse programs) and Sioux Falls. This program is primarily administered by the states in the form of grants to nonprofit organizations. Moreover, many states had carryover funds for the component programs for the treatment of alcoholism and drug abuse and mental health services. No funding cut was reported for six of the large cities in the sample.

Where cuts did occur for the large city governments in the sample, the responses varied. Local governments in Boston, Los Angeles, Newark (for mental health), and Houston ratified the cuts. In St. Louis the federal aid cut was compounded by cuts in local spending. In Cleveland, county officials administering alcohol, drug abuse, and mental health programs faced a decline in state funds in addition to a federal cut. The associate reported that the fiscal condition of the community's mental health system was weak, because "agencies never realistically planned for the formula phaseout of federal categorical money," and state efforts to release mental patients from hospitals have increased the demands on community mental health services.[7] Newark, though it ratified this cut in 1982, was considering increasing client fees as a way of raising revenue to maintain services.

Programmatic impacts of the changes in the alcohol, drug abuse, and mental health program during 1982 could only be discerned in cities affected by large cuts. In Orlando, Orange County (the overlying county that administers these programs) found itself in a bind between a new state policy to treat only the chronically and acutely mentally ill and the incentive created by federal funding cuts to treat fee-paying patients who are moderately impaired. In Los Angeles, the county is consolidating three mental health facilities into one, partly in response to a loss of a federal grant that was to have supported the staff of a new facility. Despite the partial replacement of federal funds for these public health programs in Cleveland, the county ended twenty-four-hour nursing care at a

---

7. The reference here is to the provision of the federal grant for community mental health centers whereby federal aid was phased out on a schedule set forth in the original law.

detoxification center, dropped 200 people from a methadone treatment program, closed two inner-city clinics, and ended outreach programs.

In the maternal and child health block grant, the funding changes also varied widely among cities. Again the analysis is in terms of funds for services provided in the city, and it is made difficult by the varied administrative arrangements for these public health programs. St. Louis and Cleveland experienced cuts of more than 50 percent in funding for maternal and child health services, three cities had cuts of 25 to 49 percent, and two cities had less than a 10 percent cut. Four associates reported no discernible change.

State distribution systems were an important cause of this wide range of changes. Some states chose to shift funds out of large cities so that service levels would be uniform across the state. In the case of St. Louis, the associate reported that Missouri chose to make the deepest funding cuts in urban areas, "The restructured maternal and child health program has provided increased services to medically underserved rural areas at the expense of services in St. Louis and Kansas City." The Seattle associate reported a similar shift in funds in Washington from urban to suburban and rural areas. Seattle lobbied hard to avoid the reshuffling of funds and was partly successful, reducing a 31 percent cut in federal aid to 25 percent. The Cleveland associate reported a dispute between city officials and the state over the proportion of funds from this block grant used to finance state operations. Some city officials believed the state was using the block grant programs to save positions in the state health department.

Maternal and child health received more local support than most other programs, with four jurisdictions at least partly replacing some of the loss in these federal funds. The political appeal of preventing sickness in children is strong. As a result, several jurisdictions, which were very reluctant to replace federal aid cuts, replaced cuts in this program. In Phoenix, for example, county spending on community health rose by about 17 percent in 1982; a major part of this increase was for maternal and child health programs. In Houston, where the cut in funding for city-run programs was nearly $700,000, the city replaced most of the funds cut. The Houston associate attributed this to "the political clout of minority community representatives, including the health department director." In Boston, the city partly replaced federal cuts in the lead-paint poisoning prevention program, one of the categorical programs superseded by this block grant; in Cleveland, the county did the same thing. For Orlando and Los Angeles, county governments also replaced a portion of the lost federal funds for maternal and child health.

Health services changed as a result of the 1981 changes in federal policy in ways that suggest that the health impact of the cuts will occur over a long period of time and be hard to assess. In Phoenix, Newark, and St. Louis, associates reported cuts in programs with a long-run payoff such as health outreach and lead-paint poisoning prevention. In some cities such as Seattle, the biggest impact has been on the length of time persons have to wait to receive treatment. St. Louis increased the use of lower-skilled employees to save money.

Under the preventive health block grant, nonprofit organizations receive a large portion of the funds. Most of the funds are provided to a large number of agencies for specific kinds of preventive health programs. Several cities with cuts in funds for rodent control replaced at least some of the cut or shifted other money into this area to maintain service levels. Chicago and Houston replaced cuts in rodent control funds, and Cleveland shifted community development block grant funds to cover a portion of the loss in this program. Newark is an exception to the pattern of replacement; there the city phased out its own support for the rodent control program.

Community Development Block Grant

Large cities receive community development block grant (CDBG) funds as entitlements. Their allocations are determined by a formula based on population and various indicators of urban distress and social need. In 1982, Congress cut the budget authority for the program by 13 percent,[8] decreased the proportion of the funds going to large cities from 75 percent to 70 percent, simplified the application process, and imposed a new requirement that no more than 10 percent of the funds may be used for public services, as opposed to capital projects. (Police and fire protection

---

8. Under the emergency jobs legislation passed by Congress in March 1983, more than sixty federal programs received additional funding totaling $4.6 billion. The community development block grant received an additional $1 billion in fiscal year 1983, raising spending above 1982 levels. The new funds are available until September 1985, and the normal 10 percent ceiling on public service spending is raised to 50 percent for these additional funds. Future research will examine the effects of this additional spending.

in neighborhoods undergoing development as well as social services to low-income people are examples of services that can be
funded with CDBG money.) The restriction on spending for public services can be waived by the secretary of the U.S. Department
of Housing and Urban Development. HUD also relaxed regulations requiring targeting of funds on designated "neighborhood
strategy areas."

Though states and small cities benefited from the fiscal year
1982 changes in the CDBG program, all of the large cities in the
sample lost funds, though the reduction in all cases was less than
25 percent. The cuts in 1982 allocations were softened in some cities; Los Angeles initially had a $7 million cut, but received a late
allocation of additional funds; Chicago changed its program year to
begin in July rather than October so it received a portion of its
1983 grant earlier than it would have otherwise.

Most cities in the sample ratified the cuts in CDBG funding.
Rochester and Tulsa maintained services by shifting other federal
funds into CDBG-funded programs. In Rochester, the city set up a
revolving loan fund for rehabilitation projects with the loan payments from urban development action grant (UDAG) projects and
used interest earned from CDBG funds to establish a mortgage-re-
duction program with a local bank. In Tulsa, the city merged the
city development department and the urban renewal agency. The
renewal agency had carryover funds and reserves from previous
programs, which the city used to maintain community development services. In Boston, the city's fiscal crisis forced at least temporary abandonment of many city capital projects, undermining
recently initiated efforts to use CDBG and local funds together to
promote and facilitate economic development.

Some of the program effects of the 1982 CDBG cuts are still to
be felt because the funds go for capital projects that take several
years to complete. The 10 percent limit on public service spending
from CDBG funds was not an immediate problem because of temporary HUD waivers, but cities such as Boston, Newark, Chicago,
and Cleveland that use CDBG for public services must make politically difficult reallocation decisions in the near future. The public
service limit is not an issue in growing cities such as Phoenix,
Orlando, Houston, and Tulsa, which spend less than 10 percent of
their CDBG funds on public services.

The relaxation of CDBG geographic targeting requirements on
poorer neighborhoods may have long-term impacts; Los Angeles's
experience in 1982 raises an issue other cities may face. In 1982,

the city received a cut in CDBG funding of about $5 million, or almost 10 percent. The combined effect of this cut and the termination of the neighborhood strategy area requirements under CDBG was reflected in a decision by the city to change its geographic priorities. City officials increased the amount of money available for community development by combining a portion of the CDBG funds with community services block grant funds, and solicited formal proposals for their use from community-based organizations. The city council decided to spend some of this money in council districts that did not include neighborhood strategy areas. Related to this policy shift, housing assistance increased in importance from 48 percent of CDBG funds in 1981 to 58 percent in 1982. Much of this housing assistance money is dispersed, going to homeowners for rehabilitation of single-family and multi-unit buildings.

The impact of these kinds of changes is to lessen the income and geographic targeting effect of the CDBG program. The public services funded by the CDBG grant, which were reduced in response to the federal changes, tend to be most important to the very poor, so the shift away from services hurts them, as does the geographic spreading of the funds outside low-income neighborhoods and its greater use for the rehabilitation of owner-occupied housing.

Funds provided under the CDBG program often have been used as discretionary money for a wide variety of community purposes. This practice continued in 1982; CDBG funds were used to maintain a variety of services in the face of federal cuts. In Chicago, the mayor used CDBG funds to finance a summer youth program jeopardized by CETA cuts. Rochester covered part of the cuts in housing rehabilitation funds and economic development planning with its CDBG allotment. Cleveland used CDBG funds to continue a rodent control program and for maintenance of public housing.

Community Services Block Grant

The community services block grant provides financial assistance to local nonprofit community action agencies that deliver a variety of social services, including health, nutrition, housing, and employment services, to low-income people. Associates in nine of the cities in the sample reported a loss of funds for this program.

The issue of spreading versus targeting was especially important in this case. Several associates reported that state policies for distributing these block grant funds caused greater reductions for large cities than for small cities or rural areas. In Massachusetts, the state distributed community services block grant funds by formula, weighting heavily a jurisdiction's poverty population. Under the formula, Boston stood to lose over $1 million in 1982. The state used carryover funds from previous years to provide Boston with a one-year supplement to ease the transition to lower funding. In a similar way, Chicago lost money under a new state formula; its share of all community services money in the state dropped from 70 percent to 40 percent. Here again, the state provided a one-year transition grant raising Chicago's 1982 total to 55 percent of the total funds available. In Rochester, the city lost slightly more than the state as a whole but for both the cut was about 10 percent. In other states, large cities fared better. Seven of the large cities in the sample received cuts that on a percentage basis were smaller than the cut received by the state government for this block grant. The remaining four cities had roughly the same percentage cut as the state.

All cities in the sample ratified the cut in this federal aid. In Cleveland, the cuts led to a reorganization that many local administrators predicted will increase program efficiency. That city's community action agency consolidated its operations into fewer centers and focused its efforts on employment and economic development. Centers providing many different services closed and agency officials dropped some of their advocacy and ombudsman efforts. These changes were made when Cleveland officials feared an even larger reduction in funding. Even after a late supplemental allocation of funds, the changes stayed in place and the programs that had been eliminated were not restored. The federal cut did not by itself cause this shift in program orientation and organization, but it provided the catalyst for the changes. Chicago also consolidated its community services operations by closing one-third of its neighborhood service centers and reorganizing delivery of services to youths and the elderly.

St. Louis did not do as well in adjusting to changed funding and policies under the community services block grant. During the transition to this block grant, the local community action agency closed twelve neighborhood centers due to uncertainty about funding levels. Furniture was sold, staff terminated, and offices vacated. Three months later when funding was restored, new offices had to be leased and furnished and the staff rehired. This transition was much more costly than in Cleveland or Chicago.

Elementary and Secondary Education Block Grant

The new education block grant, as previously pointed out, consolidates programs that in the past had been forward funded. Only education grants receive this special treatment. Hence the effects of the changes made in 1981 tended not to be felt in fiscal year 1982, with one exception. The exception applies to school districts that in 1981 had received large amounts of school desegregation assistance funding, which they expected to continue. Here, the effect was so large for the school year starting in September 1982 that the consequences of this cut quickly became apparent.

School districts for two cities in the sample, Seattle and Rochester, had cuts of more than 50 percent in the education programs supported by this block grant. Both school districts were still receiving large desegregation grants in 1981 and lost much of their funding with the shift to the block grant. Boston, which had a slight increase in funds in 1982, lost its desegregation assistance in 1980–81, when the desegregation aid program began to phase down.

Most cities ratified these cuts, but where court orders requiring desegregation programs were in effect, schools had to maintain these programs. Cleveland and St. Louis both had to maintain court-mandated services. Cleveland, as already indicated, resorted to emergency financing measures. The St. Louis school district shifted funds from other programs and financed a small part of its desegregation program from general revenues. In Rochester, the city replaced about 25 percent of this cut with general revenues.

Summary on Geographic Shifts of Funds under Block Grants

Many officials in large cities expressed concern that states would use their increased authority under the block grants to shift funds from large cities to suburban and rural jurisdictions. The experiences in the large cities in the sample suggest that these concerns were warranted in some programs though not in others. The health block grants show no consistent pattern of shifts in funds into or out of large cities. Most, though not all, large cities had roughly the same percentage cut as their states, and many benefited from the use of carryover funds to cushion the effects of some cuts. This spreading effect from large to smaller places was most strongly manifest for the health block grants in the case of the new block grant for maternal and child health programs. In the community services block grants only three states have shifted funds out of big cities, but in two of these—Chicago and Boston—the city losses were large. Four states shifted substantial amounts out of big cities in the education block grant programs. In this case, federal law required that funds be allocated on a formula basis, accentuating the spreading effect that occurred under state administration.

Capital Grants and Related Programs

Table 18 lists important capital and closely related operating grants to local governments and shows the impact of the fiscal year 1982 changes on large cities in the sample. Housing and mass transit grants are grouped together in this section because of the close links between the various capital and operating programs in each area.

Only a few cities experienced substantial cuts in capital and related programs, and some even had increases. This finding goes against the public perception that large cuts were made in these programs. Several factors explain this gap between funding levels and public perceptions of them.

Uncertainty was an especially important factor for these capital and related grants, and no doubt contributed to the public perception that major changes were occurring. For much of 1982, local governments were unsure of the amounts they would receive under these grants. In the wastewater treatment program, for example, Congress did not appropriate funds until August 1982. In housing programs, HUD delayed announcing allocations. As a result, many jurisdictions were unsure of the amounts of funding they would receive for more than half the year, after which they received increased funding from a supplemental appropriation enacted in mid−1982. In addition, many of these programs are discretionary project grants, so grants to a city normally vary from year to year and quick assessment of the 1982 changes is impossible. Cities also were aware that President Reagan did not get all the cuts he wanted in these programs in 1982; they feared rescissions during the year as well as more cuts in future years.

To add to the general confusion, much of the public controversy about the grants covered in this section in mid−1981 was about cuts'that did not happen at all or cuts that were not nearly as large as the president had requested. Examples are the unsuccessful efforts by the administration to cut public housing operating subsidies and urban mass transit operating subsidies, and to eliminate the urban development action grant.

Despite the strong tendency toward exaggeration in debates

Table 18. *Capital and Related Programs: Changes in Federal Aid for Large Cities, Fiscal Year 1982*

Assisted housing: capital & operating	**Public housing: operating subsidies**	**Urban development action grants**
Reduced 50% or more	*Reduced 25% to 49%*	*Reduced 10% to 24%*
Houston ($3 million)	Seattle (NA)	Cleveland ($630,000)
St. Louis ($2.5 million)		
Seattle (NA)	*Reduced less than 10%*	*No significant change*
Sioux Falls ($240,000)	Rochester ($200,000)	Boston
	Tulsa ($120,000)	Chicago
Reduced 25% to 49%		Houston
Cleveland ($730,000)	*Increased funding*	Jackson
	Boston ($7.6 million)	Los Angeles
Reduced 10% to 24%	Chicago ($12.5 million)	Newark
Orlando ($500,000)*	Los Angeles (NA)	Orlando
	Orlando ($1.3 million)	Phoenix
Reduced less than 10%	St. Louis ($2.3 million)	Rochester
Tulsa ($80,000)		St. Louis
	No significant change	Seattle
Increased funding	Cleveland	Sioux Falls
Boston ($2.7 million)	Houston	Tulsa
Los Angeles ($840,000)	Jackson	
Rochester ($2 million)	Newark (NA)	
	Phoenix (NA)	
No significant change	Sioux Falls	
Chicago		
Jackson		
Newark		
Phoenix (NA)		

Table 18, continued

**Urban mass
transportation**
Reduced 25% to 49%
Cleveland, capital ($15 million)
   operating ($2.1 million)
St. Louis, capital ($18.7 million)
   operating ($2.8 million)

Reduced 10% to 24%
Los Angeles ($614,000)*
Rochester ($1.2 million)
Seattle ($2 million)

Reduced less than 10%
Boston, operating ($3.5 million)
Chicago, operating ($4.4 million)

Houston ($5 million)

Increased funding
Phoenix ($9.1 million)
Sioux Falls ($740,000)
Tulsa ($260,000)

No significant change
Jackson
Newark
Orlando

Wastewater treatment
Reduced 50% or more
Seattle ($300,000)

Reduced 25% to 49%
Jackson ($5 million)
St. Louis ($9.6 million)

Reduced 10% to 24%
Los Angeles ($8 million)

Reduced less than 10%
Chicago (NA)

No significant change
Boston
Cleveland
Houston
Newark
Orlando
Phoenix
Rochester
Sioux Falls
Tulsa

* Cuts affected a program administered by an overlying county.

about cuts in capital grants, there were some cuts in this area. The following sections review the effects of the 1982 changes in capital and related grant programs and the responses affecting the large cities in the sample.

Assisted Housing

Assisted housing consists of two elements: public housing programs operated by local housing authorities and section 8 assistance for low- and moderate-income households. Under the former, the federal government provides funds to local public housing agencies for the construction and operation of public housing. Under the latter, subsidies are given to tenants in newly constructed or rehabilitated housing or to tenants in private-market rental units.

In the fiscal year 1981 budget, President Carter proposed allotting $30.9 billion for assisted housing. Reagan's approved 1982 budget provided for $18.2 billion; it also provided for increasing rental contributions by tenants of subsidized housing from 25 to 30 percent of their gross income over a period of five years.

Public Housing Operating Subsidies. To help public housing authorities bridge the gap between the amount they receive from tenants and the amount they must spend to operate the facilities, the federal government provides operating subsidies. In the past, such subsidies have equaled close to 40 or 50 percent of the operating costs of public housing authorities. The distribution formula is based on estimates of what a housing authority should receive in rental income. The subsidy is, in effect, the difference between the estimate of what a well-run project costs to operate and the income received from tenants.

In a supplemental appropriation signed into law in July 1982 (near the end of the fiscal year), Congress approved subsidies equal to at least 90 percent of the formula eligibility. Previously HUD had been providing these subsidies at much reduced amounts while the agency worked on a new formula; the supplemental appropriation bill increased both the amount of money HUD distributed and directed the agency to spend the bulk of these funds under the existing funding system.

Changes in public housing operating subsidies during fiscal 1982 followed no set pattern. Certain jurisdictions received increased funding, including Boston, Orlando, and Los Angeles. Other jurisdictions experienced reductions. These included Tulsa, Cleveland, and Rochester.

The jurisdictions with reductions dealt with them in a variety of ways. In Rochester, the housing authority attempted to be more efficient by centralizing operations and consolidating maintenance crews. In Tulsa, the housing authority attempted to make up part of the cut through rental increases and increased revenues from other sources. Tulsa was also able to cover $456,000, or 17.7 percent, of the cut it experienced from its operating reserve for public housing. Tulsa and Cleveland ratified parts of the cuts they received by not filling positions. Tulsa chose not to fill positions for a social service director and two counselor-trainees; Cleveland froze all employment for public housing, leaving thirty-five positions vacant during the year.

Housing authorities also made up the difference by deferring maintenance for public housing: In Cleveland, delays in funding resulted in reduced maintenance and repairs of occupied units. Units being vacated were boarded up rather than prepared for new tenants. Overall, in Cleveland, occupied units decreased both in the quality and quantity of services, with few vacated units made available for occupancy.

Section 8 Housing. The section 8 housing assistance program provides support for both the construction of new housing for low-income persons and subsidies for low-income tenants in existing housing. Under the part of the section 8 program that funds new housing construction, the federal government guarantees to the owner of certain new housing units that it will pay for a portion of the rent for a section 8 recipient, with the funds going directly to the owner. Under the existing housing program, eligible recipients in effect receive a voucher; they then find acceptable housing and receive a direct rent subsidy. Besides reducing the amount of money available for subsidies approximately in half, the Reagan administration increased the amount of the gross family contribution toward rent from 25 percent of income to 30 percent of income for new households coming onto the section 8 program during 1982, rather than spreading the increase over time as for households already participating in the housing programs.

For much of the year, allocations for the section 8 program were uncertain. Because new construction grants were cut most and these are discretionary project grants, assessing the impact of the 1982 changes was very difficult. Five associates could find no clear impact during 1982, but associates for St. Louis, Sioux Falls, Seattle, Houston, and Cleveland reported significant cuts and Boston, Los Angeles, and Rochester experienced increases. In Seattle, a sharp cut in section 8 new construction led the city to scale down two local housing initiatives. Houston also lost its section 8 funds for new construction. In Cleveland, the associate noted a loss of section 8 funding and a shift from family units to units for the elderly.

Wastewater Treatment

The wastewater treatment program provides grants to local governments for the planning, design, and construction of these facilities. Funding levels were sharply reduced in fiscal year 1981 because of a rescission in previously available funding; the fiscal year 1982 appropriation was delayed until August because of a dispute between Congress and the president. The reconciliation act ended separate funding for planning and design (these functions now are reimbursed out of construction grants), and lowered the federal share of costs, starting in 1984, from 75 percent to 55 percent.

Most localities did not know what their 1982 allocations would be under this program in the summer of 1982, as the fiscal year was ending. The late appropriation and delays in state review of the projects meant that many local governments could only speculate on the impact of these changes. Some did respond despite the uncertainty. Los Angeles faced a court order to clean up its sewage discharge and used city funds to keep construction of a facility on schedule; these funds will be reimbursed by the federal government. Orlando and Orange County (the overlying county) increased sewer fees and hookup charges and secured financing from a private developer to pay for a portion of a needed facility. These two jurisdictions also increased water conservation efforts to lessen the need for new capacity and experimented with new treatment technologies.[9]

Mass Transit

The Urban Mass Transportation Administration (UMTA) within the U.S. Department of Transportation helps states, local governments, and regional transit authorities develop and improve mass transit systems. UMTA programs provide operating assistance as well as capital grants for the purchase and rehabilitation of

9. See the description of Orlando below for more information on these changes in state and local policy.

facilities and equipment. Funding for UMTA programs had been rapidly increasing until fiscal year 1982; in that year, budget authority was reduced by 31 percent.[10] The Congressional Budget Office projected, however, that outlays in 1982 would be reduced by only 7 percent, reflecting the slow spendout rates of capital programs. Nearly half of UMTA's budget is for capital grants.

The effects of the federal changes in 1982 in mass transit grants varied at both the state and local levels. UMTA provides some grants on a formula basis, according to population size and density. The agency also provides discretionary grants, awarded on the basis of project reviews. Half of the transit agencies for the large cities in the sample received reductions in operating or capital grants or both. The cuts in operating assistance had an immediate impact, and were reflected in increases in state and local aid, fare hikes, and service cutbacks.

In most cases the cuts constituted only part of the fiscal problems facing transit authorities, especially in the older areas. Escalating fuel and labor costs, management problems, deteriorating facilities, and recession-induced shortfalls in state and local revenues were other concerns. In many cases, these concerns were more pressing than the federal reductions. The two quotes below from the associates' reports for Chicago and Boston underline this point.

In Chicago, there continues to be an unresolved political and fiscal tug-of-war between city, suburban, and state politicians with respect to mass transit—who controls it and who pays for it. Federal policies have had little to do with creating this conflict nor are they likely to have much effect on the outcome.

The Massachusetts Bay Area Transit Authority (MBTA) has a long history of fiscal, managerial, and labor crises. Events in 1981 did not significantly change this pattern. Service decreased and fares increased; labor struggles continued. The MBTA overspent its budget by $10 million. The federal cuts are the least of the problems plaguing the Boston-area system.

But from St. Louis another view is presented; the associate reported,

Less federal money to the bistate system has resulted in employee layoffs, increased rider fares, and fewer bus routes. Even though these cutbacks were precipitated somewhat by high fuel costs, poor economic conditions, and inefficient management, the greatest impact has resulted from lost federal revenue and the anticipation of additional cutbacks.

---

10. Much of this aid for future years was restored in the legislation enacted in 1982 to raise motor fuel taxes to pay for capital improvements in transportation.

The transit system in the Rochester area had a 20 percent cut in operating assistance. Carryover funds helped offset some of the reduction; however, fare increases and service cuts still occurred. For a few jurisdictions, the fiscal year 1982 cuts in federal operating assistance had little impact. The transit system serving the Phoenix area, for example, received an increase in funding, attributable to population growth within the region.

Even the transit authorities receiving about the same level of federal funds in fiscal year 1982 as in the previous year were affected by expectations of, and worries about, future federal reductions. Associates conducted interviews with state and local officials before the president announced plans to raise the federal gasoline tax by five cents a gallon to increase assistance for highway and mass transit programs.[11] The administration had originally proposed phasing out operating subsidies for mass transit. State and local officials complained that the prevailing uncertainty about federal funding for mass transit made planning difficult. The threat of a phaseout in operating assistance, for example, stimulated the consideration of a new financial agreement between Orlando and Orange County, under which the city increased its contribution to the transit authority serving the region.

Sioux Falls's transit agency expected little change in federal aid for fiscal year 1982, and the agency serving the Tulsa area received a slight increase in capital and operating assistance. However, officials from both agencies expressed concern about the effects future reductions, particularly in capital programs, would have on their planned expansion. The Sioux Falls associate said, "In anticipation of future federal aid reductions, the city is forgoing service expansion."

Economic Development

The programs of the Economic Development Administration (EDA) and the urban development action grant (UDAG) program, administered by HUD, provide grants to local governments for specific economic development projects. Awards are based on a competitive evaluation of proposals, so grants to a locality fluctuate from year to year.

The Reagan administration originally sought to eliminate both EDA and the UDAG program. In 1981, political support for the

---

11. This legislation also increased funding for federal highway aid and is discussed in chapter 3 in connection with that program.

UDAG program assured its continuation, though at a reduced funding level, and the administration settled for a sharp reduction in EDA funding for 1982. Four associates reported declines in new awards of EDA grants that were tied to the 1982 changes in the program; none identified cuts in the UDAG program.

Because these two programs have been very important in the local economic development efforts of some cities, associates reported that cities were searching for alternative funds in anticipation of future cuts in this assistance. In the short run, several cities used CDBG funds for their economic development programs; Rochester and Los Angeles were funding economic development planning positions in this way, and St. Louis considered using CDBG to finance industrial development projects. Boston and Tulsa were fortunate to have EDA money available from previous years, which they used for revolving loan programs.

Though the immediate program effects of the 1982 changes in these two capital grant programs were slight because of the long time lag between the allocation of funds and the completion of projects, many city officials expressed concern about the long-run impacts of these cuts in economic development grants. In Boston, the industrial development agency feared that the loss of EDA funds would force it to take a less active role—waiting for private developers to act rather than stimulating development. In St. Louis, the associate reported that officials feared that these cuts would curtail their economic development efforts in 1983 and beyond. In Newark, officials had enough capital projects in the pipeline to keep them busy for two years, but feared that the loss of EDA funds would make future economic development projects more difficult to sell to developers.

Summary of Local Responses

Though cities are affected by cuts in federal entitlement programs because of increased demands for other services, changes in operating and capital programs were more important to their own operations. On the whole, city replacement in operating and capital programs was lower than that of the states.[12] Table 19 lists the cities in the sample grouped by their level of replacement and lists areas of replacement for each. Though precise percentages are

12. Several states ended up with net savings, indicating an overall decline in spending from what it would have been without the federal changes, but this occurred because of the workings of the entitlement programs. This is not true for cities.

Table 19. *Replacement by Large Cities*

City	Programs in which cuts were fully or partially replaced	

Highest Replacement

Orlando	Mass transit	Social services
	Maternal and child health	Wastewater treatment
Los Angeles	Child nutrition	Mass transit
	General relief—aid to families with dependent children	Refugee assistance Wastewater treatment
Cleveland	Compensatory education	Highways
	Education block grant	Hypertension prevention
	Education impact aid	Lead-paint poisoning prevention
	General relief and emergency assistance (aid to families with dependent children)	Mental health and drug abuse Social services (daycare) Summer youth employment (CETA)
Rochester	Community development block grant	Education block grant Home relief—aid to families with dependent children
	Compensatory education	
Houston	Child immunization	Maternal and child health care
	Family planning	Mental health
	Lead-paint poisoning prevention	Rodent control Summer youth employment (CETA)

Low Replacement

Chicago	Rodent control	Social services block grant
Boston	Maternal and child health	Rodent control
Jackson	Child nutrition	
Sioux Falls	Education impact aid	Highway safety
Seattle	Maternal and child health	
St. Louis	Lead-paint poisoning prevention.	
Phoenix	None identified	
Tulsa	None identified	
Newark	None identified	

again impossible, cities in the higher-replacement group replaced 5 percent or more of the federal cuts, while those in the lower-replacement group typically replaced only very small amounts of the cuts.

A number of local governments responded to federal aid cuts by increasing fees and charges for the affected services. The imposition of increases in user fees generated revenue for transit, wastewater treatment, child nutrition, housing, and some health and social services programs. Many cities shifted CDBG funds to cover cuts in federal aid. Carryover funds were especially important in the health block grants. As with the states, however, ratification of the federal cuts was the most common response.

Private-sector replacement of the cuts in federal aid was more important for localities than at the state level. Associates in many, but not all, of the cities reported greater United Way contributions and private support of emergency food programs. Corporate replacement of federal cuts through cash donations was most important in the cities of the Sunbelt—Houston and Tulsa and to a lesser extent in Phoenix. These responses are briefly described in the city descriptions that follow. Outside the Southwest, corporate cash contributions were rare, though in Rochester and Boston the private sector assumed new roles in health and economic development planning. In all sites, associates reported general agreement that corporations and private contributors could not be expected to make up for all the cuts in federal aid.

Individual City Descriptions

As in the case of the state governments in the sample, we present individual descriptions of the responses to federal aid cuts by the large city governments in the sample. They are ordered by level of replacement.

Orlando

The federal cuts in the Orlando area were small, compared with those in other large cities. The city and Orange County, which overlies Orlando, were under little fiscal pressure at the time of the reductions. But, faced with the prospects of additional federal cuts as well as pressures from rapid population growth, both the city and county governments began to assume greater roles in financing public services. Both jurisdictions were well equipped to do so. Florida recently raised the state sales tax; the state shares the proceeds with local governments.

Although federal cutbacks in medicaid, refugee assistance, food stamps, and AFDC led to increased demands for county health and social service programs, most replacement in the area during fiscal year 1982 was for two capital grants: mass transit and wastewater treatment.

Replacement efforts in the transit area were in response to anticipated federal cutbacks, not to the actual reductions occurring in fiscal year 1982. The transit authority serving the Orlando region had federal carryover funds and was not significantly affected by the 1982 cuts. Faced with the prospect that federal transit operating assistance would be phased out by fiscal year 1985, local officials began considering additional support to the transit system. Officials agreed on a financing arrangement that dedicates portions of the county and city receipts from the state sales tax increase to transit operations. Though subject to annual approval, the plan gives Orlando a major role in subsidizing mass transit for the first time.

The fiscal year 1981 rescission and fiscal year 1982 cuts in federal authorizations for wastewater treatment grants also had a significant impact in Orlando and Orange County. Wastewater treatment is a very important local function in this fast-growing urban area and the response of these local governments to changing federal policies in this area is noteworthy. Both jurisdictions are seeking funds for the expansion of wastewater treatment facilities, since the Florida Department of Environmental Regulation in effect compounded federal cuts in construction grants for wastewater treatment facilities for some local governments. The federal program funds up to 75 percent of local construction costs, but by 1984 the federal government plans to limit grants to 55 percent. In an effort to spread its diminishing statewide allotment of wastewater treatment funds, the state's environmental agency obtained federal EPA approval to limit the federal matching rate to the 55 percent level two years before the federal change takes effect nationally.

Officials in Orlando and Orange County are preparing to finance needed wastewater facilities with reduced federal aid or without federal aid, if necessary. Sewer rates were doubled in both the city and county, and hookup fees were increased from $500 to $1,500 per connection. Both the city and the county are experimenting with conservation measures that would expand the capacity of existing treatment facilities. The city instituted a trial program with "state of the art" water conservation devices—special faucets, shower heads, and toilet dams—installing them in homes free of charge. Orange County, in addition, has worked out an arrangement with a private developer who has agreed to purchase $11 million in bonds for expansion of wastewater treatment facilities. The county created a taxing district, which encompasses the developer's property, and will tax the developer to pay the interest on the bonds. Both the county and the developer benefit. The county has a revenue stream to pay off the bonds for this facility. The developer is excused from sewer connection fees. Moreover, the wastewater treatment expansion supports growth in the area and enables the developer to proceed with the residential development. These policy innovations prompted by the fear of federal cuts were viewed favorably by state officials approving wastewater treatment grants and led them to move Orlando and Orange County up the priority ranking, increasing their prospects of getting aid.

Los Angeles

The city and county of Los Angeles both faced serious fiscal pressures in 1982. Los Angeles County is one of the few county jurisdictions in the sample that faced more serious fiscal problems than the city it overlies. This is important, because of the substantial role played by county government in Los Angeles. The county spends more per capita in the city than the city does, and because of state laws it has historically taken a strong leadership role in social programs.

Revenue shortfalls led the county to institute budget cuts and layoffs just at the time that the reductions in federal spending were occurring. The state also faced a difficult financial squeeze in this period. When Proposition 13 passed in 1978, the state had substantial fund reserves that it used to help local governments offset the effects of this tax limitation. By 1982, the reserves were depleted, and the imbalance between state revenue receipts and expenditures was growing. As the year progressed, the state was forced to enact its own cutbacks, compounding the fiscal problems of local governments. Nearly $300 milion in assistance to localities was cut in the state's budget for fiscal year 1983, which began July 1, 1982. Moreover, the state's voters and politicians continued to support limitations on public spending; in 1982 the state adopted legislation that indexed the income tax and abolished the state's inheritance and gift taxes.

To summarize, city and county revenue shortfalls, the impacts of Proposition 13, other tax limitations, and the emerging state financial crisis overshadowed federal aid cuts, although the cuts added to the financial problems of local governments in the Los Angeles area.

The programs most affected by the federal cuts were welfare, social services, education, mass transit, and health. Various replacement and coping strategies emerged in 1982. City and state funds were used to replace most lost federal aid used by the city to provide home-delivered meals for the elderly. City funds also were used to replace federal funds for construction of a major wastewater treatment facility. Because of the delay in federal appropriations for this facility, city funds had to be used to maintain construction in order to meet a court-imposed deadline that required zero sludge discharge by 1985. The city will be reimbursed for these expenditures by the federal government. City officials also used a portion of their community development block grant to offset reductions in community services funding.

The city's school system received an $8.1 million cut in federal aid for school lunches and breakfasts. State assistance for these meals was also cut. School tax revenues were used and meal prices were increased to offset these reductions.

Federal cuts in transit operating and capital assistance were more than offset by an increase in the county sales tax, designated for transit; this levy was approved in 1980 but did not take effect until 1982.

Eight thousand additional people received county general relief benefits in 1982; 38 percent of this increase consisted of people who lost federal refugee assistance benefits and were transferred to the county program. The county received a special federal grant to help cover part of these added costs. Declining economic conditions also contributed to the increase in the general relief caseload. County officials reserved slots in CETA training programs to aid these families.

Cleveland

High unemployment and diminishing sales and income tax receipts were the major concerns of Cleveland city officials in 1982. The recession had severe effects on the financial condition of the state government and the major cities of Ohio. To deal with the state's growing budget deficit and projected revenue shortfalls, the legislature enacted tax increases and spending cutbacks. The state could offer little help to the city in coping with the federal cuts during 1982, however. In fact, local governments in some instances faced reductions in both state and federal aid.

Since its widely publicized 1979 bond default, Cleveland has instituted tax increases and management improvements that are said to have improved its fiscal condition. Hence, the city was able to replace a small portion of the federal cuts out of general funds. During 1982, $1 million in city funds was used to replace the federal cuts for highway improvements and lead-paint poisoning prevention. However, city officials relied more heavily on shifting funds to reduce the effects of this federal cut.

Community development block grant money served as an important buffer against some reductions. The city used CDBG money partly to offset cuts in federal grants for rodent control, to help defray public housing maintenance costs, and to support a housing rehabilitation program similar to the federal section 312 program, which was abolished. City officials also used CDBG funds to reduce cutbacks that occurred as a result of the enactment of the community services and social services block grants. Cuts in daycare services were made up with city CDBG money along with county general revenue funds; some CDBG funds were allocated to neighborhood opportunity centers that had received cuts as a result of the creation of the community services block grant.

Cleveland also used $1 million from its CDBG entitlement to restore CETA cuts. In addition, CETA fund balances from the previous year reduced the impact of these cuts. The city's human resources department was able to transfer $230,000 to summer jobs. City officials negotiated an agreement whereby an additional $2 million owed to the U.S. Department of Labor could be used for summer jobs.

Most replacement of lost federal aid in the Cleveland area occurred at the county level. The county and state general relief program helped offset a small amount of the reductions in AFDC. During the year, county welfare administrators noted an increase in the number of people applying for general relief. This came about as a result of the way the existing county-state program works, not as a result of a conscious policy change. Families with dependents over age eighteen—one of the largest groups of people who had been previously aided under AFDC—moved to the general relief rolls.

Cuyahoga County, which overlies Cleveland, provides a number of major services in the city, and it was able to offset some federal aid reductions for social services. The county has traditionally spent more for social services in the Cleveland area than either the state or federal government, relying largely on two special-purpose tax levies to support health and human services. Cuyahoga County commissioners used general fund balances to maintain a nutrition program for the elderly that received a cut in federal aid in 1982. The county also drew on its $40 million general fund balance to increase support for daycare and mental health services. Although changes under the new social services block grant had a small effect in the Cleveland area in fiscal year 1982, officials began considering an increase in the property tax levy to replace social services cuts expected in fiscal years 1983 and 1984.

In addition to offsetting some of the impacts of the federal reductions, county funds were also used partly to restore emergency assistance benefits cut by the state. This county-state funded program has provided what amounted to a "thirteenth check" to all AFDC recipients. The allotment helped pay for clothing, utilities, and other needs. In 1982, the state enacted a law limiting benefit levels and restricting eligibility for this program, so that only families affected by natural disaster could receive benefits. The cutbacks came under severe attack from welfare recipients and social advocacy groups in Cleveland. For the coming fiscal year, county commissioners allocated $1 million in general funds to restore some of the benefits.

Federal cuts in education grants added to the financial problems of the Cleveland school system. The school district was especially hurt by the redistribution to rural areas and smaller cities of federal funds administered under the new education block grant. Most of the previous categorical grants supporting court-ordered desegregation programs were consolidated into this new block grant. Faced with the loss of $3.7 million from the previous year's grant receipts along with other federal cuts in education aid, the school district had to refinance existing state emergency loans in order to maintain its desegregation programs under the terms of the court order. The city school system is hoping to have some of these costs reimbursed by the state.

Rochester

The city of Rochester was in weak financial shape in 1982 and could afford little replacement of federal cuts. In recent years, operating costs have outpaced the growth in property tax receipts, Rochester's major revenue source. Little direct replacement occurred from city funds. City officials relied more on new uses of federal aid and the shifting of discretionary funds to reduce the impact of federal aid cuts.

Community and economic development funds served as an important source of discretionary money used to offset the effects of federal aid cuts. UDAG loan repayments amounting to approximately $450,000 replaced some of the cuts in the city's community development block grant entitlement. In turn, cuts in section 312 housing—the rehabilitation loan fund—were partly replaced with a portion of CDBG funds designated for housing improvements. These funds were deposited in a local bank, and the interest was used to write down mortgages for single-family structures, much as the section 312 federal program did before it was eliminated. In addition, the city set up a revolving loan fund with CDBG money to supplement bank loans for the rehabilitation of vacant housing in lower-income neighborhoods. A small amount of CDBG money was also used by the city to maintain planning positions, which were previously funded by grants from the Economic Development Administration.

Increases in funding from the state and overlying special-district governments helped the city cope with some of the cuts in the Rochester area. The New York State legislature approved measures that raised state transit subsidies. The increases, enacted before the reconciliation act, responded to long-term financial difficulties of mass transit operations in the state. The New York field associates indicated that while the increases were not in direct response to the reconciliation act, they were stimulated by a concern that federal aid eventually would not be sufficient to compensate for the revenue shortfalls.

The Rochester-Genesee Regional Transportation Authority received $2.7 million in additional state aid in 1982. The agency experienced a cut in federal operating assistance of $941,000; federal capital grants for purchases of equipment, new construction, or the repair of existing facilities were $246,000 lower than in 1981. The transit agency had $238,000 in carryover funds from the previous year's allocation of federal operating assistance. Still the agency had to raise fares and cut service during the fiscal year;

federal cuts in transit funding were cited as major reasons for these actions.

Rochester's school district, which encompasses the entire city, replaced some of the federal cuts in education programs. As a result of the new education block grant, the school district received $2.5 million less in federal aid than the year before. In the past, the Rochester school district had been especially active and successful in getting federal education aid for special programs that encouraged voluntary desegregation. To offset some of this reduction, the school district spent $440,000 of its own funds and is anticipating state aid increases.

Private-sector funds also were used to replace federal cuts. The health planning agency serving the Rochester region (the Finger Lakes Health Systems Agency) received a $495,000 cut in its federal planning grant. To help offset this cut, a task force was established under the United Way consisting of corporate leaders and representatives from the Blue Cross, United Way, area hospitals, and the voluntary health community. The task force worked out a temporary arrangement whereby the region's Blue Cross plan will defray the loss of federal planning funds in 1982 and 1983. The task force is also working out an arrangement to distribute the cost of health planning among beneficiaries. The Rochester associate observed that leaders of the private sector generally support efforts to replace federal planning grants. There is agreement, for example, that the planning and coordinating activities of the Finger Lakes Health Systems Agency have been effective in holding down health care costs.

Houston

The city of Houston, generally prosperous, growing, and politically conservative, was under little fiscal pressure in 1982; however, even here fiscal pressures increased as the year progressed. The worsening of the national economy and the depressed world oil market contributed to rising unemployment. Because of the devaluation of the Mexican peso, the rate of illegal immigration into Houston has escalated, placing a strain on the health and social services delivered by Harris County, which overlies Houston. By June 1982, Houston's unemployment rate had exceeded the previous high of 7 percent; the rate rose rapidly from 3.8 percent at the end of 1981.

Though Houston has historically been a low-tax city with limited public services, tax hikes were enacted by both the city and county in 1982. These were linked to services such as police, fire, hospitals, and flood control. Public officials "sold" the increases to area residents by stressing how low the taxes in Houston were compared to other U.S. cities.

The fiscal effect of the federal cuts on Houston local governments was basically a limited one, though Houston-area governments (particularly the city) made notable efforts to replace lost federal aid. Most city agencies, however, were not heavily dependent on federal aid and followed a policy of not using federal money to support permanent employees. Though the city health department experienced losses of federal aid for several categorical public health programs, these funds represented a small percentage of the department's total budget. Moreover, the department had several categorical grants that were winding down during the year and were expected to expire soon. City general revenues were used to replace a considerable portion of the funds lost by the health department. City funds were also used to offset most of the $183,000 loss in categorical funding used to support a counseling program for pregnant teenagers. Likewise, the city's $128,000 lead-paint poisoning prevention grant, which expired in December 1981, was replaced with general revenues. Cuts in federal grants for child immunization and family planning services were also replaced during the year. A $328,000 (25 percent) reduction in federal aid for maternal and child health services is expected; city officials plan on covering this loss with general revenues.

In addition, Houston officials used general revenue funds for a summer youth employment program, replacing a small amount of the federal aid lost as a result of the CETA cutbacks. City officials expect that its federal grant for rodent control will diminish, and intend to maintain this service without federal assistance. For the first time, the city allocated a portion ($180,000) of Houston's community services block grant to help support a legal services agency that had lost half its budget as a result of the federal cuts.

The Houston associate noted that, in most instances, city replacement was explained by the politically sensitive nature of a program. "The political clout of the city's minority communities was successfully exercised to prevent cutbacks in these programs."

Nonprofit organizations play an important role in delivering social services in the city. The elimination of public service employment, which was one of the largest single grant reductions in the Houston area, and cuts in federal grants for social services had a direct impact on the budgets and programs of these agencies.

Increased volunteer support and contributions from foundations, religious organizations, and private businesses lessened the effects of these cuts. The United Way agency serving the Houston area reallocated $960,000 for a special emergency fund to assist agencies affected by the federal cuts. As of September 1982, however, only four nonprofit agencies had applied for funding. Churches operated shelters, food kitchens, and clothing banks for long-time residents and recent arrivals who did not qualify for federal, state, or local assistance.

Business executives in the Houston area formed a private-sector initiative planning group and identified housing rehabilitation, daycare services, and summer jobs for youths as priorities for corporate efforts.

Chicago

Federal grants are very much in the background in the Chicago area. City officials have historically kept federal aid separate from ongoing basic city functions, treating it as money from Washington for federally identified purposes. Moreover, in 1982, the general state of the economy and its adverse impact on major revenue sources, such as the sales tax and the state income tax, was a much more important problem for local governments in the region than were the cuts in federal grants. Unemployment in the state was above 12 percent; the continuing decline in basic industries such as steel and farm equipment manufacturing contributed to economic problems in the Chicago area.

In addition, local finances during 1982 were heavily influenced by state and local electoral politics. Republican Gov. James Thompson was in the midst of a close campaign against Democrat Adlai Stevenson III for the November 1982 gubernatorial election, and Chicago's Mayor Jane Byrne, seeking a second term, was campaigning in the February 1983 Democratic primary. Both Thompson and Byrne were determined to avoid either tax increases or major public service crises.

The two darkest spots in what was otherwise a manageable fiscal picture in the Chicago area were the board of education and the Chicago Transit Authority. Little action was being taken to resolve the fundamental problems of these two overlying governments; instead, the time of reckoning was pushed ahead until after the elections. The September opening of the Chicago schools was in doubt up to the last minute because of funding problems; the mayor and the board of education patched together a special budget package. In much the same way, city and state officials bought time for the mass transit system. The legislature authorized the Regional Transportation Authority to meet cash flow needs by borrowing $100 million over a period of eighteen months.

A distinguishing feature of the local governmental structure in Chicago is the high degree to which overlying governments finance and administer services provided in the city. The impact of the federal cuts in the Chicago area was spread among a variety of agencies, many of which are outside of city government.

Overall, there was little replacement of federal money by either state or local governments. The shifting of federal funds among programs reduced some of the impact of the federal cuts.

Within city government, the main impact of federal grant cutbacks occurred in social programs. City officials have historically kept these clearly separate from basic city functions, and have used federal grants for the bulk of their support. When cuts occurred, there was no move to replace federal funds with local money.

The effects of reduced federal capital grants were delayed because of the availability of funds from prior-year federal commitments. The federal interstate transfer program for highways, for example, provided an important source of funds for the Chicago area. In 1979, state and local officials received the Federal Highway Administration's approval to cancel a $2 billion appropriation for the Crosstown Expressway. City officials in Chicago are counting on applying half of this amount primarily to mass transit extensions and bridge repairs. Transfer funds are subject to annual appropriation, however, and there is some concern that the Reagan administration may try to slow down and stretch out these expenditures.

As in other cities, officials in Chicago relied on community development block grant funds to make up some federal aid reductions, especially those in the CETA program. Chicago's community development block grant entitlement for fiscal year 1982 was scheduled to be reduced by $5.8 million, from $128 million in 1981 to $122.2 million. However, the impact of this cut was nullified as a practical matter when HUD permitted Chicago to move the beginning of its community development block grant program year forward from October 1 to July 1, 1982. Chicago's receipt of fiscal year 1983 funds on July 1, 1983 had the effect of double funding the program from July to October 1982.

Since the beginning of the CDBG program in 1974, Chicago has frequently used these federal aid funds for ongoing operating functions—snow removal, trash cleanup, extra police services, and social services. During 1982, CDBG funds were used to fill gaps in a variety of programs and to offset some federal cuts. Often this meant shifting funds away from previously planned programs. Chicago spent $5 million in CDBG funds to subsidize housing rehabilitation loans, bringing interest rates down to 5 percent for low- and moderate-income borrowers. These funds were combined with the receipts from a $25 million city revenue bond issue for home improvement loans. The subsidized loans had few takers, however. Most of the funds went for a city cleanup campaign.

Also in 1982, Mayor Byrne announced a "public-private venture fund" whereby private donors would match $2 million in CDBG funds to "help fill the gap created by the federal cuts in social services." The plan never got very far; CDBG funds earmarked for it eventually were used for a youth employment program, offsetting some CETA reductions. All totaled, approximately $3.2 million in CDBG funds was redirected for youth employment. Most of the jobs made available were in the city's streets and sanitation department, where workers were hired for tree-trimming, vacant lot cleanup, and rodent control. Similarly, a one-time $300,000 federal grant for juvenile justice and delinquency prevention helped offset some of the CETA cuts by providing 631 half-time jobs to youths between age fifteen and eighteen who had had contacts with the police.

During fiscal year 1982, Mayor Byrne continued to use CDBG funds as an emergency fund—not just for city agencies. The Chicago Housing Authority received $4.5 million; $16.8 million in CDBG funds went to the Board of Education. The allocations helped both agencies respond to pressing financial problems unrelated to the federal cuts.

Boston

Boston's fiscal condition in 1982 was dominated by local revenue concerns rather than the effects of the Reagan domestic program. Proposition 2 1/2, passed by Massachusetts voters in November 1980, limited property taxes to 2.5 percent of assessed property value, severely restricting the city's primary revenue source. In a separate action in 1980, the Massachusetts Supreme Judicial Court supported a property owner who sued to lower his assessment. The court ordered the city to repay about $50 million in past tax overpayments.

After about a year of fiscal chaos, the state legislature in 1982 gave Boston the authority to issue $50 million in bonds to pay these court-mandated payments. The legislature also approved four new tax sources. Two of them, a county deed-transfer tax and a tax on new hotel rooms, are temporary diversions of state taxes. The other two are a tax on condominium conversions and a special fire service charge. The city will also sell its convention center to a new state authority to raise more revenue. Unfortunately, these devices and new sources of revenue may not raise as much revenue as officials had originally hoped. One factor easing the strain in 1982 was that state aid to the city was increasing.

Because Boston has been active in seeking federal grants, especially for economic and community development, it will be affected in a serious way by the reductions in federal aid for these purposes. For capital programs, however, the impact of federal cutbacks is not immediate, and the cuts themselves have been smaller than originally expected.

Despite these ameliorating circumstances, some of the cuts in other Boston programs were major ones. Education and·training programs were the hardest hit. CETA programs were cut by $8.9 million, of which $5.4 million was for public service employment. The cuts in education programs were smaller. They were also less noticeable, because of the magnitude of the other problems faced by the public school system. Compensatory school aid was cut by about 15 percent, but part of this reduction was due to declining school enrollment. The state allocation of federal desegregation money declined sharply for the second year in a row, from $4.8 million in 1981 to $1.6 million in 1982.

The city did not have the resources to replace federal aid cuts. In the CETA programs, city officials tried to increase private-sector involvement, with some success, but there was no political support for increased local funding of public schools.

The response of the housing authority to federal cuts was also constrained. Boston is heavily reliant on housing grants. About one-fifth of the city's housing stock is federally assisted. Cutbacks in the housing rehabilitation loan program, which were substantial in Boston, caused major concern—again not for the immediate future, but for the long term. As for CETA and education programs, there was no replacement.

In transportation, as in housing, federal aid losses were longer run. Thus, while federal cuts were not a big factor in 1982, officials were concerned about future impacts. The mass transit operating grant was cut by about 10 percent; this cut was offset by an increase in state aid.

Federal grants for health programs also were reduced in Boston. Rodent control lost about one-fifth of its federal funds. The city replaced some health funds, notably for the lead-paint poisoning prevention program.

In sum, the main effects of the Reagan domestic program on Boston will occur in the future, after money in the pipeline runs out. Losses in operating programs have been more immediate than in capital areas. The city has made only minor replacements because of its serious fiscal problems.

Jackson

In 1982 the city of Jackson was experiencing moderate fiscal stress. The city's fiscal problems were caused in part by the recession, which reduced sales tax revenues below the amount that had been projected when its fiscal year 1982 budget was enacted. City officials used general revenue sharing funds as operating funds in the street department in order to cover the revenue shortfall. To raise more revenue for fiscal year 1983, the city raised the property tax assessment rate, increasing its local tax revenues by 5 percent. This additional revenue was used in the city budget; none went to the school district. As a further revenue measure, the mayor planned to seek authority from the state legislature for cities to levy an additional one-cent sales tax. Because the city's resources were already stretched to meet existing financial and program obligations, the city was unable to replace funds lost from federal programs.

The biggest loss of federal funds for Jackson was in the CETA program. The area lost $2.8 million in CETA funds for other than public service employment, of which $600,000 was administered by the city and $2.2 million was administered by the Capital Area Training and Employment Consortium. Funds received under programs consolidated into the new education block grant were reduced by one-third. Another education program, the compensatory education program, was cut by 6 percent.

The urban mass transportation operating grant was cut slightly, a cut which the city compounded by reducing its contribution by 6 percent. Child nutrition funds for school meals were cut by 2 percent, which was made up by raising school lunch prices. In the social services area, daycare aid was cut by 4 percent; the state compounded this by withdrawing a like amount of state funds.

Aside from these programs, capital grants were also affected by the 1982 federal budget reductions, although in this case the effects were prospective, not immediate. At the same time, Jackson was in the process of issuing bonds for capital programs. The city planned to float a $30 million capital improvements bond issue in early 1983. City officials hoped to avoid having to levy a tax increase to finance bond repayments by using a surplus in its bond and interest fund and by aggressive cash management. Because the city has an ambitious capital improvement plan, there was concern about possible future reductions in capital grant funds from Washington. In the past, Jackson has made heavy use of federal aid for capital projects. In 1982 the city completed major projects funded by the urban mass transportation and federal aid to urban systems grants. The only near-term effects of federal cuts for Jackson in capital programs in 1982 were minor. In 1982, the city did not receive an anticipated $5 million in an environmental protection grant for wastewater treatment because of late federal appropriations. However, the city did expect to receive this money eventually. The city lost $500,000, or 10 percent, of its CDBG grant.

Sioux Falls

Sioux Falls was facing little fiscal stress when the federal budget cuts were enacted. Unemployment was at 3.8 percent in July 1982. Despite these pluses, there were clouds on the city's fiscal horizon.

The federal budget cuts were not large or important for Sioux Falls, nor were they a major political issue. Some important operating grants were cut in Sioux Falls and in the overlying county, Minnehaha. For the CETA program, the combined city-county losses, including the elimination of the public service employment program, totaled nearly $200,000. Funding for the work incentive program to train AFDC recipients was also eliminated. The state took over part of the program, providing jobs for welfare recipients.

A number of other operating programs also experienced cuts. Education impact aid was cut by about one-third. The school district replaced these federal funds, but the amount involved—$108,000—was dwarfed by the size of the overall school budget—$28 million. Compensatory education received a large cut, which was not replaced. Many health programs received some reduction in funding. Federal funds were reduced for the maternal and child health services, urban Indian health, and the primary care block grant. For programs included in the primary care block grant, a fee increase helped to offset some of the cut. One health program—the alcohol, drug abuse, and mental health block grant—gained in both federal and state funds, as well as increased county matching funds.

Among community development and social services programs, the community services block grant lost all but its carryover funds. The shift to block grant funding brought about major administrative changes. Southeastern Human Development, a six-county antipoverty agency, lost most of its funds when the state assumed a new and larger role in the delivery of community services. Thus, while funds to the state were cut by less than half, some local community services agencies, as in this case, were reduced by much more than that. The state is considering establishing a statewide community services agency to replace local ones, but so far has not done so. Other community programs that lost money were legal services and family planning.

Capital programs also had some reductions. The housing rehabilitation loan program was eliminated, and CDBG funding was reduced by 10 percent.

Almost no replacement of federal programs occurred in Sioux Falls. The federal budget cuts did not affect the city as severely as city officials had expected. The associate summarized the situation as follows,

The impact on this jurisdiction was modest in fiscal year 1982, but will increase by 1983 and 1984 even if no additional reductions occur. As surpluses are absorbed, further postponements become impossible and existing, already adopted cuts will take effect. Reductions generally will be ratified by local governments. The exceptions will be some hardware programs, primarily transportation and community development, where replacement may occur. Replacement in social service areas by jurisdictions in this area will be minimal and highly selective.

Seattle

Seattle's financial condition was relatively sound at the beginning of fiscal year 1982, but the city was hurt as the year progressed by the recession, inflation, and state-imposed revenue limitations. As a result, the city's fiscal problems and the related deterioration of economic conditions in Washington State came to overshadow the effects of the 1982 federal budget cuts.

The state legislature prevented the city from pursuing the

strategy it had planned for the provision of city services. City officials had defined what they considered a minimum level of services that local governments should provide, and planned to raise the needed taxes and fees to fulfill these responsibilities. In order to raise revenue, in 1980 city officials imposed a hotel and motel tax and a business and occupations tax on services. In 1981, city officials increased the general business and occupations tax and added a surcharge. They also raised utility rates and used other available taxing authority to supplement local revenues. The legislature undercut these efforts in April 1982, when it prohibited cities from imposing a surcharge on the business and occupations tax, put a lid on the growth of this tax, denied the city authority to levy a hotel and motel tax, and capped growth of the utility tax rates. These measures reduced Seattle's revenues and made it impossible for the city to respond to federal aid cuts.

The most important reductions in federal aid in Seattle were in operating grants. The largest amount of money lost was from the CETA program. In addition to the elimination of the public service employment component, CETA funding for training and related labor market services was cut by more than 25 percent. Education programs also sustained major reductions. The education block grant funds took a cut of 80 percent, and compensatory school funds were cut by 14 percent. Seattle's allocation under the social services block grant declined 30 percent, even after carryovers were used. Health programs also lost funds, especially the maternal and child health block grant, where funding dropped by 45 percent. This cut was partly offset by local funds. This was the only program to receive local replacement funds.

Transportation programs, both operating and capital, also experienced reductions. Federal aid for urban highway systems was reduced by 15 percent; UMTA grants for mass transit administered by King County were cut by 20 percent for operating and capital purposes together.

Housing and community development grants were also reduced. Community development funds declined by $2.7 million or 17 percent. The loss of CDBG money adversely affects housing in Seattle because the city had allocated nearly half of its CDBG money to improve existing housing and to build new low-income housing.

Looking ahead, Seattle officials expected a number of capital grants in future years. The city has made heavy use of federal grants for capital improvements such as wastewater treatment, housing, and various transportation grants, including special bridge funds. City officials are very concerned that after the funds committed to the city are exhausted, they will not be able to obtain additional grants.

In sum, Seattle was unable to replace more than a thin sliver of lost federal funds with local funds because of its rapidly worsening fiscal and economic conditions in 1982. At the same time, Seattle bore a disproportionate share of the 1982 federal budget reductions in Washington State, because the state legislature increased the proportion of federal aid going to suburban and rural areas under several of the new block grants at the expense of Seattle.

St. Louis

St. Louis, as described earlier, is distinctive among the cities in the sample because of its lack of an overlying county government that could assume some of the burdens resulting from the federal aid cuts. The city of St. Louis is geographically and politically separate from St. Louis County, and the county operates no programs within the city.

Partly because almost all population and economic growth in the area has occurred outside the city's borders, the city has long-standing and serious financial problems. City officials anticipated a deficit for their 1983 budget. Serious fiscal problems also existed at the state level; state expenditures in recent years have outpaced general revenue, and Missouri's newly elected Republican governor embarked upon a series of state cutbacks just as the federal cuts were unfolding.

With St. Louis's fiscal woes augmented, federal cuts in general were ratified; little replacement was possible. City funds partly replaced the loss in federal funds for a lead-paint poisoning prevention program. In 1981, the federal categorical grant for this program totaled $522,000, providing nearly 43 percent of the program's budget. In 1982, the city's allotment for the program was reduced to only $45,000. City officials increased the amount of city funds going to the program, shifted CDBG money to it, and relied on carryovers, thus making up almost half of the loss in federal aid.

Though the city lacks an overlying county government, there are two special districts which are important for this analysis.

St. Louis's school system, which is coterminous with city boundaries, also had to make up for losses in federal aid. The biggest reduction in education funds came in grants that supported court-ordered desegregation programs. To maintain these pro-

grams, school officials transferred approximately $7.5 million from
the general operating budget, cutting expenditures in other program areas. Finally, the regional transit system was plagued in
1982 by many financial problems, including federal aid cuts. The
federal reductions were cited as a major reason for an increase in
bus fares as well as for cuts in service and the layoff of 400 workers.

Phoenix

Phoenix and Maricopa County, which overlies it, were in good
fiscal condition in 1982. City officials were concerned about
declining revenues, but no major tax increases were enacted, nor
were deficits incurred. The county's diversified economy continued to grow during the year and benefited from new defense contracts. The federal cuts had only what can be characterized as a
mild impact.

The largest reductions for both the city and county resulted
from the elimination of CETA public service employment and the
cuts in CETA training programs. Carryover funds in the job training programs helped cushion these reductions. Carryover funds
also helped reduce the impact of cuts in maternal and child health
services, which are provided in the Phoenix area by county health
clinics. The county's health department also experienced cuts in
grants for family planning, primary care services, and child
immunization. Several nonprofit organizations and religious
agencies experienced relatively large cuts in grants for refugee
resettlement.

In other programs, agencies in the Phoenix area received
increases in federal aid. The transit agency serving the region
received an increase in operating assistance, which was largely
attributed to population growth and the use of 1980 census figures
in the federal distribution formula. State administration of the
preventive health block grant brought unexpected new federal
money into the county for a hypertension program.

Even though the cuts were limited and the city and county
governments were in relatively good fiscal condition, there was little replacement in the Phoenix area in 1982. Maricopa County
increased its spending for community and health services, but the
increase was not tied to any specific federal aid reduction. In
some programs, replacement was not needed because of the availability of carryover funds.

Another reason for limited replacement was the prevailing attitude of Phoenix officials toward federal grants. As a general rule,

city officials have been wary of federal aid, reluctant to become dependent on these funds by using them for basic city services. As long as federal funds are available, the city generally accepts them and even works to obtain what it is entitled to receive. Once funds are reduced, the city has taken the position that the activities involved reflect federal priorities; they are federal programs.

Arizona firms and nonprofit organizations have attempted to build on the state's tradition of voluntarism and private action to help maintain important services. Local firms increased their efforts to encourage volunteer support for nonprofit organizations, and a newly formed United Way agency worked to link volunteers with agencies needing assistance.

Tulsa

The city of Tulsa enjoyed economic health and fiscal stability for most of fiscal year 1982, although there was a decided falling off by the end of the year. For the housing authority, transit authority, school district, city department of development, and the urban renewal authority, generally good economic conditions helped build sizable fund balances, which enabled the city to continue to finance operations in 1982 at normal levels of activity. The impact of reductions in federal funds that pass through the state was partly offset by special state appropriations. Thus, the impact of the fiscal year 1982 changes on people, programs, and government agencies was minimal.

The effects of the recession became more significant at the end of the federal fiscal year. In July and August of 1982, collections from state sales taxes, largely earmarked for welfare and social service programs in the state, declined for the first time in a decade. Local property tax revenues were also affected, which caused problems for schools and county health programs.

The city of Tulsa faced few federal aid cuts. The biggest federal aid cuts occurred in the CETA programs and in EDA grants. Other capital programs were cut, notably CDBG and section 8 housing subsidies. A few operating programs—compensatory education, maternal and child health, and housing operating subsidies—also received cuts.

The city was able to shift funds to cover most of its federal losses. Shifting money from the general fund balance and from general revenue sharing enabled the city to reduce the impact of the federal cuts that did occur under CDBG, CETA, EDA, and its alcoholism program. The urban renewal authority and the city

development department, which between them administered
most federally aided capital programs, were merged in order to
make the best use of the carryover funds available to these agencies. The housing authority used operating reserves and interest
income to keep its programs on schedule. The use of these
reserves meant that, although HUD contributions decreased from
1981 to 1982, total expenditures increased.

Contributions of businesses and nonprofit organizations lessened the effects of the federal cuts. Local businesses contributed
$318,000 to a public health clinic serving northside Tulsa, replac-
ing federal aid lost under the new health block grant programs.
The city financed a home energy conservation program with $2
million from a utility company, $2 million from the city's commu-
nity development block grant entitlement, and $20 million from a
bond issue. The Tulsa Area United Way increased its annual fund
drive by $300,000, established a special "safety net fund" for non-
profit agencies hard hit by the reductions in federal aid, and
received pledges totaling $400,000 to help offset future federal
cuts.

Local officials expected that more serious cutbacks in federal
funds, particularly for transportation, would soon hit Tulsa.
Declining sales tax revenue along with concern about growing
capital needs prompted a search for new revenues. A transportation advisory committee endorsed a city gasoline tax. At the same
time a campaign was launched to change the city charter so that a
simple majority of voters, rather than the currently required 60
percent plurality, would be able to approve public utility and general obligation bonds. The associates said that the Reagan domestic program in the form of real or threatened cutbacks was a major
stimulus to this search for new revenue.

Newark

Newark is the most economically and socially distressed city in
the sample. In fiscal terms, however, the city is relatively better off
than might be expected, in large part due to the strong supervisory
role over local finances played by the New Jersey state government.

Federal aid cutbacks in Newark were not a big issue locally in
1982. There were some significant cutbacks in the employment
and training, health, and social service areas, but city administrators conceded that even these cuts were smaller than they had initially expected. Moreover, because of overlapping fiscal calendars,

prior-year surpluses, and the money saved through staff attrition, program effects of federal aid cuts could be minimized in most cases.

Few cuts were made in capital programs as a result of the 1982 budget. The community development block grant, predominantly a capital program, received a budget cut of $1.1 million or 6.3 percent. Other capital programs, including housing, economic development, and transportation, did not receive large cuts. These programs had enough money and work in the pipeline to keep essentially on schedule in 1982.

Most of the major cuts occurred in operating grants. As in other jurisdictions, the largest losses were in the CETA program. The city, a CETA prime sponsor, lost $7.6 million in public service employment funds. Other funds were cut by $3 million. Other programs that sustained relatively large reductions were the community services block grant and nutrition for the elderly, both of which were cut by one-third. Other nutrition programs that sustained cuts were summer nutrition and meals for children in Head Start. Compensatory education, with a cut of $2.5 million, had the next-largest loss of money after CETA. Health programs also were cut. In addition, the program for feeding infants and pregnant women, preventive health programs, rodent control, and lead-paint poisoning prevention all sustained cuts.

There was no replacement of lost funds by the city. In fact, for the rodent control program, the city compounded the federal cuts. The associate reported that the biggest and most serious effect of the federal aid cuts on the city of Newark in 1982 appeared to be psychological: a dampening of expectations and heightened pessimism about the future of government programs and finances.

Concluding Comments

The analysis to date indicates that state governments were more likely to replace cuts in federal operating and capital aid than were the large cities in the sample. (Cuts in entitlement programs do not affect localities in most cases.) Of the fourteen cities we studied, five—Orlando, Los Angeles, Cleveland, Rochester, and Houston—replaced significant amounts of federal cuts. Although we classify them as "highest replacement," this term simply shows how they compare with the other cities; replacement on the whole was not high or widespread for the large-city governments studied.

Because large cities vary widely in fiscal and economic conditions and in governmental structure, the cities in the sample selected different programs in which to replace federal cuts and relied on different sources of funds with which to make the replacements. In a number of the large-city areas studied, state governments replaced lost federal aid for local programs.

The analysis in this chapter focuses on what local governments did—cities, counties, school districts, and various types of special districts. In Orlando, in a high-growth area, the focus of attention was capital programs and needs, and the importance of avoiding any adverse effects from cutbacks in federal aid for capital purposes. In Cleveland, the significant reaction was the replacement of lost federal aid by Cuyahoga County; most of the replacement that occurred was for social service programs. In Rochester, many types of local governments were involved in the replacement that occurred in a variety of program areas. In Los Angeles, education, transit, and a number of other federal grants were affected by the replacement decisions of both the city and county governments. In Houston, on the other hand, the city was much more active than the county in replacing federal grants.

The overall picture is one of delays in federal aid cuts taking effect, low levels of replacement by local governments, and the shifting of some federal aid and other funds to cope with federal aid cuts.

5. Suburban and Rural Jurisdictions: Cuts and Responses

When most people think of federal aid to local governments, images of New York, Chicago, Detroit, Newark, and other big cities come to mind. In fact, in 1981, nearly as much federal aid went directly to cities with populations of under 50,000 as to those with more than one million people, and nearly half of the people living in cities live in those with less than 50,000 population.[1] Even though per-capita federal aid for these smaller communities is much less than for the largest cities with their large numbers of poor people, small cities and rural areas deserve attention in studies of federal aid. Surprisingly little has been written about federal aid to smaller cities and rural areas, their use of federal aid funds, and their responses to changes in federal aid.

This chapter shows how several smaller communities use federal aid and how they were affected by the changes in federal aid policies that took effect in 1982. By necessity this analysis must be more tentative than the reports on states and large cities. The twenty-six jurisdictions studied here make up a very small portion of all suburban and rural governments; there are nearly 20,000 municipalities with fewer than 50,000 people.

This chapter discusses the following main conclusions:

1. Suburban and rural jurisdictions show great variety in demographic and economic characteristics, making generalizations difficult; but for most, federal aid is much less important than for states or large cities.

---

1. U.S. Bureau of the Census, *City Government Finances in 1980-81* (Washington, D.C.: U.S. Government Printing Office, 1982), tables 3 and 4.

2. For small jurisdictions, revenue sharing is the most important federal grant program. It was unaffected by the reconciliation act, but allocations to individual jurisdictions did change because of changes in their income, population, or tax effort. Most smaller jurisdictions segregate revenue sharing funds from other revenue and use it for one-shot projects rather than continuing programs, so they found it easy to adjust to cuts in revenue sharing funds caused by changes in the operation of the allocation formula.

3. A number of the suburban jurisdictions in the sample received considerably more federal aid than others. Some of these jurisdictions were large enough to be entitlement jurisdictions for community development block grant (CDBG) funds, while others actively and successfully sought project grants because of their community needs, capacity to compete for funds, and political ideology.

4. Most federally funded entitlement and operating grants are received by overlying governments or nonprofit organizations rather than small general-purpose governments (cities and towns). This meant that unless a suburban or rural jurisdiction in the sample was exceptional and received appreciable amounts of CETA public service employment funds or education project grants, the cuts felt by the city and town governments were likely to be modest. Some of the smaller governments in the sample did not have federal aid cuts in fiscal 1982; a few received increases in federal aid.

5. The increases in federal aid that occurred were principally in the new block grants. A jurisdiction that had previously not participated in the superseded categorical programs may have received more federal aid because the state adopted a funding allocation formula under the new block grant that distributed federal money to more suburban and rural jurisdictions. This spreading effect away from large cities was most common in the education block grant.

6. Suburban and rural governments rarely replaced federal cuts, although some governments and nonprofit organizations did raise user fees to continue affected services.

The Sample of Jurisdictions

The variety of smaller jurisdictions is one of the major themes of this chapter; the composition of the sample captures this diversity. Within the sample is a New England town with traditional town meeting government (Middleton, Massachusetts), a predominantly Hispanic community in south Texas (Weslaco), a wealthy Sunbelt community with a large retirement and resort population (Scottsdale, Arizona), and poor inner suburbs such as Orange, New Jersey, and Chelsea, Massachusetts. The sample includes one of the nation's few almost entirely black suburbs—Robbins, Illinois— which is also one of the country's poorest suburbs. It also includes two western counties, reflecting the importance in some areas of counties as service providers outside of large cities.

The smaller governments studied are divided first between suburban governments located near a larger central city and rural cities, towns, or counties. Within each category, the sample units are further divided by per-capita resident income. Income level is an important factor in understanding differences in the relative size and importance of federal grants and the effects of the 1982 cuts.

Suburban Jurisdictions

The idea of a suburb is one of the hardest to define in urban studies. The nature of communities changes over time as values, income, and technology change, making it difficult to devise definitions that adequately reflect changing settlement patterns. The Census Bureau defines a "metropolitan" area as a central city of more than 50,000 in population plus all contiguous counties in which at least a certain percentage of residents commute to the central city. This definition means that many small outlying places—often freestanding communities or predominantly rural places—are treated as suburbs.

The sample for this study was drawn to capture the kinds of variations that we regard as most important for suburban governments. At the same time, the choice of places to be studied reflects practical considerations. Almost all suburbs in the sample are located near the large cities being studied, permitting the field researchers for the city to also cover the suburban jurisdiction.

Table 20 presents information on the thirteen suburban jurisdictions in the sample, divided into economically distressed, middle-income, and relatively well-off jurisdictions, and an overlying county. Each group is discussed below.

Table 20. Suburban Jurisdictions in Sample

Jurisdiction	Population	Region	Percentage growth in population, 1970–80	Per-capita income, 1979	Percentage of residents in poverty, 1979
Economically distressed					
Chelsea, Massachusetts	25,431	Northeast	-17	5,389	21
El Monte, California	79,494	West	14	5,002	20
Orange, New Jersey	31,136	Northeast	-4	4,681	31
Robbins, Illinois	8,854	N. Central	-8	4,695	28
Middle-income					
Bixby, Oklahoma	6,969	South	75	7,545	7
Katy, Texas	5,660	South	93	8,775	6
Redlands, California	43,619	West	20	8,545	10
Relatively well-off					
Cleveland Heights, Ohio	56,438	N. Central	-7	9,233	8
Greece, New York	81,367	Northeast	8	9,069	4
Scottsdale, Arizona	88,622	West	31	10,346	6
Webster Groves, Missouri	23,097	N. Central	-16	9,801	4
Winter Park, Florida	22,339	South	2	10,083	13
County					
King County, Washington	1,269,749	West	9	9,588	8
U.S. average			14	7,313	12

Economically Distressed Suburbs. These four jurisdictions in many ways resemble central cities; they have large low-income populations and problems with deteriorated housing. Three of the four lost population in the 1970s; El Monte, California, gained population, partly because it annexed adjacent territory. Three of the four are near-in suburbs; Robbins, Illinois, which is twenty-five miles from downtown Chicago, is the exception. All have substantial minority populations. Chelsea, Massachusetts, is 16 percent Hispanic and black; El Monte is 62 percent Hispanic; Orange, New Jersey, is 57 percent black and 6 percent Hispanic; and Robbins is 99 percent black. All the governments except El Monte's were under moderate or extreme fiscal pressure; El Monte was under little fiscal pressure, in large part because of its fiscally conservative municipal administration and low levels of public services.

Middle-Income Jurisdictions. Two of the three jurisdictions in this group—Bixby, Oklahoma (twenty miles outside of Tulsa), and Katy, Texas (thirty-five miles outside Houston)—are fast-growing, but still small, cities. Before the influx of commuters in the 1970s, both were rural and predominantly agricultural. Redlands, California, the third jurisdiction in this group, is larger in population and experienced most of its growth before 1970, though it continued to grow during the 1970s. All the cities are predominantly white; Bixby and Katy are more than 90 percent white, while Redlands is about 80 percent white. None of these three local governments faces serious fiscal problems.

Relatively Well-Off Suburban Jurisdictions. Except for Scottsdale, Arizona, these five jurisdictions are older, established suburbs with substantial populations (the smallest, Winter Park, is 22,000). All are relatively close in, within five to ten miles of the central city of their metropolitan area. Scottsdale, the only rapidly growing jurisdiction, is a fast-growing retirement and resort community.

Four of the governments in this group were in a relatively good fiscal position in 1982, rated as having little or no fiscal stress. Only Webster Groves, Missouri, was rated as under moderate fiscal stress. Scottsdale, Webster Groves, and Greece, New York, are over 90 percent white. Cleveland Heights, Ohio, is an integrated suburb; its population is three-fourths white and one-fourth black. Winter Park, Florida, consists of three main communities: a black community, a bedroom community of people who work in Orlando, and a retirement community.

Overlying County. King County, Washington, is the over-lying county for Seattle and suburban communities in the metro-politan area. The county has a population of over 1.25 million, of whom about 500,000 live in Seattle. Although the population of Seattle declined by 7 percent during the 1970s, the number of King County residents outside the central city increased by about 25 percent. The county's population is 85 percent white. In 1982, the county's fiscal situation was better than that of Seattle even though during the year fiscal pressures in the county increased noticeably as unemployment rose.

Rural Jurisdictions and Smaller Cities

The rural group includes thirteen small communities outside a metropolitan area or on the metropolitan fringe, plus Rapid City, South Dakota, a freestanding smaller city. These jurisdictions are grouped together because they are more isolated from large central cities than the suburban jurisdictions; they have lower population density and strong ties to agriculture. Here again, the census definition is not satisfactory, since "rural" generally applies to places of less than 2,500 inhabitants. Table 21, which lists the jurisdictions in this group, divides them by income level.

Economically Distressed Rural Jurisdictions. The five jurisdictions in this group all have populations of fewer than 20,000, ranging from 2,996 in Wilburton, Oklahoma, to 19,331 in Weslaco, Texas. All of these communities have a high rate of pov-erty, ranging from 16 percent in Casa Grande, Arizona, to 36 per-cent in Weslaco. The population of all of the economically distressed rural jurisdictions grew by more than 20 percent during the 1970s; Casa Grande grew by 42 percent.[2] Four of the cities in this group have substantial minority populations. Casa Grande is 41 percent Hispanic and 4 percent black; Grenada, Mississippi, is 44 percent black; Weslaco is 79 percent Hispanic; and Winter Garden, Florida, is 16 percent black and 4 percent Hispanic. Only Wilburton, which is 95 percent white, lacked a substantial minor-ity population. Four of the cities were under little fiscal stress; Wilburton faced moderate to extreme fiscal stress.

---

2. There is no relationship between income levels and growth in the 1970s for nonmetropolitan areas in general. See Calvin Beale, "The Population Turnaround in Rural Small-Town America," in W. Browne and D. F. Hadwiger, eds., *Rural Pol-icy Problems: Changing Dimensions* (Lexington, Mass.: Lexington Books, 1982).

Table 21. *Rural Jurisdictions and Smaller Cities in Sample*

Jurisdiction	Population	Region	Percentage growth in population, 1970–80	Per-capita income, 1979	Percentage of residents in poverty, 1979
Economically distressed					
Casa Grande, Arizona	14,971	West	42	5,748	16
Grenada, Mississippi	12,641	South	27	5,452	26
Weslaco, Texas	19,331	Southeast	26	3,904	36
Wilburton, Oklahoma	2,996	South	20	4,766	25
Winter Garden, Florida	6,789	South	32	5,896	23
Middle-income					
Lincoln, Illinois	16,327	N. Central	-7	7,167	8
McConnelsville, Ohio	2,257	N. Central	7	6,602	12
Middleton, Massachusetts	4,135	Northeast	2	7,948	7
Rapid City, South Dakota	46,492	N. Central	6	6,960	11
Tupelo, Mississippi	23,905	South	17	6,800	14
Washington, Missouri	9,251	N. Central	9	7,170	5
Yankton, South Dakota	12,011	N. Central	1	6,634	9
County					
Walla Walla County, Wash.	25,618	West	8	6,817	12
U.S. average			14	7,313	12

Middle-Income Jurisdictions. Four of the seven jurisdictions in this group—McConnelsville, Ohio; Middleton, Massachusetts; Washington, Missouri; and Yankton, South Dakota— are very small, with populations of 12,000 or less. The population of these four communities has been stable in the last decade, with growth of less than 10 percent. All four are at least 95 percent white. All are rated as under little fiscal stress. Lincoln, Illinois, is a slightly larger city with a population of 16,327. It is a middle-class city and is almost entirely white. Lincoln's population declined by 7 percent between 1970 and 1980, and the community is rated as being under little to moderate fiscal stress.

Rapid City, South Dakota, and Tupelo, Mississippi, both middle-income jurisdictions, are freestanding population centers, which are larger than the other jurisdictions in the rural part of the sample. Tupelo, with 23,905 residents, is the population center of its county. The population is 18 percent black. Tupelo experienced growth of 17 percent during the 1970s. Rapid City is the second-largest city in South Dakota. Its population of 46,492 is 90 percent white and 8 percent American Indian. Officials of Rapid City had anticipated population growth more rapid than the 6 percent it actually experienced; they expected the population to reach 50,000, which would have qualified the area as a standard metropolitan statistical area (SMSA) by 1980. Both Tupelo and Rapid City were rated as being under little fiscal stress.

County. Walla Walla County, Washington, is much like Tupelo and Rapid City. The city of Walla Walla is the local population center, with 25,618 residents. The county has 47,435 residents. The county's population is predominantly white, with 5 percent Hispanic and 2 percent black, and middle income. Walla Walla County was rated as being under little fiscal stress in fiscal year 1982.

The Role of Federal Aid

Federal aid is less important to nearly all the suburban and rural governments in the sample than it is to the large cities and states. Typically, these communities are not involved in federal entitlement programs, are not eligible for operating and capital grants distributed by formula, and in many cases choose not to compete for project grants for which they are eligible. The next section describes which grants are most important to these jurisdictions and why, and explains why some local officials do not seek federal funds.

Important Federal Grants for Small Cities and Towns

Few federal grants are important in all the jurisdictions in the sample. Revenue sharing, distributed by formula to over 39,000 general-purpose governments, was received by all of the jurisdictions in the sample. For the smaller jurisdictions it was often the government's only important source of federal funds; most other federal grants were received intermittently for specific projects in the form of competitive awards. According to the associate for Winter Garden, Florida, "Federal funds meant little to Winter Garden in any direct way. If all such funds disappeared tomorrow, only revenue sharing would be missed."

Adopting a cautious approach, most of the smaller jurisdictions in the sample do not treat even revenue sharing as a stable source of funds, even though the program has been in existence for more than a decade. These jurisdictions separate revenue sharing funds from other local funds, and use revenue sharing for one-shot capital or equipment expenditures. In Katy, Texas, for example, the associate reported that the city sees revenue sharing as a gift. "This allows the city to avoid any long-term commitments to service programs, allocating revenue sharing money primarily for long-term equipment purchases." Similarly, in Middleton, Massachusetts, revenue sharing has been used primarily for capital expenditures, such as new equipment for the police and fire departments.[3]

School districts for the smaller communities in the sample typically receive federal funds which, as in the case of revenue sharing, are distributed on a formula basis. Despite the long concern about federal involvement in education, these smaller school districts tend to have a strong continuing fiscal relationship with the federal government, often under formula grants that provide a continuous flow of federal aid for operating purposes. The programs that aided the school districts in the sample governments during fiscal year 1981 include compensatory education, child nutrition, and the special milk program. Only the special milk program was eliminated in 1982. In places with federal installations, education impact aid was also found to be an important source of revenue.

Because they have populations above 50,000, four suburban jurisdictions in the sample are eligible for community develop-

3. See Richard P. Nathan, Charles F. Adams, Jr., and Associates, *Revenue Sharing: The Second Round* (Washington, D.C.: The Brookings Institution, 1977), for further discussion of this point.

ment block grant funds distributed by formula, and so do not have to compete for these funds. These jurisdictions are Scottsdale, Arizona; El Monte, California; Greece, New York; and King County, Washington. They use their annual allotment in a variety of ways reflecting their differing needs and fiscal capacities. Scottsdale, a relatively wealthy community, has used community development funds primarily for public works projects, including a landscaped lake and a park around the city hall. Greece, a less prosperous community, has used its community development funds for housing rehabilitation and preservation. Housing rehabilitation is also important in El Monte.

The importance of receiving community development funds automatically as an entitlement city is illustrated by Rapid City's distress at discovering that its 1980 census population fell below 50,000. Rapid City began receiving project grants for community development in the mid-1970s after a major flood. In 1979, the federal government accepted the city's claim that it had reached 50,000 in population, and the city became a CDBG entitlement city. When the 1980 census count indicated that Rapid City had only 46,000 residents, the city lost its entitlement status and more than $200,000 a year in CDBG funds. The lower population count also affected its revenue sharing grant, which dropped by $70,000.

The actions of Orange, New Jersey, an economically distressed suburb, illustrate the lengths to which jurisdictions may go to maximize their grant receipts under federal formula grants. In Orange, federal grants have largely come from general revenue sharing and the community development block grant. The associate reported the following policy decisions:

The city has protected itself from anticipated cuts in these two programs in two ways. With respect to revenue sharing funds, in September 1982 the voters elected to change the name of the "City of Orange" to "City of Orange Township" so that under federal regulations the "township" could qualify for additional revenue sharing funds. The city expects to receive an additional $400,000 in fiscal 1983 over what it received in 1982 because of the change in its legal status. In fiscal 1981 Orange chose to receive community development funds from the overlying urban county rather than compete for the small-cities community development grant. This change raised receipts by about $200,000. These steps were taken to offset the loss of another federal formula grant, the special program of antirecession grants begun in 1976 and terminated in 1978.

Aside from revenue sharing and education grants, most of the smaller jurisdictions in the sample receive federal aid only intermittently. Most of the federal grants affected by the 1981 reconciliation act normally go to higher levels of government—as discussed in more detail below—or are distributed as project grants. These project grants can be important sources of funds for meeting local needs, though some of the governments in the sample chose not to compete for them.

A community's choice of whether or not to apply for a project grant is based on three factors: the political ideology in the community, community needs, and its capacity to compete for grants. While those accustomed to thinking in terms of large cities may assume that every jurisdiction seeks all available federal aid, the experiences of the smaller jurisdictions in the sample show that this assumption is not valid.

Political conservatism was the main reason why several small jurisdictions in the sample did not participate in federal programs. In El Monte, California, for example, a coalition of conservatives dominates the city council, sets services levels fairly low, and generally applauds President Reagan's budget reductions. In Casa Grande, Arizona, according to the associate,

The community is conservative in its view of the role of government. Casa Grande believes in a limited role for government and a limited use of federal funds by municipal government. Because of this, Casa Grande has historically been cautious about accepting federal aid.

The Tupelo, Mississippi, associate reported that city officials are "suspicious" of federal aid and seek to avoid involvement except for one-shot capital projects.

Officials of some conservative communities preferred to limit federal aid to capital projects because they believe that the federal government is unreliable as a funding source. By accepting federal aid only for discrete capital projects, and by keeping federal funds separate from local operating budgets, officials hoped to limit their community's dependence on federal funds. These jurisdictions did not want to face political pressure to replace lost federal aid. In Weslaco, Texas, according to the associate, "A major fear of many officials is that federal funds and programs might turn into burdens, which the city must assume if and when federal money is no longer available."

Other communities in the sample do not face the types of problems that lead cities to seek federal assistance. In Scottsdale, for example, income is high and the level of publicly provided social services is low. The city assists nonprofit social service providers, but feels local government involvement in these kinds of programs is both unnecessary and undesirable.

Still other communities cannot compete effectively for federal grants or properly administer them on their own if they are awarded. On occasion, small and poor jurisdictions, such as Robbins, Illinois, and Grenada, Mississippi, received technical assistance on grant application and administration from organizations outside the city, but they do not have the capacity on their own to succeed at the "grantsmanship" game on a continuing basis.

The experience of Washington, Missouri, is typical of city governments that have not actively participated in federal grants. The associate reported,

Washington, Missouri is an old, established river town of 9,251 people, most of whom are working-class or middle-class German Catholics. The relative isolation of Washington from contemporary urban problems, coupled with its relative prosperity and strong German work ethic, all combined to maintain its independence from federal funding through much of the Great Society period. CETA funds and jobs were sparse and the city's participation in CETA was not welcomed by its citizens. Federal grants were sought and utilized for capital expenditures (e.g., water and sewer projects), but no long-term dependence was established through these capital projects. When Washington failed to receive a federal grant requested for constructing a swimming pool, the city voted a bond issue to carry out the project.

The small communities in the sample that have actively sought federal funds are primarily very poor suburbs with problems much like those of central cities. Orange, New Jersey; Chelsea, Massachusetts; and Robbins, Illinois, are all active participants in federal programs. Only El Monte, California, among the economically distressed suburbs is restrained in its attitude toward federal aid, although as a community development entitlement city it automatically received this federal aid. The efforts of Orange to garner federal aid have already been described. In Chelsea, the city officials actively sought housing rehabilitation and economic development funds in an effort to revitalize the community. Chelsea used small-cities community development funds for housing rehabilitation and commercial renovation, and used an urban development action grant and an Economic Development Administration grant for public facilities supporting new development. The associate reported that "federal grants are a necessity for drawing new industry into the city." The city is also a CETA subgrantee under the balance-of-state prime sponsor, and has administered a large public service employment program and a training center.

Robbins deserves special attention because of the magnitude of its problems. Most of the federal funds received by Robbins actually go to Cook County, an overlying government. Cook County, in turn, consistently allocates a large percentage of its federal aid funds to Robbins. The village and the county have developed a relatively stable working relationship in this regard. Under the CDBG program, the associate reported, "Cook County seems to have taken quite seriously the mandate of targeting CDBG funds. So Robbins, at the bottom of the socioeconomic scale, has been a major beneficiary." More than one-tenth of Cook County's allocation since 1975 has gone to Robbins—more than $10 million. The village used most of the money for streets, sewers, storm drains, and its water system. The village also participated in the CETA public service employment training programs, using funds channeled through Cook County. At the peak of the public service employment program in 1977–78, about half of all village workers were paid with CETA funds.

For small-community governments, federal capital grants are important actual or potential sources of funding. Most small communities in the sample sought and accepted capital aid. The officials of these jurisdictions appear to have a preference for capital grants because they are for discrete projects that do not involve long-term commitment and because federal funds can relatively easily be kept separate from other local funds. The capital grants most heavily used in the suburban and rural jurisdictions in the sample were for wastewater treatment plant construction, community development, housing, and transit systems. Capital programs were particularly important to jurisdictions that were growing or anticipated growth in the near future, and to poor jurisdictions with deteriorating infrastructures.

Some jurisdictions chose to avoid all federal aid, including capital assistance. Bixby, Oklahoma, for example, preferred to undertake capital projects on its own rather than accept federal grants. The town manager in Bixby, referring to an Environmental Protection Agency treatment grant, was convinced that "the city can do all it needs without the 75 percent federal money and it can do so more rapidly." The Bixby associate described another instance where the city avoided federal aid because the trouble of applying outweighed the benefits: "The city manager is proud of a drainage ditch project in which he withdrew a grant application, hopped on a bulldozer, and eliminated the problem that was the reason for the grant application in the first place."

Aid to Overlying Governments and Nonprofit Organizations

Small cities and towns often do not administer federal operating grant programs; this is normally done by overlying governments, and in other cases federal aid is paid directly to nonprofit organizations. Participation in federal programs at higher levels reduces the need for cities and towns to get directly involved with the federal government under these programs.

The community services program in Washington, Missouri, for example, is administered by the Jefferson-Franklin Community Action Corporation, a community action agency serving two counties. The agency administers eight federal human service programs ranging from weatherization to child health care. Similarly, in Lincoln, Illinois, a five-county community action agency administers a variety of programs, including Head Start, maternal and child health programs, and programs for senior citizens. A multicounty consortium administered CETA programs for Lincoln; health programs are administered by the county health department.

Two factors help to explain why most federal aid programs are not administered by small general-purpose governments: efficiency and federal administrative requirements. For reasons of efficiency, programs that require a professional staff can be more easily administered at the county, multicounty, or state level in areas of low population density. In South Dakota, for example, social services and housing assistance are administered by the state rather than by a local or even regional organization. The state has such a small population (690,000 in 1980) that centralizing this program makes sense. In other states, social services are administered by large nonprofit agencies. Community services are usually delivered at the county level or by regional nonprofit organizations. In Redlands, California, the San Bernardino County community services agency provides community services. Large nonprofit organizations provide such services in Chelsea, Massachusetts; Orange, New Jersey; Yankton, South Dakota; and Walla Walla County, Washington.

Health services are frequently provided by counties; Redlands, California; Winter Garden and Winter Park, Florida; Webster Groves and Washington, Missouri; McConnelsville, Ohio; and King County, Washington, are examples. In South Dakota, health services, like social services, are provided by the state. In other states, certain health services are provided by regional health agencies. Nonprofit agencies usually provide the federally aided alcoholism and mental health services.

Some federal programs are structured to be administered by higher levels of government in suburban and rural areas. For example, CETA regulations stipulated that participating governmental bodies had to be states, units of general local government having a population of 100,000 or more, "consortia" of local government units at least one of which had a total population of 100,000 or more, or units of local government considered eligible by the secretary of labor because of special circumstances. To participate in CETA, small cities and towns either had to join a consortium or be served by the state government. Similarly, in mass transit, most operating subsidies and capital grants are only available to "urbanized areas" of 50,000 population or more. Small jurisdictions can receive federal aid for mass transit through the special program for rural and small urban areas, but these funds are allocated to states, which in turn usually distribute them to regional transit agencies.

Because most operating and entitlement grants and some capital grants are received by higher-level governments, small general-purpose local governments tended to be relatively unaffected by the changes made in federal aid programs in 1982. The associate for Webster Groves, Missouri, explained, "This minor impact of the 1981 reconciliation act on the city of Webster Groves is a reflection of the fact that most of the major federal grants in St. Louis County are administered by county officials, not those of the county's ninety-two municipalities."

Entitlement Grants

None of the smaller jurisdictions in this study administered entitlement programs. Changes in AFDC, food stamps, and medicaid, therefore, did not directly affect these governments. These programs are, however, very important to the people who live in many of the poorer jurisdictions in the sample. In the economically distressed suburbs in the sample, 20 percent or more of the residents were in poverty in 1979, with Robbins, Illinois, topping the list at 31 percent. In the rural economically distressed jurisdictions, the percentage of residents in poverty ranged from 16 to 36 percent. With unemployment increasing due to the recession during the study period, economic conditions in these poor jurisdictions deteriorated. Public assistance in general, and federally funded entitlement programs in particular, became even more important. The Wilburton, Oklahoma, associates, for example, reported that "income security programs are a vital part of the economic base of Latimer County."

Cuts in Federal Grants

Revenue Sharing

For most smaller jurisdictions, the revenue sharing program is the most important federal grant; the reconciliation act of 1981 did not change this program. However, grants to individual jurisdictions did change, caused by changes in local population, tax effort, and income. The sample includes some suburban and rural jurisdictions with increases and some with decreases. The 1980 census count in Rapid City, South Dakota, as discussed earlier, led to a 10 percent decline in revenue sharing funds in 1982. Katy, Texas, experienced a cut of about 11 percent or $7,500, because the city's per-capita income increased. Katy officials had monitored the legislative situation for the revenue sharing program; they had expected substantial cuts or even elimination of this program. They viewed this modest cut as a pleasant surprise. Yankton, South Dakota, on the other hand, experienced an increase in funds of $11,000, or a 7 percent increase. El Monte, California, also received a $150,000 (9 percent) increase in revenue sharing funds.

Despite the importance of revenue sharing compared with other federal grants in small jurisdictions, the impact of the cuts that did occur was modest. Because most of these smaller governments segregated revenue sharing funds and used them for one-shot projects, they could adjust easily by either scaling down the aided projects or making up for the cut with increased local revenue. Even in Rapid City, with its $70,000 cut, city officials expected the problems created to be minimal because the money had always been used for one-shot projects.

Capital Grants

Next to revenue sharing, actual or expected cuts in capital programs were of the most concern to local officials in the smaller jurisdictions in the sample. Many of these jurisdictions had received grants for capital projects or had benefited from federally funded capital projects undertaken by overlying local governments. As in the large cities, the effects of the cuts on capital grants distributed on a project basis were difficult to discern in any given fiscal year. Grants normally fluctuate from year to year; moreover, these smaller jurisdictions only occasionally apply for these funds. For example, Washington, Missouri's wastewater treatment grant ended in 1981 and the city did not seek to renew it.

Despite problems in identifying cuts, field associates in some of the suburban and rural jurisdictions did identify cuts in capital grants. Changes in the wastewater treatment program affected a number of jurisdictions. After having received a design grant, King County, Washington, did not receive an anticipated construction grant in 1982 of $4 million in federal funds. The state decided to finance this particular sewer construction project with state funds, but required a local match of $1.8 million. Greece, New York, was affected by the termination of grants for the planning and design of wastewater treatment facilities. In 1979, Greece received a planning grant with the expectation that it would receive a follow-up grant for design work. In 1981, the planning was nearly completed, and local officials were so sure they would receive the design grant that they signed a contract for $50,000. In 1982, they learned that their design grant was a casualty of the 1982 changes, and canceled the project.

In Winter Park, Florida, the Environmental Protection Agency's new policies for regional wastewater treatment projects caused a change in the city's plans. The city intended to rely on its own secondary treatment plant for wastewater treatment, but was strongly encouraged to join a regional treatment district in order to receive continued EPA support. Other jurisdictions in the sample received increases in wastewater treatment grants. Officials of Katy, Texas, had expected a small decrease in their EPA grant, but instead received a slight increase; in Tupelo, Mississippi, 1982 funding under a multiyear grant exceeded the 1981 amount.

Changes in two capital grant programs will have future effects in small jurisdictions, but the effects were hard to discern in 1982. The Economic Development Administration has provided grants for rural development since the 1960s; the major cut in its budget will mean fewer capital grants to small cities and towns. The field associates did not identify specific cuts in funding connected with this change during 1982, but noted concern among many local economic development officials.

On the other hand, there was an increase in the share allotted to small cities under the community development block grant program. This, coupled with the state takeover of administration of this part of the CDBG program, may have the ultimate effect of offsetting all or part of the cut in EDA grants. Because of delays in implementing the new block grant, however, field associates in most small jurisdictions did not identify effects of these program changes in 1982.

Some associates reported large cuts in planning grants from the Economic Development Administration. Because many smaller governments lack the expertise to plan complex projects, or to apply for and implement federal capital grants, these cuts can be important. The associate for Casa Grande described the impact of these cuts in southern Arizona:

The role of this region's multifunction planning agency has definitely been diminished. The loss in funds has resulted in a fairly even, across-the-board cut in programs. The director is concerned whether the agency can survive. At present, this planning agency is attempting to provide a minimal level of technical assistance to small municipalities. The need for such assistance appears to be much larger than they are now able to provide. Regional planning agencies in rural areas do not duplicate planning at the local level; theirs is often the only planning that takes place.

Despite the variety of experiences in 1982, many field associates reported that local officials were concerned that the 1982 changes in policies affecting federal capital grants may have important future impacts. For example, the Middleton, Massachusetts, associate reported that town officials considered themselves lucky to have already received federal capital grants for infrastructure, but were concerned that the 1982 changes might affect their chances for future grants. The associate for Yankton, South Dakota, summarized the effect of the 1982 changes in capital programs for his small jurisdiction:

Since federal funding is not used to support continuing programs but rather is used for one-shot projects, the loss of federal funds in the short run required very little adjustment. The real impact will be long run, as the lack of funds for construction—highways, wastewater treatment plants, and the airport—result in a deterioration of facilities.

This long-run impact might prove to be especially important to towns that anticipate future growth or to poor communities that cannot afford to finance capital projects locally.

Operating Grants

On the whole, for the suburban and rural jurisdictions studied, the most important cuts in 1982 were in operating grants. This was especially the case for the poorer and larger suburban jurisdictions and for overlying governments. For jurisdictions participating in CETA programs, the effects of the cuts in public service employment and training funds were similar to those experienced by states and large cities. In each of the four economically depressed suburbs studied, the CETA cuts were the largest. Chelsea, Massachusetts, a subgrantee under the balance-of-state prime sponsor, lost over $1 million in CETA funds. In El Monte, California, elimination of the CETA public service employment program and certain youth programs was partly offset by an increase in adult training funds. In Orange, New Jersey, the county administers the CETA program; public service employment cuts were coupled with a more than 50 percent cut in training funds. Robbins, Illinois, lost more than fifty public service employment workers, forcing a drastic cut in the staff of the village government.

Rural jurisdictions and very small suburbs were much less affected by the CETA cuts because few of these jurisdictions participated in the public service employment program. Local officials in several sites said that they dropped out of the CETA jobs program after their early participation, because they felt the workers were not productive or required too much supervision. For example, city officials in both Tupelo, Mississippi, and Bixby, Oklahoma, said that their city did not benefit from public service employment workers because of their poor work attitudes.

The public service employment program had two goals: increasing local governments' capacity to provide public services and helping disadvantaged workers. According to the field reports, local officials in many small jurisdictions judged the program almost exclusively on the first criterion and felt the output of these workers was too low to make participation in the program attractive. However, in a few jurisdictions, mostly the poorest ones, the loss of CETA employees had a noticeably adverse effect on social and other services. CETA workers were frequently employed by nonprofit organizations, and the simultaneous loss of these workers and other federal funds hampered the ability of some of the agencies to maintain service levels and in some cases even caused them to go out of existence. This same point is made in chapter 4 on large cities.

Under block grants, some jurisdictions experienced cuts while others received increases. The geographic spreading of federal funds under state administration of the new block grants, discussed in chapter 4 with respect to large cities, led to increases (or less than average cuts) in funding for many of the suburban and rural jurisdictions in the sample. In some programs there were increases. In the education block grant program, school districts that had not participated in the superseded categorical project grant programs had increases in funding. Most of the suburban and rural jurisdictions studied received the same or more education block grant funding for this reason. The associate for Scottsdale, Arizona, reported a 233 percent ($133,000) increase in funding:

The Scottsdale school district has had a philosophy of not aggressively pursuing federal funds. With the block grant funding, however, Scottsdale has benefited from a formula based on enrollment. Consistent with its conservative approach to federal grants, Scottsdale officials chose to use the funds for discrete projects with the idea that the block grant may not exist in the future. The district does not want to become dependent on the funds.

In the community services block grant program, small communities in states such as Illinois and Massachusetts gained funds as the states shifted dollars out of large cities. In Robbins, Illinois, for example, the associate reported an increase in community services funding.

The community services block grant is an example of how a cut enacted in Washington does not necessarily carry through to the local level. The state government decided to distribute community services block grant funds to all counties, not just those with existing community action agencies, and to apply a formula based on the number of families below the poverty line. Under this new distribution system, Cook County got a significant increase from $866,000 in calendar year 1981 to $1,143,000 in 1982. Most of this increase was apportioned among nine community services centers, including one in Robbins.

The associate for Chelsea, Massachusetts, reported a small increase in community services block grant funding for the local community action agency, as funds were shifted out of Boston when the state took over the program. Some associates did report cuts in community service funding for the suburban and rural jurisdictions studied. In Redlands, California, for example, funding of the overlying community action agency declined by 33 percent.

Funding cuts were common for the health block grants, but here the picture is mixed. Associates also noted some increases. Because most health programs are administered by overlying governments that also receive state funds, associates often had difficulty determining federal funding figures. In Walla Walla County, Washington, federal funding for the community health center dropped 75 percent while other funding for mental health and alcoholism treatment was unchanged or rose slightly. Webster Groves, Missouri, had a mixture of cuts and increases; programs administered by St. Louis County under the maternal and child health block grant lost about 15 percent of their funding while preventive health programs were funded for the first time. In contrast, in Casa Grande, Arizona, and King County, Washington, health programs were among the most severely cut by the 1981 reconciliation act. In Casa Grande, maternal and child health funds, administered by the Pinal County health department, were cut by one-fourth. Federal health funding in King County also declined one-fourth.

This variety of experiences should not be a surprise. During 1982, states had some carryover funding to cushion the effects of the cuts, and were still considering spending priorities and geographic reallocations of funds under the new block grants. Because some states are further along in this process than others, and because states will make different decisions about how to spend the available funds, there is no necessary reason to expect the range of experiences of the smaller local jurisdictions to narrow over time.

Entitlement Grants

Although changes in entitlement programs and other federal income-security programs did not affect the governments of most smaller jurisdictions, they had a major impact on the low-income and poor residents of those jurisdictions. In fact, many city and town administrators believed that the major impact of the federal budget reductions of 1981 was on recipients of entitlement grant funds. This was particularly true in distressed jurisdictions with substantial numbers of residents below the poverty line, such as Chelsea, Massachusetts; El Monte, California; Orange, New Jersey; Robbins, Illinois; Casa Grande, Arizona; Grenada, Mississippi; Weslaco, Texas; Wilburton, Oklahoma; and Winter Garden, Florida.

The associate in Orange observed that the loss of funding for entitlement programs had a strong impact on city residents.

The share of county cutbacks in food stamps and AFDC payments in Orange is estimated to amount to $1 million and $1.9 million respectively. Unemployment is a serious problem in the city. Approximately 25 percent of the city's population consists of senior citizens. This group has been adversely affected by the reductions in food stamps. Its members have also been hurt by the increases in medicare deductibles and increases in tenant contributions to rent for subsidized apartments. The former director of Senior Citizens Services in the city also said that the loss of CETA workers had affected services provided to the poor and senior citizens.

Similarly, the associate for Grenada emphasized that reductions in entitlement programs had the most impact on residents. In Weslaco, the associate focused on cuts in entitlement programs. "Cuts in food stamps combined with tighter AFDC and medicaid rules seriously affect the poor and working poor in Weslaco."

Responses of Suburban and Rural Jurisdictions

The suburban and rural jurisdictions in the sample overwhelmingly ratified the federal budget cuts that affected their finances and operations. There were several reasons for this. One involved political ideology. Residents and officials of the more conservative small jurisdictions believed that government, both federal and local, should provide only basic services. Such governments were not likely to replace funds for services they regarded as nonessential or extra services. Other jurisdictions lacked the fiscal capacity to replace lost federal funds, whether their residents and officials wanted to do so or not; taking on additional financial burdens was out of the question. An extreme example of such a jurisdiction is Robbins, Illinois. The associate reported,

According to Robbins officials, village finances are continuously in a precarious state. The village has not yet failed to meet a payroll, but it has come close. Robbins cannot finance major capital projects on its own, since it has no bond rating and no prospects of getting one.

Other jurisdictions, while not in such extreme fiscal straits, nonetheless were unable to raise new revenue to cover additional obligations. In Orange, New Jersey, the associate reported that, "The local property tax situation is not good. Tax ratables continue to decrease and the tax rate as a result has steadily increased over the past decade. It now ranks among the highest in the state."

Leaders in several cities and towns resisted tax increases because they believed that a tax increase during a period of federal cutbacks and state tax-limitation measures would not be accepted by their residents. El Monte, California, for example, had the legal capacity to raise new taxes despite California's Proposition 13, but the city council believed that the political climate was not right for a tax increase. Winter Park, Florida, was also in good fiscal shape, yet chose to reduce its property taxes and replace the lost local revenue with the town's share of revenues from a state sales tax.

Greece, New York, and Rapid City, South Dakota, replaced some cuts in federal education aid with local funds. In Greece, the school district lost $20,000 in compensatory education money but maintained services by shifting state special education funds and increasing local spending. This local response to compensatory education illustrates the prevailing attitude in these smaller jurisdictions that federal aid is unreliable.

The district views its compensatory education program in the context of its overall education remediation program. According to the assistant superintendent, "We planned as if we would not get a nickel. If title I aid comes, that helps us financially but not programmatically. We intend to meet those needs."

In Rapid City, South Dakota, the school district lost about $180,000 in education impact aid, a cut of 87 percent. Because this program is the only federal education aid program that is not forward funded, the town faced an immediate decision about how to respond and chose to increase local taxes to maintain services. With these exceptions, small jurisdictions did not replace federal money.

Some jurisdictions and nonprofit organizations chose to raise user fees to continue federally aided services. A number of jurisdictions in the study were already in the process of reducing their reliance on taxes and turning instead to user fees as a way of funding government services; federal aid cuts gave them additional reasons to move in this direction. A few of the smaller governments made up for cutbacks in capital grants for wastewater treatment facilities by increasing water and sewer fees and sewerage hookup fees. Winter Park, Florida, and King County, Washington, are examples of jurisdictions that increased user fees for this purpose.

Increased user fees are often the only way nonprofit organizations can cope with losses in federal funds without cutting services. These organizations frequently raised fees or imposed new fees for health programs.

6. Effects of Regulatory Changes on States and Localities

by Catherine Lovell

President Reagan's domestic policies are not limited to the spending reductions that have been described in the other chapters of this book. Administrative changes to reduce federal regulation of state and local governments have also been advanced as an important part of the president's program.

Although the actions of "watchdog" interest groups and rulings by the courts slowed deregulation in a number of areas, the administration can claim considerable progress toward its goal of easing federal requirements on states and local governments. Notwithstanding its focus on regulatory reform, however, certain of the administration's major substantive goals, such as reducing welfare dependence, take precedence over its deregulatory goals. In these areas—for example, AFDC and school nutrition programs—federal requirements under grant-in-aid programs have become stricter rather than more flexible.

This chapter examines how the Reagan administration has implemented its regulatory policy in relation to state and local governments, and presents a preliminary evaluation of the success of its deregulation efforts.

Deregulatory Strategies

The Reagan administration, like the Carter administration, has responded to complaints about the growth in the number and complexity of federal regulations affecting state and local governments. Much of the growth came about as a result of the increase in

Financial support for this part of the research was provided to Professor Lovell, University of California, Riverside, by the National Science Foundation. The chapter was prepared with the assistance of Michael Givel and Thomas C. J. Calhoun.

numbers of federal grants since the mid-1960s and the growth in the 1970s of direct federal grants to local governments.[1]

As the size and number of grants grew and as Congress and federal agencies tried to correct what were seen as problems in program administration, regulations grew more numerous and more complex. Federal agencies responded to questions of statutory interpretation, problems in management, and allegations of abuse by adding new regulations or expanding old ones. By 1980, about 90 percent of the federal regulations that affected state and local governments were imposed as conditions of federal aid. Many state and local government officials had come to feel that prescription and compulsion had taken the place of the negotiating relationship with the federal government that they preferred. These officials insisted that they could administer programs better and at less expense with fewer restrictions.

The Reagan administration has attempted to ease the regulatory burden on state and local governments through three basic approaches:

• *Removing the federal government's need to be involved in regulatory activity.* This approach stems from the assumption that much federal regulatory activity is economically or socially harmful and intrusive and that, so long as the federal government manages or funds programs, regulatory activity is inevitable. To reduce federal regulatory activity, this approach calls for the government to reduce the number of federal programs.

To some extent this approach was enacted in the 1981 Omnibus Budget Reconciliation Act. The administration was able to eliminate some programs and cut others, but Congress failed to approve the administration's more far-reaching proposals advanced in Reagan's 1982 state of the union message for transferring federally funded programs to state control. The act also included several provisions that were expected to reduce federal regulation by creating new block grants. Many policy analysts argue that block grants involve less supervisory activity than the categorical grants that they replace.

In other existing programs, however, regulations have increased federal control over programs administered by state

1. For an earlier discussion of this topic, see Catherine Lovell, "Federal Deregulation and State and Local Governments," in John William Ellwood, ed., *Reductions in U.S. Domestic Spending: How They Affect State and Local Governments* (New Brunswick, N.J.: Transaction Books, 1982).

and local governments. This point applies especially to tightened regulations on eligibility and costs under federally aided income-maintenance programs.

- *Strengthening executive oversight of agency rule making.* This approach rests on the assumption that federal agencies have a proclivity to overregulation, because they develop strong biases from their functional perspectives. In this view, agencies are insensitive to cost impacts and other consequences of their regulatory actions, because they know little about the activities of other agencies and have no grasp of how programs actually operate. These assumptions underlie the efforts of the Reagan administration to control agency actions through guidance from the president and his appointees.

- *Reducing enforcement intensity of existing regulations.* This reform approach is also based on the assumption that regulatory actions are intrusive and inflexible and also that regulatory relief can be obtained by relaxing enforcement and introducing more flexibility into program administration. A further assumption underlying this approach is that the total body of federal regulations is now too large to amend quickly or easily.

The Reagan administration has made no effort to use two other possible approaches to regulatory reform that have frequently been advocated. One such approach would attempt to make regulatory actions more effective, as well as less restrictive, by having agencies open the rule-making process to greater input from those affected by the rules. The second would try to constrain the presumed tendency of federal agencies to overregulate by increasing congressional oversight of regulatory actions.[2]

As the American Enterprise Institute noted in an analysis of President Reagan's first two years, the dominant thrust of the administration's regulatory policy was administrative change carried out by the executive branch.[3] In the area of federal grants, the three approaches listed above were used by the Reagan administration in fiscal year 1982 with varying degrees of success in accomplishing its goals.

The following sections discuss the deregulatory aspects of the new block grants, report on some of the results of strengthened

2. *Ibid*, pp. 110–18.
3. American Enterprise Institute, *Working Paper in Government Regulation* (Washington, D.C.: AEI Center for Study of Government Regulation, December 9, 1982).

executive oversight of the agencies involved in rule making for federal grants, and present preliminary findings on changes in the enforcement intensity of regulations relating to federal grants-in-aid.

Deregulation with Block Grants

The block grants to the states enacted or expanded in 1981 were seen by the Reagan administration as a major step in grant deregulation as well as in the decentralization of domestic policy-making. Compared with the categorical grants they replaced, the block grants have far fewer programmatic and procedural conditions attached to them. Under most of the new block grants, state governments have greater authority to set priorities, allocate funds, and design reporting and management systems. The reconciliation act also changed two older grant programs, medicaid and the community development block grant (CDBG), by giving states and localities greater discretion on how to spend funds.

By contrast, the reconciliation act imposed more complex requirements in categorical public assistance programs such as aid to families with dependent children (AFDC), food stamps, and school lunch programs—changes that reduced state and local discretion. Under all three programs, regulatory changes tightened eligibility rules and set up more controls on eligibility screening and record keeping. In the child nutrition program, for example, the reconciliation act required schools to collect the social security numbers of the parents of the children applying for subsidized lunches. California is the only state that so far has refused to follow that directive. In medicaid, the reconciliation act also required states to implement cost and fraud control programs or lose federal aid.

In general, however, procedural rules affecting states and localities have been made more flexible under Reagan. As the associate from Illinois said, "The main effect of the regulatory changes has been less interference with complex, nit-picking, and inflexible rules."

Federal agencies have exempted block grants from OMB Circulars A-102 (setting forth administrative and financial requirements for grants to state and local governments) and A-87 (which provides uniform rules for determining the costs applicable to grants). States, under the block grants, have the flexibility to use their own laws and procedures governing property acquisition and procurement standards and determining allowable costs. Many states are continuing to use the federal standards, however, until they are sure their procedures will be accepted by federal auditors. In some cases where states are temporarily continuing to administer categorical programs that are being phased into the new block grants, they are required to follow federal rules.

The block grants created in the 1981 reconciliation act require states to obtain independent audits every one or two years and to use the Comptroller General's "Standards for Audit of Governmental Organizations, Program Activities and Functions" in conducting such audits. Under the block grants, federal agencies must rely on state audits if they have been conducted in accordance with the Comptroller General's standards. State audit plans for these grants are still evolving.

For most of the block grants, federal agencies had not as of mid-1983 prescribed the format states should use in submitting applications and annual reports. States were told to use their discretion in interpreting requirements under the reconciliation act. The administration's position is that federal agencies will defer to state statutory interpretations.

The degree of latitude that states perceive varies among the block grants. It also varies from state to state. The heads of state agencies implementing these programs were found to have widely divergent views on where they stand. The associate for Massachusetts reported,

The latitude allowed in the health block grants provided an opportunity for state review and reevaluation of all programs and resulted in better synchronization of state and federal funds. The federal data requirements on the mental health grant, however, go beyond what the staff required in the past, and these differences are still being negotiated with Washington.

On the other hand, the Massachusetts associate reported that, for the social services block grant,

administratively not much has changed. Instead of a "preexpenditure report," the Department of Social Services had to write an "annual plan"; instead of being audited annually, they will be audited every two years; and while they theoretically no longer have to provide eligibility information to the federal government, federal officials have implied that state administrators would be well advised to keep this kind of information on file.

Speaking about procedural requirements, the associate for Ohio reported that for the alcohol, drug abuse, and mental health block grant,

the federal requirements for disbursement of funds are very strict. Federal rules require an invoice each month indicating projected cash needs. Previously the state used a lump-sum arrangement. The federal government generally has increased monitoring and reporting requirements in this case.

The associate for New Jersey noted that, for the social services block grant, the state is determining the data requirements, not federal agencies; the state is simplifying forms and hoping to get better information from localities.

The consensus among state officials seems to be that while they like the greater program flexibility of many of the block grants, the full "benefits" of deregulation have been less than expected in the procedural area. Federal agencies have reduced program requirements in some areas, giving the states more policy flexibility, but they still require extensive and detailed paperwork and reports for audits and financial reviews. The states are still not sure just what to expect in the way of audits from federal agencies. The Illinois associate, for example, said,

There is anxiety on the part of state officials about the ambiguity of some federal rule changes and about the unwillingness of federal agencies to issue interpretations. The anxiety stems from the possibility that audit exceptions may be issued against them later by federal auditors strictly interpreting federal requirements.

It is apparent from the field reports that the Reagan administration has not provided clear signals to state and local governments on deregulation. On the one hand, it has encouraged governments to back off on record keeping and reporting, yet many state officials feel the administration has not given them sufficiently clear assurances that later federal auditors will accept less detailed documentation of program operations. This uncertainty has prevented many state and local agencies from obtaining the full benefits of reduced record-keeping and reporting requirements and greater programmatic discretion in the use of funds. As a consequence, many risk-averse officials stick with old, often burdensome, procedures or at least move slowly to make any changes. In New Jersey, for example, the associate reported,

When the state took over federal programs under the block grants, the state in many cases simply adopted the federal regulatory apparatus in order to ease the transition and concentrate staff time on absorbing the budget cuts. In many instances federal regulations did not change. For example, the assurances required under the block grants are seen as simply a continuation of the kind of state compliance with federal mandates that was previously required.

Associates noted confusion in a number of programs. For example, under the CDBG program many officials of large cities are pleased with the new streamlined application and reporting processes, but anxious about the possibility of future federal audits and are maintaining extensive monitoring and record-keeping procedures. Similar concerns were expressed for the compensatory education and education block grant programs. Reflecting a common attitude, New York officials were concerned that some-day federal officials would ask for material that the state officials thought they were not required to keep.

The Reagan administration's policy of decreasing regulations has led it to experiment with so-called nonbinding guidelines for program administration, that is, letters of explanation from agency officials rather than formal regulations. This approach has produced confusion on the part of state and local officials. Education programs provide the clearest examples of this approach. In Tulsa, for example, local administrators were eager to take advantage of increased flexibility in compensatory education programs but were uncertain how to interpret the "nonbinding guidelines" issued to implement the program changes. Federal officials would not provide further interpretation of the statute. Again, being risk adverse, local educators usually decided to stick with the tried and true ways of doing business. Other associates reported that program officials are nervous about future auditors who would not hesitate to give definite interpretations of these requirements and hold program officials accountable.

Summing up the situation in their jurisdiction, the Tulsa associates reported that local officials had apparently developed the following decision rule: "Move fast on federally mandated changes, as in welfare. On everything else, where discretion is greater, be sure we have correctly read the mandate."

These state concerns make sense. The 1981 reconciliation act assigned the General Accounting Office (GAO) a special mandate to monitor the block grant programs. Staff members of the GAO completed their first report in August 1982; this report presented the GAO's early observations on block grant implementation based on data collected from a sample of thirteen states.[4] Although spokesmen have said that the GAO does not want to "chill discretion by the states,"[5] there is always potential for some members of Congress to use GAO findings to press for new controls or disciplinary action.

The GAO plans to issue reports on each block grant, on each of the thirteen state governments being monitored, and on a sample of local governments. The reports will cover the implementation

4. General Accounting Office, *Early Observations on Block Grant Implementation,* publication GAO-GGD-82-79 (Washington, D.C.: GAO, August 24, 1982).

5. Remarks by Paul Posner, Intergovernmental Planning Coordinator, General Accounting Office, at a national conference sponsored by the National Assistance Management Association, Washington, D.C., March 8, 1983.

of the grants, their service impacts, and institutional changes in the states resulting from the initiation of these new block grants. These reports will also discuss more specific aspects of the implementation of the new block grants, such as the enforcement of cross-cutting requirements, how the states handle information management, and how states are implementing specific compliance and fiscal audits. The full GAO reports are due the Congress by January 1984. Spokesmen for GAO have said these reports will simply present what is happening under the block grants, and not evaluate how well the states are doing. The GAO officials realize that their work constitutes the only substantial federal presence in the states in relation to the block grants and that states are concerned about these reviews because of their traditional fears of GAO audits.

Effects on Local Governments

For local governments, the impact of deregulation became manifest more slowly than at the state level. The clearest benefit to local governments came in the new elementary and secondary education block grant, which combined twenty-nine programs into one block grant with increased flexibility in the use of funds and an attendant cut in specific requirements. For other block grants, however, local governments in many states are waiting for state administrative agencies to issue final regulations. State agencies have been slow in carrying out their planning processes, often waiting to incorporate the recommendations of task forces and advisory committees. Some state agencies simply reissued the old federal regulations until they could make decisions on a new approach. From Illinois, for example, the field associate reported,

The replacement of federal rules with state rules is an ongoing process—a slow and time-consuming approach. The state has a highly developed administrative rule-making process that requires careful review and approval by a joint legislative commission. OMB Circulars A-102, which established uniform financial and other administrative requirements, and A-87, which provides uniform rules for determining the costs applicable to grants, have not yet been replaced. They will be reevaluated in the future.

Mississippi has also adopted the financial practices specified in Circular A-102 on cost determination, and there is evidence that the state will be stricter with the local governments than the federal government has been in enforcing its accounting rules. New Jersey required compliance with the circulars on financial and administrative requirements and on cost determination, as an interim measure, but later allowed its agencies more flexibility.

Local government officials view regulatory changes in various ways, depending on the grant in question and whether the local government had previously received federal funds directly from Washington or indirectly through the state. In the rural town of McConnelsville, Ohio, for example, local officials said the elementary and secondary education block grant gave them "a genuine sense of greater local autonomy as compared to the old categorical programs." The non–block grant medicaid rules, by contrast, have caused "a big increase in paperwork in connection with verification of client eligibility, and the accounting system has been changed under state requirements to make it more burdensome." The associate for Ohio said that the state has imposed more rigorous auditing rules on local governments, primarily to ensure conformity with federal laws and regulations.

Under the new block programs for small-cities community development and community services, associates found that new state regulations often were perceived by local officials as being at least as restrictive as the previous federal rules. Ten states in the sample picked up the small-cities portion of the CDBG program in fiscal year 1982. In these states, monitoring and audit requirements are unusually detailed, suggesting that from the local perspective regulatory relief may not materialize at all. The same finding applies to the community services block grant. The field associate reported on Oklahoma:

The state Department of Economic and Community Affairs staff developed extensive guidelines to ensure that funds were spent appropriately and were accounted for. The state staff is understandably concerned that it be able to give evidence of effective administration to the federal Department of Health and Human Services (HHS). The result may have been an increase rather than a decrease in administrative red tape, at least as viewed by the local community action agencies.

From Florida, associates reported a similar experience.

In the state Department of Community Affairs, officials indicated that while federal reporting requirements to the states have become less demanding, the state's requirements to local governments have become greater. For example, in the community services block grant program the state was given a great deal of flexibility in administration by the federal government. However, agency officials note that because of strict state legislation regarding this block grant, the state guidelines and rules do not leave much flexibility to local grantees. An advisory committee has been appointed to propose revisions of these rules.

Chicago officials said that in their view state regulations involve more administrative control over grantees than the federal regulations. Similarly, local officials in Casa Grande, Arizona, said that the state takeover of the program had increased paperwork requirements. Reflecting a somewhat cynical view and the fears of local governments, the associates for Tulsa reported that "the overall effect of the new block grant so far has been to replace long federal guidelines and regulations with long state guidelines."

Obviously, state and local governments would prefer to receive federal money with few or no strings, but this is not likely to happen. State officials are aware that both Congress and their own legislatures must be accountable to the taxpayers. These officials know that interest groups that support particular programs are on the lookout for noncompliance with federal statutes and the misuse of federal funds. Such groups often use the courts to press their points, as described later in this chapter.

To summarize, regulatory activity takes place in a complex legal and political environment. While the OMB and some federal agencies have attempted to give more flexibility to the states under the Reagan administration, local officials are aware of the limits on the flexibility that federal agencies can allow and, in turn, on the flexibility that the states can allow local jurisdictions.

Increased Executive Oversight of Agency Regulations

The second way that the Reagan administration has attempted to advance deregulation has been to give the OMB extraordinary powers to oversee the regulatory activities of federal agencies. The staff of OMB works with the President's Task Force on Regulatory Relief; the two entities together have exerted a strong influence on federal agencies to maximize state and local government flexibility. The OMB reviews all new regulations before they are published in the *Federal Register*. However, the extent to which the expanded role of the OMB has affected the content and quantity of regulations is difficult to determine, because OMB officials review and approve rules before they are proposed publicly. In several instances that are publicly known, OMB's role has been a very strong one, and the rules that have emerged after negotiations between OMB and the rule-making agency have strongly reflected OMB's efforts to make changes consistent with the administration's ideology.

The rules issued for the large-cities portion of the community development block grant are an example of the OMB role. For more than a year after President Reagan signed the 1981 reconciliation act that reauthorized and amended this program, OMB and the Department of Housing and Urban Development (HUD)

negotiated regulations to implement the legislative changes.[6]
The proposed CDBG regulations finally were issued on October 4,
1982. The regulations as they emerged—with one exception—gave a great deal of flexibility to the states on issues involving eligible activities, the income group to be aided, program
targeting, citizen participation, and various procedural matters. In
this case, OMB officials substantially revised HUD's initial draft.

The final regulations for the revised small-cities community
development block grants to the states were also delayed for many
months while three-way negotiations took place among OMB,
HUD, and the congressional subcommittee that oversees community development programs. In this case, also, OMB severely
edited HUD's initial draft of regulations.

Questions have been raised publicly about the OMB oversight
process. In November 1982, the General Accounting Office issued
a report critical of the way OMB was implementing the general
requirements for cost-benefit analyses of major new regulations.[7]
The preparation of such analyses was first required under President Ford's Executive Order 11821 (November 1974) and again by
Executive Order 12044 (March 1978) issued by President Carter.
Under President Reagan's Executive Order 12291 (February
1981), the costs and benefits of "major" regulations must be analyzed. Unless otherwise required by law, the most cost-effective
alternatives must be chosen. These analyses are intended to
improve the cost-effectiveness of major federal regulations by
requiring agencies to consider the consequences of alternative
strategies.

The GAO found that regulatory analysis has not achieved its
potential for improving regulatory decision making. According to
its report, many of the regulatory analyses that were reviewed,
including several approved by OMB, did not provide adequate
support for their conclusions. *The Regulatory Eye*, a Washington
newsletter for business and government officials interested in
regulatory activities, suggested that "the net effect of the clearance
process is not of sharply improved regulatory analyses but far
stronger intervention by the White House and OMB in the regula-

6. Paul R. Dommel, Leonard S. Rubinowitz, Michael J. Rich, and Associates,
Deregulating Community Development (Washington, D.C.: U.S. Department of
Housing and Urban Development, draft, February 1983).

7. Report by the Comptroller General to the Chairman, Committee on Governmental Affairs, United States Senate, on Regulatory Analysis (GAO/PAD-83-6),
November 2, 1982.

tory activities of the agencies."[8]

The OMB has also attempted to increase its power over federal agencies to reduce paperwork requirements. It proposes not only to review agency information-gathering activities initiated since the Paperwork Reduction Act was passed in 1980, but also to review paperwork requirements in existence before the act was passed.[9] There is a question, still unresolved, as to whether the OMB has the legal authority to review existing paperwork regulations. The Office of the Legal Counsel in the Justice Department has concluded that the Paperwork Reduction Act does not apply to existing agency regulations. The issue may ultimately have to be resolved in the courts.

The President's Task Force on Regulatory Relief, headed by Vice President George Bush, in 1981, its first year of operation, targeted about a hundred regulations for review and possible modification; twenty-five of these regulations affected states and local governments. By the end of 1982, the task force had completed action on fifteen of them. The agencies themselves, under pressure from the task force, initiated reviews of additional regulations.

The task force has had mixed results. A court decision prevented the implementation of proposed changes of special interest to state and local governments involving the interpretation of the Davis-Bacon Act. This act, originally passed in 1931, requires that construction workers on federally aided projects be paid the "prevailing wage" for the area. It has been criticized for driving up costs of such projects because of the way the Department of Labor has calculated the "prevailing wage."

In May 1982, the Labor Department published new rules revising the Davis-Bacon Act. The rules would have changed the method by which prevailing wages are calculated and provided expanded authority for contractors on federally aided projects to employ semiskilled helpers. In July 1982, the AFL-CIO Building and Construction Trades Department, joined by its constituent unions and the International Brotherhood of Teamsters, won an injunction against the Department of Labor to block implementation of the new regulations. A U.S. District Court judge found that the new regulations represented an "abrupt change of a long-

---

8. *The Regulatory Eye*, vol. 4, no. 11 (January 1983).

9. Notice of proposed rule making appeared in the *Federal Register*, September 8, 1982.

standing administrative position" interpreting the act, and that under the new regulations "workers would be forced to accept lower wages, a change for which they would have no legal avenues of redress." The request to permanently stay the new regulations had not been heard by mid-1983.

Another administration deregulation attempt of special importance to state and local governments was stopped as a result of interest-group pressure. The attempt involved the Department of Education's proposed changes in regulations implementing the Education for All Handicapped Children Act. The proposed changes would have allowed schools to evaluate and place children in special education programs without parental consultation or consent; eliminated a rule requiring a school to place a handicapped child in an appropriate program within thirty days after evaluating the student's needs; abolished requirements for related services; eliminated the requirements that handicapped children participate in classroom and extracurricular activities with other children; and reduced the requirements for documenting procedures and submitting data to supervisory agencies. When organizations of parents and educators mounted a vigorous campaign of protest, this proposal was withdrawn.

In an attempt to restrain future interest-group lobbying efforts, OMB issued a new Circular A-122 in January 1983. The circular proposed to restrict lobbying by nonprofit organizations and defense contractors that receive federal grants and contracts. The purpose was to prevent federal money from being used either directly or indirectly for political purposes. A barrage of public criticism greeted the issuance of the rule, however, and it was withdrawn for revision.

In another deregulatory action affecting schools, the Department of Education rescinded guidelines issued in 1974 that required schools to provide equal educational opportunity for students with limited English-speaking ability. Schools are no longer required to abide by federally prescribed remedies; each school district can decide how to teach children with little or no facility in the English language. Unless the Bilingual Education Act is amended, litigation clarifying what is required in bilingual education under federal law will undoubtedly be attempted.[10]

One of the earliest reviews by the Bush task force resulted in the revision of rules requiring mass transit systems to be accessi-

10. American Enterprise Institute, *Working Paper*, p. 28.

ble to the handicapped. Under Section 504 of the Rehabilitation Act of 1974, the Department of Transportation had required expensive measures, such as lifts on new buses and elevators at subway and train stations. Under the new regulations, many of the most expensive and controversial requirements were deleted. Operators of transportation systems are now allowed to decide how they should make "special efforts" to help the handicapped. An Urban Institute study of how local agencies are meeting this obligation found large savings of money and, at the same time, mixed results in terms of the impact of the new policy on the access of the handicapped to public transportation.[11]

Also of special interest to state and local governments was the Bush task force's review of OMB Circular A-95, which required federal agencies to use clearinghouses established by states and local governments (usually councils of local governments) to ensure that federally supported projects were properly coordinated with all parties affected. The clearinghouses were required to review all federal grant applications. President Reagan abolished the A-95 process in July 1982, allowing elected state and local officials to decide for themselves which federal grant and development programs to review and how to do it. Reagan's executive order also requires federal agencies to allow states to simplify and consolidate federally required state plans. The administration, in a related area, has encouraged states to reduce or eliminate their involvement in special-purpose planning agencies, such as health planning agencies.

Other intergovernmental regulations that the Bush task force reviewed involved (1) the elimination of the Agriculture Department's cost-accounting requirements for the school lunch programs; (2) revisions to give states more flexibility under the home-weatherization program; (3) revisions to the regulations for environmental reviews of projects funded by the community development block grant; (4) revised Department of Transportation rules permitting states to design their own procedures and criteria for resurfacing, restoring, and redesigning highways; and (5) the elimination of certain Army Corps of Engineers requirements affecting state-run dredge and fill programs and the simplification of others.

---

11. Michael Fix, "Effects of Changes in 504 Regulations," paper presented at the annual conference, American Society for Public Administration, April 16–19, 1983.

Enforcement of Regulations

A third approach taken by the Reagan administration to regulatory reform involves the close scrutiny and reevaluation of the extent to which existing requirements are enforced. After a law has been passed and administrative regulations have been issued, federal agencies enforce them with varying degrees of seriousness and vigor.

Monitoring and enforcement activities of agencies are the most difficult aspect of the federal regulatory process to observe and document. It is especially hard to separate the effects of changes in administrative strategy involving the enforcement of regulations from the effects of budget cuts. Clearly, regulatory reform has to take into account the processes for interpreting statutory intent and establishing the rules to implement it. Such measures as cutting back on enforcement activities, reducing the size of agency staffs through budget cuts, and changing the nature of the goals the enforcement personnel pursue can be effective methods of reducing federal regulatory activity as well.

Much of the controversy about the Reagan administration's deregulatory policies and actions centers on the question of how seriously and vigorously federal agencies and OMB are enforcing certain "cross-cutting" regulations, particularly in the environmental, civil rights, and health and safety areas, which extend beyond the boundaries of individual programs and agencies.[12] Such cross-cutting requirements apply to states and local governments receiving all types of federal grants. As conditions of the aid, they are obliged to administer the grants in a way that also helps to carry out national policy objectives that are not a direct and intrinsic part of any particular grant program.[13]

Typically, one federal agency is designated as the "lead agency" for a cross-cutting policy; its role is to coordinate the efforts of the other agencies in enforcing these regulations. For example, the Department of Justice is the lead agency on cross-cutting regula-

12. See National Wildlife Federation, *The Full Story Behind the EPA Budget Cuts* (Washington, D.C., 1982); Friends of the Earth, *Ronald Reagan and the American Environment: An Indictment* (San Francisco, 1982); Leadership Conference on Civil Rights, *Without Justice: A Report on the Conduct of the Justice Department in Civil Rights in 1981–82* (Washington, D.C., 1982).

13. For a full explanation of cross-cutting requirements, see, Advisory Commission on Intergovernmental Relations, "Generally Applicable National Policy Requirements for Grant Programs," in *Categorical Grants: Their Role and Design* (Washington, D.C., 1977), A-52.

tions to carry out provisions of the Civil Rights Act and title IX of legislation prohibiting discrimination on the basis of handicap.

Under the new block grants, a large part of the enforcement of cross-cutting regulations has been assigned to the states, although they have been given little guidance about federal intentions for enforcement. There is evidence that the administration has not always been certain of the enforcement posture that it wants the states to take.

In civil rights, for example, it was the administration's view that the federal agencies that have enforced most civil rights laws in the past had been overly intrusive and rigid.[14]   The Justice Department, as the lead agency on civil rights, has prepared new regulations for coordinating the activities of the other agencies in civil rights enforcement, but the proposed regulations have been held up in OMB since August 1982.[15]   One controversy has arisen in this area over the efforts of the Civil Rights Division of the Justice Department to prevent the Equal Employment Opportunity Commission from requiring the heads of all federal agencies to develop multiyear affirmative action plans, including goals and timetables to guide personnel actions affecting the programs of their agencies..

Policies to prevent discrimination against the handicapped is another area in which the administration's actions have caused controversy. The Justice Department early in 1982 circulated a draft of revised regulations on discrimination against the handicapped that would have weakened regulations previously adopted by the Department of Health, Education, and Welfare (when it was the lead agency for these regulations). These regulations set penalties for federally aided governments and private institutions if they were found to be discriminating against the handicapped. The HEW regulations had been used as a standard by other executive agencies. In March 1983, the Justice Department dropped its effort to revise these regulations because of strong protests mounted by organizations representing handicapped persons.

The OMB's ambiguity on enforcement of cross-cutting rules is illustrated by a recent OMB publication. In November 1982, OMB sent each state a copy of its *Directory of Generally Applicable Requirements and Administrative Management Standards,*[16]

14. Michael Wines, "Administration Says It Merely Seeks a Better Way to Enforce Civil Rights," *National Journal,* June 5, 1982.

15. *The Regulatory Eye,* vol. 4, no. 9 (November 1982).

which lists each generally applicable requirement, describes the scope of its application and the applicable compliance mechanisms and court rulings. The directory collects all the cross-cutting requirements in one place for the first time, but it leaves undefined the role of federal agencies in enforcing these requirements. The underlying message to the states seems to be, "You decide how seriously you wish to take each of these requirements and make the best guess you can as to how federal agencies will monitor your actions."

The Reagan administration is blowing an uncertain trumpet on this issue. The general legal counsel of OMB has argued that most cross-cutting rules do not apply to the block grants, because the block funds given to the states become state funds and therefore are not subject to national laws. The administration has not publicly decided to accept this opinion and appears still to be considering what the agency role should be in applying the cross-cutting rules to block grants.

Some of the cross-cutting requirements are specifically mentioned in the reconciliation act as applicable to the block grants. For all but two of the block grants, the act cites civil rights statutes prohibiting discrimination on the basis of race, color, national origin, age, and handicap, as well as title IX of the Education Amendments of 1972, which prohibits sex discrimination. The reconciliation act specifically states that environmental laws and the Davis-Bacon Act are applicable for the small-cities community development block grant. Ambiguity remains as to whether cross-cutting rules not specifically mentioned in the reconciliation act apply.

According to the GAO, the process for deciding these issues is that, if a federal agency administering a block grant believes that a particular requirement applies, it seeks general administration agreement from the Interagency Block Grant Implementation Task Force led by OMB.[17] In the meantime, while the administration's policy is being decided on a case-by-case basis, some federal agencies are requiring assurances of compliance from the recipient jurisdictions. To add to the uncertainty, groups interested in stronger enforcement of various cross-cutting laws often ask the courts to step in. In response to such a suit, a federal judge

16. Office of Management and Budget, *Directory of Generally Applicable Requirements and Administrative Management Standards for Federal Grant Programs* (Washington, D.C.: U.S. Government Printing Office, November 1982).

17. Report by the Comptroller General on Regulatory Analysis, p. 42.

in March 1983 ordered the Department of Education to more actively monitor the efforts of grant recipients to prohibit sex discrimination.[18]

Few field associates noted major changes in enforcement intensity at the state and local levels. Many associates report uncertainty about which requirements are applicable to the new block grants, who is to enforce them, and how the states should enforce those they deem applicable.

The Texas associates reported that civil rights and environmental organizations feared a weakening of enforcement by the state, but state and local officials said that nothing had changed. The Missouri Advisory Committee to the U.S. Commission on Civil Rights investigated how federal and state agencies had been enforcing rules on nondiscrimination under the new health and social services block grant programs, and concluded that the oversight activities of the federal Department of Health and Human Services were not sufficient. The study found that reviews by state departments were slightly more extensive than past federal efforts, but were still inadequate.[19]   From Mississippi, an associate reported that the governor had taken the position that he wished to enforce the cross-cutting rules, but that the machinery was lacking and the money to put it in place was unavailable.

Concluding Comments

Results of regulatory changes in intergovernmental programs during the first two years of the Reagan administration are mixed. States have more flexibility in deciding how to run many programs and have more leeway as to the procedures they follow in administering them. On the other hand, the administration has shown that its goals of reducing federal spending and narrowing welfare dependence take precedence over deregulation. The administration has demonstrated these priorities by imposing tighter guidelines on eligibility for entitlement programs, such as AFDC, food stamp, and the school lunch programs. Local officials maintain that they have little more flexibility; as far as they are concerned, the new block grants, for example, have simply meant the replacement

---

18. *Adams* v. *Bell*, Federal District Court, Washington, D.C., March 10, 1983.

19. Missouri Advisory Committee to the United States Commission on Civil Rights, *State and Federal Civil Rights Enforcement in Missouri—Nondiscrimination in the New Health and Human Services Block Grant Programs*, October 1982.

of federal rules with state rules.

Whether increased authority for the states is good or bad depends on who answers the question. Most organizational theorists and most state and local government officials welcome the increased flexibility. In fact, there is wide agreement on the need for more flexibility, more common sense in enforcement, less complexity, and less redundancy.

But some observers are uneasy about the shift from federal responsibility to state autonomy. Groups representing the handicapped, minorities, and women, and those favoring environmental protection are accustomed to concentrating their efforts in Washington. It is much more difficult for them to organize and press their views in fifty states. These interest groups still have influence. Many are turning to the courts to attempt to continue and strengthen federal enforcement of laws they favor.

The courts can roll back or prevent deregulatory actions by federal agencies. A number of associates indicated that coalitions are also forming to bring suits in state courts to prevent state deregulation and, in some cases, to strengthen regulatory programs and activities. The administration is increasingly aware of the power of interest groups, as its defeat in the attempted rewriting of the handicapped education rules and other such incidents illustrate.

The first two years of the Reagan administration's attempts to deregulate grant programs have shown once again the complexity and incrementalism of the American intergovernmental system. The administration's first year was a period of new initiatives and administration optimism in the regulatory area; in the second year, constraints were strongly felt as a consequence of judicial review and political pressure from members of Congress and coalitions of interest groups. The administration's greatest success in its terms has not been in actually changing regulations, but in changing the way agencies enforce them. On the whole, delays or inaction in enforcement of existing regulations, particularly for cross-cutting regulations, have resulted in a less intrusive federal presence in the states. This experience has shown that, if they use their power strategically, presidents can achieve their policies through administrative action or inaction.

7. Toward a Theory of Federal Aid Replacement

The focus of the analysis in this first report on the field data for the full fiscal year 1982 is on the extent to which state and local governments and nonprofit organizations have replaced federal aid cuts. By now, we should not have to assert or prove that this is hard to do. The findings in this volume are presented in terms of general magnitudes rather than precise numbers that indicate that x dollars were cut and y percentage of the cuts were replaced with state and local revenues raised in specified ways. The principal finding, however, is clear—namely, that the overall level of replacement of federal aid cuts was modest at both the state and local levels. In this chapter we explore the implications of this finding and present a preliminary theory to explain replacement behavior where it occurs.

The first question about the implications of this finding of modest replacement concerns its macro-effect: What does this finding indicate about the extent to which President Reagan has succeeded in reducing the role of government in the American economy, particularly in domestic social programs? The answer suggested by the initial findings is clear: Reagan is succeeding to a degree that is impressive for the chief executive in our political system.

The longer-run effects of Reagan's domestic policies remain to be studied, and one of the purposes of this research is to do precisely that. But the early returns tell us a lot. The size of the domestic public sector in the U.S. economy appears from what we have learned to be smaller than would otherwise have been the case without the considerable political energy devoted by the Reagan administration and its supporters to the policy changes studied in this research. These changes have reduced the size and scope of federal social programs, and this reduction has not to any substantial degree been offset by state and local actions to increase the amount of taxes and other revenues these governments collect to support social programs.

There are many aspects of this central issue that require further study—for example, the degree to which federal aid cuts have been restored at the national level since 1982; the ways in which state and local governments respond to cuts in social service programs that have not yet had their main effect due to the use of carryover funds (e.g. under the new block grants); and the willingness of state and local governments in the future to take on responsibilities that the federal government is eschewing. Longitudinal field research, as indicated, is one way to get at these issues. Another way, which we also plan to pursue, is to use national statistics on economic activity and government finances to study the shifting of shares between the public and private sectors (or at least between the defense and social sectors), using econometric modeling techniques.

A major premise of the field research studies we have done over the past ten years is that it is desirable to blend these two approaches—field evaluation and statistical modeling. In previous studies, we have referred to this blending as the "complementarity" approach to the evaluation of national domestic policies.[1] Essentially what is involved is using the insights obtained from the field analysis to build a better mousetrap for statistical modeling. We plan to do this, and hope to be able to do this in a way that will enable us to separately assess the effects of the Reagan program within the domestic public sector in major functional areas of activity, such as health, welfare, education, and capital infrastructure spending.

The Reagan presidency has already been characterized by many observers as a watershed presidency. The more precise meaning of statements like this, the nature and degree of the changes that have occurred, and their effects on people and institutions are important subjects for social scientists to tackle. Our basic research purpose is to pursue the issues subsumed in this

---

1. Charles F. Adams, Jr., and Dan L. Crippen, "The Fiscal Impact of General Revenue Sharing on Local Governments," Department of the Treasury, Office of Revenue Sharing, A-79; and Charles F. Adams, Jr., Robert F. Cook, and Arthur J. Maurice, "A Pooled Time-Series Analysis of the Job-Creation Impact of Public Service Employment Grants to Large Cities," *Journal of Human Resources*, vol. xviii, no. 2 (Spring 1983), pp. 283-94.

discussion and to present the findings in a careful way, and on as timely a basis as we can, in the expectation that such information will be useful in the political process.

This first report on the 1982 field data presents the fiscal and programmatic effects of the 1982 cuts and changes in federal aid in order to help policymakers and interested citizens assess and understand the events of the current period. The report also presents emerging theoretical lessons. A number of useful generalizations are discussed that help us think about the future, specifically about whether and under what conditions cuts in federal aid are likely to be replaced by state and local governments. Chapters 3, 4, and 5, which discuss the responses of state and local governments to the cuts in federal aid made in the 1982 budget, emphasize the following three main findings:

1. The overall level of replacement of the federal cuts was modest at both the state and local level.
2. The replacement rate varied from jurisdiction to jurisdiction.
3. Replacement of federal cuts in entitlement programs providing cash or cash-substitute benefits (AFDC and food stamps) was the lowest among all types of programs, while replacement in operating grant programs was higher. Though the cuts in capital programs in most jurisdictions were relatively small in 1982 compared with the cuts in entitlement and operating grants, some governments made efforts to secure alternative financing for capital projects that were (or appeared to be) threatened by cuts in federal aid.

The rest of this chapter is organized into three parts corresponding to the findings listed above. Each section briefly reviews the evidence supporting the finding and presents hypotheses interpreting the possible future significance of the responses to federal aid cuts in fiscal year 1982.

Low Overall Replacement

Most of the cuts in grants to state and local governments in the sample were ratified—that is, they were passed along to the recipients of benefits and services under the programs affected by federal budget cuts. The most active state in replacing federal aid (Oklahoma) restored an estimated 25 percent of the cuts; two states (Massachusetts and New York) were found to have replaced 10 to 20 percent of the cuts. Most states replaced less than 10 percent of the cuts. Replacement was generally low in large cities, and virtually nonexistent in most suburban and rural jurisdictions.

The economic and political conditions that prevailed in 1982 help to explain this modest overall level of replacement. The national recession reduced state and local government receipts from income and sales taxes and increased the costs of some welfare programs. Many field reports emphasize the importance of the recession in shaping governmental responses to federal aid cuts.

The year 1982 also brought two states, California and Massachusetts, face to face with the consequences of state and local tax cuts enacted in the late 1970s and early 1980s. California's Proposition 13, enacted in 1978, placed a ceiling on local property taxes of 1 percent of assessed value. State aid was used to compensate for the resulting losses in local tax revenue, but by 1982 this drain on the state treasury combined with later cuts in state income taxes had brought the state government to the brink of insolvency. Massachusetts also confronted the need to deal with a statewide constitutional limit on local taxes; the state increased state aid to relieve local fiscal pressure caused by Proposition 2 1/2, which cut local property taxes and limited their future increase.

The nature of the federal programs cut served in some cases to limit, or at least discourage, state and local government actions to replace lost federal aid. Most of the cuts were in programs that redistribute resources from taxpayers as a whole to low-income people. The AFDC and food stamp programs redistribute tax revenues to provide cash and cash-substitute payments to eligible low-income recipients. Medicaid does the same thing by providing low-income people with an entitlement to medical services they otherwise could not afford. Even many of the operating grants that were cut redistribute income in the sense that they raise tax revenues to pay for health services, social services, education programs, and employment and training programs that primarily benefit low-income people.

Many state and local government officials oppose income redistribution by their governments, and as a result could be expected to be hesitant about replacing federal aid cuts in social programs. To understand why even liberal officials of state and local governments might feel this way, consider what would result if a state or city were to raise its taxes to pay for redistributive programs for the poor when other jurisdictions did not do so. Wealthier taxpayers would have an incentive to leave the jurisdiction to escape the increased taxes needed to pay for these services, and poor people would have an incentive to move in or remain in order to receive this aid. This point, of course, needs to be considered in overall terms: The state and local jurisdictions that provide the highest income-support benefits and the most extensive social services, and that devote the highest proportions of their own revenue to doing so, are the ones most likely to be affected in the manner just described.

When redistributive programs are financed by the federal government and provide relatively uniform benefits in real terms throughout the country, both wealthier taxpayers and recipients have less of an incentive to change their behavior because of the financing arrangement for these programs. Taxpayers must take the dramatic step of leaving the country to avoid the tax, and recipients receive equal benefits everywhere. In the same way, the incentives are weaker when states and large counties redistribute income than when cities and towns do so.

Liberals have based arguments for federal government programs to aid the poor on this reasoning. Conservatives often act, or appear to act, on the basis of this reasoning, when they urge that income redistribution programs be handed over to state and even local governments. They realize such changes are likely to reduce the redistribution of income by government, and argue that this is desirable as a means of increasing incentives for individual self-support. The federal budget cuts and increases in state and local responsibility for redistributive programs that occurred as a result of the 1981 reconciliation act appear to have produced precisely this result: reducing total government spending on programs to aid the poor below what it would have been otherwise.

Considerations related to political tactics also contributed to state and local decisions not to replace the federal aid reductions enacted for fiscal year 1982. State and local government officials faced a dilemma in 1982. If they acted to replace federal cuts—even in programs that they regarded as valuable—they would have undercut their own arguments that federal aid is vitally needed to support these services. By replacing federal aid cuts, they unavoidably would have supported President Reagan's contention that federal programs can and should be turned over to state and local governments. Our observation is that this strategy consideration did have an effect on state and local decision making about how to respond to federal aid cuts, especially in liberal jurisdictions, though its weight cannot be determined. As the next section indicates, political ideology as a whole appears to have a role in determining replacement behavior. Jurisdictions with a politically liberal ideology—that is, one that supports spending for social programs—were more likely to replace federal aid cuts for these programs.

Differences in Replacement Among Jurisdictions

Despite the generally low level of replacement of federal aid cuts, there were differences in net overall replacement among the jurisdictions in the sample for this study. Oklahoma, New York, and Massachusetts replaced the highest proportions—more than 10 percent—of the federal aid cuts. Arizona, California, Florida, New Jersey, and South Dakota replaced from none to less than 10 percent of the cuts. Six states—Illinois, Mississippi, Missouri, Ohio, Texas, and Washington—were found to have realized savings in state spending due to federal cuts.

For the large cities, there were similar variations. Five cities replaced noticeably more of the federal cuts than the others in the sample: Orlando, Los Angeles, Cleveland, Rochester, and Houston. Orlando and Los Angeles were slightly ahead of the others in this group. The remaining nine cities replaced some federal aid cuts, though generally in very small amounts. Differences in rates of replacement are not apparent in the suburban and rural governments in our study because of the overall low level of replacement. We concentrate on states and large cities in this analysis since they more clearly illustrate the nature and role of the factors that influence replacement behavior.

The states that realized savings because of the federal aid cuts did so not by deliberate action, but because they simply allowed federal restrictions of AFDC and medicaid eligibility to be translated into reductions in state spending on these programs. Large cities, on the other hand, did not face this kind of option, because most cities do not have the responsibility for financing the AFDC or medicaid program. There was some compounding of cuts in particular programs by the large city governments in the sample, but we found no cities with net reductions in local spending as a result of such compounding.

The next two sections present an explanation of the differences in replacement rates and efforts for the states and large cities in the sample.

State Replacement

Differences in state replacement behavior are associated with two key variables: the degree of fiscal pressure under which the state government operated in 1982 and the state's political ideology. This finding is not surprising or hard to explain. These two factors indicate whether in the period of the study a government had the resources to restore grant-in-aid funds cut by the federal government, and whether there was local political support for doing so. Table 22 lists the states in the sample grouped by their rate of replacement; it also shows both the fiscal pressure rating for each state and the dominant political ideology. In the first two groups of jurisdictions shown, the states are listed from those with greatest replacement to those with least replacement; under the "net savings" heading, the states are listed alphabetically.

The fiscal pressure rating system used in table 22 was developed in the previous field network evaluation study of the public service employment program to analyze the balance between the service demands and revenues of a jurisdiction. The field research associates chose the appropriate category for their jurisdictions based on two types of information. First, they analyzed financial data for the preceding five years, considering such information as end-of-year cash balances, unrestricted fund surpluses, rate of growth of taxes and expenditures, fund deficits, short-term borrowing, changes in the tax base, and bond ratings. Second, they made a qualitative assessment of the capacity of a jurisdiction to expand activities and add programs based on interviews with officials and analysis of the political situation of the jurisdiction.

The classification of political ideology used in table 22 is based on per-capita state and local spending on public welfare programs.[2] States spending more than $300 per capita are classified as liberal, those from $200 to $300 as moderate, and those below $200 as conservative.

We found that liberal ideology alone does not lead to replacement, nor does the lack of fiscal pressure. It appears the one factor must be strong, while the other must be at least in the intermediate range.

Three of the six states with net savings—Mississippi, Ohio, and

---

2. Data are from U.S. Bureau of the Census, *Governmental Finances in 1980–81* (Washington, D.C.: U.S. Government Printing Office, 1982), and include both state and local government spending. Included in this category are AFDC, medicaid, and general relief programs, among others.

Table 22. *State Replacement and Characteristics*

State	Fiscal pressure[a]	Political ideology
Highest net replacement		
Oklahoma	Little	Moderate
New York	Moderate	Liberal
Massachusetts	Moderate	Liberal
Some state net replacement		
New Jersey	Little	Moderate
Florida	Moderate	Conservative
Arizona	Moderate	Conservative
California	Extreme	Liberal
South Dakota	Moderate	Conservative
Net savings		
Illinois	Moderate	Moderate
Mississippi	Moderate	Conservative
Missouri	Extreme	Conservative
Ohio	Extreme	Moderate
Texas	Little	Conservative
Washington	Extreme	Moderate

a. The ratings for fiscal pressure are defined as follows:

Extreme fiscal pressure. Own-source revenue and anticipated external sources of revenue are insufficient to meet the demands for essential services. Essential services are not defined as all existing services; this is a limited concept. Furthermore, there is no apparent and generally used revenue source available to increase own-raised revenue in the relative near term, on a one-year basis.

Moderate fiscal pressure. Anticipated own-source revenue and external sources are insufficient to support the existing level of services. Therefore, the maintenance of the current level of services requires positive action, i.e., use of a new tax source, a significant increase in nominal tax rates, or the reduction of service levels.

Little fiscal pressure. Anticipated internal and external revenues (using existing sources with possible small nominal rate increases) are expected to cover anticipated expenditure increases and even meet some new, but limited, service demands.

Washington—have one factor with a strong or high rating in the terms of this analysis (conservative ideology or fiscal pressure) and the other with an intermediate rating. Missouri, also a state with net savings, is an unusual case, having both extreme fiscal pressure and a conservative political ideology. It is the only state in the sample where both factors point strongly in the same direction. This is not surprising; few states with low spending suffered extreme fiscal pressure during the recession and few with high spending completely avoided it. In Texas, the state's conservatism is so strong that net savings occurred despite its low-fiscal-pressure rating. Illinois, with moderate ratings on both factors, is less of an exception than might appear from table 22. It had some (but very low) net replacement, and the fiscal pressure it faced (rated here as moderate) increased soon after the observation period ended.

The states in the middle category present a variety of situations. New Jersey is close to the percentage cutoff for the highest replacement category. Florida is a growing state, which is becoming increasingly more moderate politically. This shift to a more moderate political stance in Florida appeared to be linked to the state's decision in 1982 to raise the sales tax, increase spending for public health, and maintain state AFDC and medicaid spending in the face of federal aid cuts. Arizona, despite its political conservatism, replaced federal cuts, but the increases in state spending came in large measure as a result of higher spending for education, because of a state-aid distribution formula that automatically increased aid to schools as other revenue declined. Arizona also replaced some federal aid cuts for highways; in this case there was an increase in revenue from an earmarked tax. In California, the states's liberal political ideology rating was tempered by its serious fiscal problems in 1982, attributable to the arrival of the day of reckoning on Proposition 13 and other tax-cutting measures. South Dakota increased spending on medicaid, which was enough to put the state in the intermediate replacement category, because the state's savings under AFDC were relatively small.

Most economic models of grantee responses to changes in federal aid use per-capita resident income to measure capacity. Our analysis here, and in previous studies, places emphasis on fiscal pressure, defined in a way that takes into account the functional responsibilities and financial system of the recipient jurisdiction. We believe fiscal pressure is a better measure of capacity than per-capita income in considering short-term responses to changes in federal aid. When considering longer-run adjustments to changes in federal aid, income may well be the relevant measure of fiscal capability. However, in the short run, political and institutional limitations on revenue sources and tax rates affect a government's ability to provide the particular types of services that federal aid supports. The measure of fiscal pressure used here captures these factors.

Replacement in Large Cities

Table 23 shows the large cities in our sample according to two net replacement ratings—"highest" and "low" replacement. The jurisdictions are listed in order of degree of replacement.

The relationship between the replacement rating, on the one side, and the degree of fiscal pressure and political ideology, on the other, is not as clear as the relationships at the state level. Two of the cities in the highest replacement group are classified as being under extreme fiscal pressure. Three of them fit the pattern discussed for the states, namely of having either a liberal ideology or little fiscal pressure, and an intermediate ranking on the other factor. In the low-replacement group, the relationship between replacement and the combination of fiscal pressure and political ideology is clearer, with most (but not all) cities having either extreme fiscal pressure or a conservative orientation.

The exceptions to the general pattern observed for the states help to bring out an essential additional point about the large cities, namely, the varying role of overlying governments, such as counties or special-purpose governments. This factor affects replacement behavior, and helps to explain a number of the cases that deviate from the explanation for state governments. The rating of the role of the overlying government in table 23 is the same as that developed in chapter 4. It measures the relative importance of overlying governments as service providers.

All of the cities in the highest-replacement group have active (i.e., strong) overlying governments. Only Chicago among the lower-replacement cities has a strong overlying government. All of the sample cities where overlying governments play a weak role have low replacement.

In jurisdictions with a strong role for overlying governments, many of the federal cuts actually affected these overlying governments more than they affected the city government. In such cases, it is the overlying government that faces the question of whether to replace federal cuts, and the fiscal condition of this overlying government becomes an important factor.

In Rochester, for example, Monroe County and the regional transportation authority administer key federally aided programs. Both have a wider geographic scope and are in better fiscal condition than the city of Rochester. Much of the federal aid replacement for Rochester was made by these overlying governments. The overlying counties for Orlando and Cleveland were experiencing relatively little fiscal pressure in 1982; they contributed to the

Table 23. *Large City Replacement and Characteristics*

City	Fiscal pressure	Political ideology[a]	Role of overlying governments
Highest replacement			
Orlando	Little	Moderate	Strong
Los Angeles	Extreme	Moderate	Strong
Cleveland	Moderate	Liberal	Strong
Rochester	Extreme	Liberal	Strong
Houston	Little	Moderate	Strong
Low replacement			
Sioux Falls	Little	Conservative	Weak
St. Louis	Extreme	Moderate	Medium
Chicago	Moderate	Moderate	Strong
Boston	Extreme	Moderate	Medium
Tulsa	Little	Conservative	Weak
Phoenix	Little	Conservative	Medium
Seattle	Moderate	Moderate	Medium
Jackson	Moderate	Conservative	Weak
Newark	Moderate	Liberal	Weak

a. This rating is based on information contained in the field reports.

replacement found for these cities, especially in the case of Cleveland. This is why Cleveland, although it had a recent and well-known bout with financial disaster, ranks in the highest-replacement category.

Newark, with moderate fiscal pressure and a liberal political ideology, seems out of place at the bottom of the low-replacement group. Its low replacement appears to stem in part from its recent serious fiscal problems. Having had a brush with fiscal insolvency in 1975-76, it adopted a fiscally very conservative stance. Newark also has a weak overlying government in terms of the role it plays in Newark. The state supervisory role over local finances in New Jersey is a strong one, which may have prevented it from being as active in replacing federal aid cuts as otherwise might have been the case.

Another important factor in explaining replacement behavior for federally aided services in large cities is the role of the courts. The Los Angeles situation illustrates this point. The city of Los Angeles in 1982 was bound by a consent decree to stop discharging sewage sludge into the ocean by July 1985. Faced with this

deadline, the city could not wait for the appropriation of wastewater treatment grants, and spent $6.7 million of its own money in
1982 on the construction of a major waste treatment facility. (The
city eventually will be reimbursed by the federal government for
this expenditure.) Court action also affected the finances of the
countywide transit district in Los Angeles. In 1980 voters
approved a county sales tax for transit. The tax was challenged as
violating Proposition 13. Litigation continued through 1982, when
the court approved the tax. Court orders also influenced the
replacement behavior in Cleveland and St. Louis, where the
school districts were required by desegregation orders to maintain
certain educational services despite cuts in federal aid.

The analysis in this section begins with a discussion of the reasons for the generally low level of state and local replacement of
federal aid cuts found in fiscal year 1982. It is followed by our
interpretation of the reasons why some jurisdictions in the sample
replaced more of the federal aid cuts than others. Future field
research will test these conclusions. It is possible that, as national
economic conditions improve, there will be a generalized increase
in the replacement of lost federal aid. Other factors — for example,
political factors or simply the passage of time — may cause generalized changes in replacement behavior. There is likewise a possibility that the differences in the rates of replacement by the
sample governments will become larger or more muted. We need
to be alert to these possibilities.

Varying Replacement Behavior by Type of Program

There were differences across types of programs, as well as by
jurisdiction, in the replacement behavior of the sample governments. For entitlement programs, most states ratified cuts in
AFDC, food stamps, and medicaid. They replaced some cuts in
operating grants, and in some cases began to act to maintain capital
spending even before threatened federal cuts actually affected
federally aided construction activities. Local governments are not
ordinarily involved in policymaking for federally aided entitlement programs, though a few were found to have partially
replaced AFDC cuts with increased local spending on such programs as general relief and emergency assistance. Most replacement behavior by local governments, however, was for operating
and capital grants.

Several factors contributed to the greater support for operating
and capital grants as opposed to entitlement programs. The previ-

ous discussion of income redistribution programs helps explain this finding. The more redistributive a program is, the less likely a state or local government is to replace federal cuts in that program. Furthermore, since all eligible persons must receive entitlement benefits, spending is difficult to control and fiscally hard-pressed governments were hesitant to get more deeply involved in these programs.

Variations in the degree of political support also contributed to the patterns of replacement observed. The more discrete and visible a federally aided program is, and the greater the political salience of the problem it addresses, the more likely it is to receive state and local support. This factor has its counterpart at the national level. Conservatives tend to support broad (i.e., noncategorical) grants as a way of reducing the overall political support for spending. Programs such as AFDC (addressing the general problem of insufficient income) and the community services block grant (addressing the multiple service needs of low-income communities) fared poorly as candidates for replacement in the sample jurisdictions. But this issue is a complex one. Programs that are part of a block grant, such as health services for mothers and children, daycare, and rat control programs, were frequent candidates for replacement.

Part of the reason for the political appeal of certain kinds of social service programs as opposed to others is a reflection of the organization and character of the providers. This point is very important for social programs. The larger the stake providers have in a given social service, the more likely it is to win support in periods of retrenchment like the current one. A number of the operating grant programs that were cut in fiscal 1982 benefited from organized lobbying by the providers of the services being funded. This was especially important for health programs. Likewise, in the social services area, certain programs (like child daycare and home care for the aged) were singled out for replacement, often partly for this reason.

Many of the providers of these public health and social services are skilled professionals, and in many states they have well-organized and politically strong "trade" associations. This factor tends to have the greatest effect where a parallel state program exists. For some health and social services aided by federal grants, state financial support often exceeds federal aid, so the service providers involved are accustomed to lobbying at the state level.

Among the federal grants cut in 1982, CETA and the community services block grant received the least political support; service providers had received most of their funds from the federal government and had focused their attention in the past on federal officials and agencies. They were as a result not in a good position to lobby at the state level for the replacement of lost federal aid in 1982.

The discussion in this section about state and local political support for the services provided under federally aided operating grants raises important questions, alluded to earlier, about the form of federal aid instruments. While there appears to be some evidence for the point that is frequently made that the broader a grant is, the less likely it is to have grass-roots support, one should not overgeneralize. Form is not everything. In some cases, a block grant (e.g., the social services block grant) may support services, like child daycare and home care for the aged, that have a strong, effective constituency. It well may be that these constituencies would get more money under a categorical grant. But it is also possible that we will eventually decide that social-program constituencies strongly influenced the funding patterns, both nationally and locally, under block grants in a way that increased spending beyond what it would have been had aid instead been provided in a more categorical form. This is an important subject for continuing scrutiny in the research.

Capital grant programs have both specific and general political support, reflecting the growing concern about state and local infrastructure needs. These programs often received generalized political support because they benefit all income groups in a community. Unlike entitlement grant programs, many capital programs benefit middle-class residents, who are likely to be among the most active voters. Builders and their suppliers are also strong supporters of capital spending by government. Several states and large cities in the sample increased spending and fees for federally aided capital purposes in anticipation of threatened cuts. This anticipatory replacement behavior differs sharply from the widespread ratification behavior found for federally aided entitlement programs.

This discussion needs to include income-transfer programs. Typically, these programs have no (or hardly any) organized constituency support. Welfare rights groups representing AFDC, medicaid, and food stamp recipients were virtually nonexistent in most of the states in the sample for this study, and were not influential where they did exist. The politics of these grant programs tend to be played out instead at the national level. Liberals often argue that providing cash welfare benefits allows recipients to purchase the goods and services most valuable to them, and that this is therefore the best and most efficient way to help the poor. In-kind aid is seen as not necessarily fitting the needs of a particular person or family. The lack of support for AFDC and food stamps found in this study suggests that on the whole politicians and voters are suspicious of the principle of consumer sovereignty when applied to the poor.

Change and Continuity

The state and local government reactions to cuts in federal aid in 1982 reported in this volume came as responses to new national policies. Nevertheless, this behavior is in many ways consonant with the findings of earlier studies on how state and local governments behaved when federal grants were increasing.

When federal aid was growing during the 1970s, what public discussion there was of this subject was concerned with the degree to which rising federal aid was causing cities and states to become *dependent* on Washington. Often without probing deeply enough, analysts asserted that the more federal aid a government received, the more dependent or "hooked" it became on federal aid. Some analysts speculated about how, like drug addicts, these governments would suffer withdrawal symptoms—pain, hardship, and unhappiness—if and when federal aid was withdrawn.

There are places and cases where this nice metaphor fits, but it is by no means a good way to generalize about how federal grants affect state and local governments. Earlier studies we conducted revealed a strong tendency for state and local governments to avoid becoming dependent on federal aid. They accomplished this by keeping federal grants off to one side, and identifying the affected programs as clearly federally aided—as "their" programs (that is, the federal government's) that presumably would not have been undertaken absent federal aid.

This approach, we observed, is rational behavior, for a number of reasons. One reason is the unpredictability of federal aid. If a state or local government expects that at some time in the future federal aid will be cut or the rules basically changed, then it is unwise to subsume that aid in its regular budget. The elimination or substantial reduction of this federal aid would create strong pressure for a tax increase to replace the federal support being provided. Another motive for treating federal grants separately is that in some cases the officials of the recipient jurisdictions do not share the purposes, or feel as strongly about the goals, of a particular federal grant. Still a third reason for treating federal aid separately is that various federal laws and regulations require that federal aid be a supplement to the jurisdiction's own resources and not be used to substitute for state or local revenue.[3]

In this context, it is not surprising that the most common response to the fiscal 1982 federal aid cuts was to cut the services affected. The pain, hardship, and unhappiness were felt primarily among low-income individuals and families and the nonprofit organizations that provide services to low-income people—not at the level of governments.

Programs that had strong political support, often in the form of influential constituencies of skilled providers, were the main candidates for replacement. The same applies to programs with a communitywide incidence, like grants for major capital projects. The more a program was regarded as something the federal government was responsible for, the less likely it was to be a candidate for the replacement of lost federal aid.

The issues for federal grants have changed and the national government's policies have changed, but in these terms the politics of federal aid have not changed. There is, to summarize, both change and continuity—*change* in the types of decisions to be made, and *continuity* in the basic factors that influence the behavior of recipient state and local governments under federal grants-in-aid.

In an early paper on this research, one of the associates wrote about the effect of the Reagan cuts and changes:

What seems enduring in the history of American government is the federal-state-local assistance relationship. The understanding, tolerance, and anticipatory behavior required to make this unique arrangement work does not seem in danger of dramatic change in Arizona. From this early, admittedly limited, perspective, the old federalism seems alive and well.[4]

---

3. For a longer discussion of these points, see Richard P. Nathan, "State and Local Governments under Federal Grants: Toward a Predictive Theory," *Political Science Quarterly*, vol. 98, no. 1 (Spring 1983), pp. 47–58.

4. John Stuart Hall, "The Reagan Domestic Program in Arizona Context," paper prepared for delivery at the 1982 Annual Meeting of the American Political Science Association, Denver, Colorado, September 2, 1982 (processed), p. 14.

Appendix
Report Form

Note: Following is the text of the report form used by field associates in preparing their reports. Part 1, "Baseline," was used for preliminary reports on states and large cities submitted in February 1982, and for reports on suburban and rural jurisdictions submitted in October 1982. Part 2, "Changes," was used for reports on all jurisdictions submitted in October 1982.

Part 1: Baseline

1. The Fiscal Setting

Please assess the fiscal pressure on this jurisdiction as of September 30, 1981. In making your assessment, you should use the terms and criteria developed for the field evaluation study of the CETA public service employment program:

- *Extreme Fiscal Pressure.* The current level of service has been cut to essential services. (We distinguish between "existing" and "essential" services.) This means that own-source local revenue and anticipated external sources of revenue may be insufficient to meet the demands for even essential services, and there is no apparent and generally used revenue source to increase local own-raised revenue in the relative near term—that is, looking ahead one year.

- *Moderate Fiscal Pressure.* Anticipated own-source local revenue and external sources will be insufficient to support the existing level of services. Therefore, the maintenance of the

205

current level of services in the jurisdiction requires difficult positive action, i.e. use of a new tax source, a significant increase in nominal tax rates, or the reduction of service levels.

• *Little Fiscal Pressure.* Anticipated internal and external revenues (using existing sources with possible small nominal rate increases) are expected to cover anticipated expenditure increases and even meet some, but limited, new service demands.

• *No Fiscal Pressure.* The jurisdiction is experiencing increases in existing surpluses or adopting tax reduction measures. There is no difficulty in meeting expected demands for public services (both essential services and desired existing and new services) with existing internal and external revenue sources and tax rates.

We would like you to consider two kinds of information in reaching your conclusion. The first is financial data for the preceding five years, which would include: end-of-year cash balances and unrestricted fund surpluses; rate of growth of taxes and expenditures; the presence or absence of fund deficits; the use of short-term borrowing; increases or decreases in the tax base; the bond rating or any recent changes in the bond rating; and increases or decreases in nominal tax rates. Please take into account any recent public referenda on bonding or spending. A second kind of information we would like you to consider is assessments by local officials of this jurisdiction's capacity to expand activities or add new programs or services.

2. Local Tax or Expenditure Limitations

What is the recent history of budget and/or tax limitation measures in this jurisdiction? Were major fiscal constraints legislated prior to Proposition 13 (June 1978)? Have Proposition 13-type tax or budget limitations been the subject of recent elections? If so, who initiated this action? What was the outcome (percent for and against)? Discuss in general terms existing state and local limitations that have affected spending and programs in this jurisdiction.

3. *Public Employment*

Please discuss the condition of public employment in this jurisdiction. Have there been recent layoffs (not counting CETA; see next question), hiring freezes, reductions or decreases in force? If there have been layoffs, freezes, or limitations of force recently, please discuss the reasons for them. Are they the result of federal program reductions (real or anticipated), state and local politics, voter-mandated ceilings, the weakening of economic conditions, management efforts to improve productivity, or some combination of these and other factors? As emphasized in the introduction to this report form, we would like your answer to this question for local jurisdictions in the sample to take into account major overlying governments where important changes in public employment levels and policies have taken place.

4. *CETA—Public Service Employment*

Please discuss the way the elimination of CETA—PSE jobs has affected the condition of public employment in this jurisdiction and major overlying governments. How was the elimination of PSE accomplished? What were the major effects on public employment and the provision of public services in this jurisdiction?

5. *The Governmental Setting*

We ask you to write a statement on the main actors in policy and budgetary decision processes and their relationships to each other for the sample jurisdictions and, where appropriate, to refer to overlying local governmental units. We are interested in knowing who are the most influential persons in policy making and finance in relation to federal grants-in-aid. We ask that you subdivide your statement to discuss the following:

a. *The Executive.*

b. *The State or Local Legislative Body.*

c. *Agencies and the Bureaucracy.* We are most interested in agencies that administer federally assisted programs. Which ones are they? How are they organized? Which political actors within the agency and outside of it are especially influential?

d.   *Interest Groups.* Again, what we are interested in is the groups most involved in decisions about federally aided programs.

e.   *Other Groups and Individuals.* This part of the question has two purposes. One is to elicit information about other groups, for example political parties and churches, that do not get treated in sections a-d. The second purpose is to ask you which external actors are especially important in the decision process, especially with respect to federally-aided activities. It is here that we expect you to treat federal agencies and officials and, for localities, state agencies and officials who have been especially important in local decision processes with respect to federal grants.

6. The Budget Process

Next, we ask you to write a statement about the budget process for the sample jurisdiction, where appropriate referring to overlying local jurisdictions. In your statement please indicate:

a.   The fiscal-year period.

b.   Key dates and documents.

c.   How federal aid is treated in the budget process, and who is responsible for allocation of this aid. Does the legislature (council) appropriate federal money or approve federally funded positions? Or are federal funds and federally funded positions kept separate, with federal funds automatically passed through to designated agencies?

d.   How and when revenue estimates are made and revised.

e.   How capital funds and accounts are treated.

f.   We would also appreciate having information about the organization and quality of budget documents.

7. Initial Response to Reagan Program

Section 7 asks you to discuss the way in which the jurisdictions in the study responded to the Reagan program as it unfolded. We would like you to cover:

a.   The point of view of key public officials and interest group representatives. Please discuss their predictions and expectations in the weeks and months immediately after the Reagan budget reduction proposals were announced.

b. Whether key public officials and interest group representatives were well informed, and the nature of any planning done to prepare for these federal policy changes. How much and what kind of publicity was given to the changes and their likely impacts on local programs?

c. Preparatory or anticipatory steps taken. (This is likely to be a very important subject in your analysis.)

d. Also please include any changes made to current-year revenue estimates and projections for future years resulting from provisions of the Economic Recovery Tax Act of 1981.

Please be sure to describe executive or legislative planning committees, new legislation (including tax changes made to offset provisions of the Economic Recovery Tax Act which affect state and local revenues), executive orders related to the Reagan policies, and new political coalitions which developed in response to the Reagan program. State-local relations are of particular interest to us.

8. Initial Effects

Section 8 is the most important part of the report form for the preliminary report.

For the first quarter of the federal fiscal year, we ask that you discuss the effects on this jurisdiction of the Reagan domestic program. Of course, we do not expect the information for the February submission to be provided in as much detail as what will be submitted in Part II of the report form at the end of the fiscal year.

We ask that you organize your analysis of the initial effects of the Reagan program to discuss the following functional areas in the following order:

a. Income Security
b. Health
c. Education, Training, and Social Services
d. Community and Regional Development
e. Transportation
f. Energy
g. Other Major Changes

Under each heading, please *number and separately discuss* each of the major federal policy changes that have had what you consider to be an important effect, or are likely to have one, in the jurisdiction(s) you are studying.

We make the assumption that if you do not discuss a program change at the federal level, this change has not had, and is not at the moment expected to have, an important effect in the jurisdiction(s) you are studying.

We want you to include in your analysis federal program changes where federal funds have been cut, but services have not been affected, due to the substitution of state or local funds for federal aid.

If you can at this stage, we would like your narrative to include two other subjects: (1) the population groups in the community most affected by the changes you discuss; and (2) emerging institutional effects that you can flag now and which you plan to consider further in part II of your full first-round report.

9. Block Grants

Section 9 asks you to discuss the way block grants have been treated by the jurisdictions in the sample. We would like you to take a *different approach* for state and local jurisdictions as described below.

1. *States:* We ask that you provide information on:
    a.   When the state "picked up" the block grants (most have)—and, if not, why not, and whether they expect or plan to do so at a later time.
    b.   The nature of the planning process, including the debates (if any) relating to the allocation and use of block grant funds. Who was involved—the legislature, recipient groups, task forces etc?
    c.   For each of the block grants, please discuss the approach to be used for:
        • the allocations among programs, places, and recipients;
        • policies for the services provided;
        • administrative structures and systems;
        • the regulatory process;
        • transfers within the blocks; and
        • the way matching requirements are being met.
2. *Localities:* We ask that you write a short statement about the actions, attitudes, and perceptions of local officials in relation to the state's handling of block grant funds. Have there been local reactions to state actions on block grants? Your statement should cover (a) attitudes towards state policy, (b) expec-

tations about changes that the states may yet make in the affected programs, and (c) political activity designed to influence the distribution and use of the block grant funds.

10. Expected Longer-Range Effects

Looking ahead, and based on the information in sections 8 and 9, what are likely to be the most important *generalized effects* of the Reagan domestic program—fiscal, programmatic, incidence, and institutional— in fiscal year 1982?

Part 2: Fiscal Year 1982 Changes

Note: In reporting their findings for the full fiscal year 1982, associates completed a "major program change form" (see figure 1) for each change that had important effects in their jurisdictions. Following is the portion of the report form for the full fiscal year that provides instructions on completing the change forms.

Instructions for Major Program Change Forms

You should prepare a separate program change form for each major program change. As in part 1, you will define what constitutes a major program change. However, we expect that you will include both local and state programs in which there has been a big change in either dollar amount or the percentage of total federal aid received, plus programs in which the dollar change was relatively small, but the local or state impact was great.

We make the assumption that if you do not discuss a program change that has occurred at the federal level, this change has not had, and is not at the moment expected to have, an important effect in the jurisdiction(s) you are studying.

Major program change forms should be completed for the level of government that directly administers a program, as well as for a government that provides substantial financing for it. Thus, you may find it necessary for AFDC to have both a state program change form and a county change form, if the county administers the program. In such instances, it will be helpful for the state associate and the local associate to coordinate their work.

At the state level, a separate program change form should be completed for each block grant. Block grants at the local level will require a program change form if you determine that the impact of the reduction in funding or change in policy was of major consequence in fiscal year 1982.

Major Program Change Form, FY 1982

Jurisdiction _____ Associate _____

Program Change Number _____ Service Provider _____

Program, & where appropriate, components	FY '82 Change in Federal Aid dollars percent	Change in Other Revenue dollars percent
_____	_____ _____	_____ _____
_____	_____ _____	_____ _____

Fiscal Effects
Pattern: Ratify _____ Compound _____ Replace _____ Augment _____

Employment Effects

Programmatic Effects

Incidence Effects

Institutional Effects

Regulatory & Administrative Changes

Function or Program Areas

We ask that you submit the major program change forms grouped by function or program area, with a cover page for each function or program area. The purpose of the cover page is to have you point out interrelations of the changes made in a broader functional or program area and to discuss any explicit or implicit strategy in this area.

Following are suggested groupings. You may vary these groupings.

1. Income security
2. Social services
3. Health
4. Education
5. Employment and training
6. Community and economic development
7. Transportation

Our purpose here is to organize our analysis at three levels: major program changes; functional or program areas of logically grouped major program changes; and the overall changes for the sample jurisdiction.

Some program changes will not fit into logical categories, and you should just submit them individually.

The next sections discuss the purpose of each part of the major program change form.

Organization of the Major Program Change Form

The form first provides for basic identifying information about the program change being reported.

Funding Information

The form then asks for the change in funding that has occurred in the program being reported. In some instances, involving major regulatory or administrative changes, there may not be a change in funding. You should also assess whether there has been a change in other funding, either to mitigate federal reductions or to add to them. The two types of reported dollar and percentage changes should combine to give a net change to the program. While the changes for operating and entitlement programs should be estimated on an expenditure basis, unless some other basis seems easier or more appropriate, capital grant changes will have to be on a contract authorization basis.

Because of differences in fiscal years, governmental account practices, and sources of program funding, it will be necessary for you to estimate the change in funding for each program reported. Our purpose is to compare the change in funding in the 1982 federal fiscal year (October 1, 1981 to September 30, 1982) to what would have occurred in the absence of the Reagan domestic program. We want to focus on changes that occurred as a result of changes in the economy. Since the federal fiscal year does not align with most state and local fiscal years, you will have to make the best approximation you can of the magnitude of the effect of the changes in the domestic policy of the federal government in fiscal year 1982. Your estimate will often involve a prorating from two different fiscal years. We know this type of quanitification can be difficult, but we ask that you estimate changes as accurately as possible. In particularly difficult cases, you may want to attach a separate explanation of how you arrived at your estimates or to call us to consult about decision rules. We believe it is important to report dollar changes by program so that the change in program can be related to the jurisdiction's budget.

Fund Changes By Type of Grant

Your estimates of changes and the analysis of effects will be different for different types of grants. Generally speaking, we will probably want to distinguish among operating, capital, and entitlement grants. Within operating grants, the analysis will often vary for formula and project grants. We will also need to take into account the special situation involving newly created (and genuine) block grants.

When several previously separate categorical grant activities have been combined into a block grant, we would like your estimate of the reduction in each of the previous categorical grant areas, after the state allocation of the grant.

Entitlement program dollar changes require that you estimate what amount would have been received but for the changes. In many cases the actual amount received may be higher because of the recession, but you should try to determine how much higher it would have been if there had not been specific actions taken to reduce spending under the entitlement.

Capital grants require you to estimate future reductions in program plans. These reductions will generally not be on an annualized basis, but instead will be on a project or program planning period basis. Just let us know the basis on which you show the reduction if it is not annualized.

For formula and continuing grants, you should be able to estimate changes in amounts from what would have been received but for the changes. However, for intermittent categoricals, such as UDAG, you may have to evaluate whether there was a reasonable expectation of receiving a grant if federal policy had not changed.

Analysis of Effects

The next part of the program change form asks for information about the effect of the change in the "traditional" (for us) categories: fiscal, employment, programmatic, incidence, institutional, and regulatory and administrative.

Under *fiscal effects*, we want to know how the government has responded financially. We use a framework here of four fiscal effect categories. Has the jurisdiction *ratified* the federal cut by reducing total spending accordingly; *replaced* it by increasing its own spending, to maintain total spending; *compounded* it by decreasing its own spending, as well as the federal portion; or *augmented* the program by increasing its spending beyond the previous combined federal and state and local spending? If you check off more than one of these four fiscal effect categories, please indicate in approximate terms (e.g., ten-percentage-point brackets) the proportion you would attribute to each. This point would apply, for example, where part, say half, of a federal budget cut is ratified and half is replaced.

We are also interested in how federal policy changes have affected the overall finances of the government. In many cases the fiscal effects may involve a rearrangement of funds so as to ratify some cuts while using state and local savings to replace other losses. If so, please try to describe the whole series of changes and the strategy—explicit or implicit. This may be done most appropriately on the cover pages for the groupings of change forms as described above.

We also ask in the fiscal effects area, and in the other areas as well, that you point out any differences that you ascertain between the initial effects and what occurs later in the budget process. We are already aware, on the basis of your part 1 reports and our field visits, of cases in which decisions you reported on in question 8 of part 1 have been changed later in the jurisdiction's budget process.

Under *employment effects*, please discuss changes in state and local public employment that result from changes in the Reagan domestic program. Please indiciate if any of the government reductions were offset by nongovernmental hirings (primarily the nonprofit sector), or if governmental hirings were caused by nongovernmental reductions.

Programmatic effects should include changes (or the lack thereof) in the *nature* of the service provided. For example, these may be categorized as follows:

1. No change was made in the program.
2. There were decreases in the quantity or quality of the service.
3. The price of the service was increased, for example, through the use of user fees or sliding scales for service costs.
4. Access to the service was restricted through tightened eligibility rules, etc.
5. The administrative processes or systems were changed in a way that reduced costs, but not the service level.

Incidence effects refers to the effects of the changes in services that occur in terms of who or what groups are most affected by the changes. We especially would like information about the numbers of people affected, and their characteristics. We would like you to classify people by income groups, racial or ethnic characteristics, or geographic area.

Under *institutional effects,* you should provide information on the way the provision of the affected programs and services is organized and which organizations and decisionmakers are responsible for their delivery. For example, a particular change may bring about an expanded role for governments (state and local); the greater involvement of elected officials or of some subset, like legislators; a reduced or increased role for program officials; less involvement of nonprofit organizations and community groups, etc. This section may include, for example, information about changes in the structure and procedures of the organizations that provide services, shifts of clients to different service providers, or changes in the groups that make allocation decisions. We are especially interested here in the ways in which you believe, or it is alleged, that federal policy changes made in fiscal year 1982 have increased or decreased the efficiency or productivity of state and local governments.

Regulatory and administrative should include effects on programs that were caused by either program or procedural changes resulting from federal actions. These can be changes resulting from the reconciliation act, regulations, or administrative action.

At the local level, the effect may result from state changes caused by federal action.

Index to Major
Federal Aid Programs